The Potosí Mita,
1573-1700

The Potosí Mita, 1573-1700

COMPULSORY INDIAN LABOR
IN THE ANDES

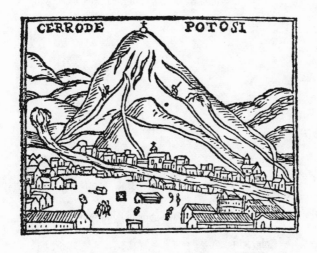

Jeffrey A. Cole

Stanford University Press, Stanford, California
1985

Stanford University Press
Stanford, California

Printed in the United States of America

Published with the assistance of the
Andrew W. Mellon Foundation

The illustration on the title page is entitled
"The first representation of the cerro of
Potosí, published by Pedro Cieza de León in
his *Crónica del Perú* (Seville, 1553)." It is taken
from Luis Capoche, *Relación general de la
Villa Imperial de Potosí* [1585].

Library of Congress Cataloging in Publication Data

Cole, Jeffrey A.
  The Potosí mita, 1573–1700.

  Bibliography: p.
  Includes index.
    1. Indians of South America–Bolivia–Potosí (Dept.)–
  Employment–History. 2. Forced labor–Bolivia–Potosí
  (Dept.)–History. 3. Indians of South America–Bolivia–
  Government relations. 4. Silver mines and mining–
  Bolivia–Potosí (Dept.)–History. 5. Spain–Colonies–
  America–Administration. 6. Potosí (Bolivia : Dept.)–
  Economic conditions. 7. Encomiendas (Latin America)
  I. Title.
  F3319.1.P6C65   1985   331.6'99808414   84-40331
  ISBN 0-8047-1256-5

*In honor of
Jane Elizabeth Larrabee Cole,
1922–1982*

Preface

BITTER DEBATE swirled about the mita during most of its 250-year existence. The draft labor system was identified by its enemies as a form of servitude worse than slavery and was accused of depopulating the provinces subject to it. Its defenders denied that it was responsible for the demographic decline in Alto Perú and argued that the mita was necessary to produce the silver upon which the Spanish Empire was so dependent. The arguments of the two factions were destined to play major parts in the formation of the Black and White Legends of the nature of Spanish American colonization.

Despite being one of the principal bones of contention in a heated historiographical controversy, the mita did not, until recently, receive the careful historical analysis that it required.* Some early articles, such as those of Alberto Crespo R. and Jorge Basadre, offered broad sketches of the system that were, we should note, remarkably accurate. But too many other studies merely parroted the claims made about the mita during the colonial period. The problem was not a lack of source materials, but rather too many, spread throughout the South American and European continents. Investigators were forced either to content themselves with broad interpretations based on a few sources or to write highly specific works restricted to a very short time frame and subject.

This is not to say that larger studies were not planned. Silvio Zavala, Marie Helmer, and Alberto Crespo R. are among those who contemplated the task of writing a comprehensive history of the

---

* See Keen, "The Black Legend Revisited," Hanke, "A Modest Proposal," and Keen, "The White Legend Revisited."

mita, but each eventually passed the torch to others.* Peter Bakewell, Enrique Tandeter, and I are among those who have sought to carry that torch forward. Bakewell and I have corresponded over the last few years and divided our work so that we do not tread too heavily on one another's toes; he has chosen to focus on the period from 1545 to 1640 and the relationship between free and forced labor at Potosí, whereas I have looked primarily at the seventeenth century and focused my attention on the mita per se and its administration. Enrique Tandeter, meanwhile, has confined his energies to the latter half of the eighteenth century, for which dependable quantitative data (of the sort that specialists on the Hapsburg period can only dream about) are abundant. By spreading the work load onto more shoulders, we have begun to piece together the history of the mita, within the wider contexts of colonial Potosí and Alto Perú.

Our work has been made easier by the development of research tools—computers, microfilm, xerography, etc.—and the appearance of archival guides edited by Lewis Hanke, Gunnar Mendoza L., John TePaske, and others. Benefiting from the efforts of these scholars and recent technological advances is a virtual army of investigators, many of whom have participated in a three-year program piloted by Tandeter and Olivia Harris.† Through such cooperative ventures as this, it seems certain that our knowledge of Potosí and of Andean America in general will grow rapidly during the next decade. It is my great hope that this book will be an important contribution to that cause.

THIS STUDY of the Potosí mita is a revision of my dissertation, "The Potosí Mita under Hapsburg Administration. The Seventeenth Century" (University of Massachusetts, Amherst, 1981), but it is a very different treatment of the subject. The original work employed a chronological format and was overly careful to present sufficient documentation to support each argument. The result was painfully

---

*Silvio Zavala has provided us with his research notes in the three volumes of *El servicio personal de los indios en el Perú*.

†The first conference (1982) concerned "Market Penetration and Expansion, 16th–20th Centuries"; the second (1983) dealt with "Reproduction and Transformation of Andean Societies, 16th–20th Centuries"; and the third (1984) was dedicated to "Resistance and Rebellions, 18th–20th Centuries." This series was funded by the Joint Committee on Latin American Studies of the American Council of Learned Societies and the Social Science Research Council.

long, with the evidence serving best to obscure the theses. The account of the mita offered here is thematic, with considerable amounts of detail sacrificed in favor of clarity of argument.*

In addition, the present text includes figures and tables that did not exist in the original. Some of these are the product of subsequent research and others are visual representations of data that earlier took prosaic form. Nevertheless, the primarily qualitative methodology of the earlier work remains; it remains because the data produced in Alto Perú during the sixteenth and seventeenth centuries were affected not only by unsystematic compilation and other irregular accounting techniques, but also by a desire to deceive as often as to enlighten. More derivative forms of quantitative analysis would, at this juncture, only compound the errors and biases in the sources.

I have also held fast to my belief that the Hapsburg administration of the mita is as interesting as the history of the *mitayos* themselves. Thus, in the chapters to follow, fully half of the text is devoted to the Hapsburg regime's efforts to administer the draft labor system. Similarly, though I have endeavored to present as complete a view of the impact of the mita on the Indians of Alto Perú as possible, I maintain that the effects of the regimen on the mining guild (*gremio de azogueros*) of Potosí and the other players in its drama are just as important and worthy of study. And as the administration of the mita and the daily lives of the mitayos were inexorably linked, if not in the way intended by the administration, the one cannot be considered without the other.

The result is what some may consider an "old fashioned" institutional history. I agree; but I hasten to point out that we have needed such a history of the Potosí mita for some time. This is not to say that revisions will not follow, but revisionism requires that there be something to revise. This book will not be the final statement on the subject—it is not my last word on the subject—but it is an overview that will serve as the backdrop for more specific studies, including quantitative investigations that bear in mind the biases involved in the production of the data. In the meantime, Latin Americanists will have at their disposal an overview of the mita and its impact on Alto Perú in the sixteenth and seventeenth centuries.

---

*This book also incorporates subsequent reinterpretations of source materials and corrections of errors in the thesis. This study replaces the accounts and interpretations in the dissertation and my previous articles, "An Abolitionism" and "Viceregal Persistence."

THIS BOOK has benefited from the cooperation and assistance of a great number of individuals and institutions. Research was made possible by financial assistance received under the Mutual Educational and Cultural Exchange [Fulbright-Hays] Act of 1961 (PL 87-256), and from the Tinker Foundation, Inc. The selection of the mita as a dissertation topic and the availability of extensive microfilm holdings on the subject in the United States may be attributed to Professor Emeritus Lewis Hanke. For my ability to read manuscripts, I am indebted to Professor Hugh M. Hamill, Jr., of the University of Connecticut, who took me on as his research assistant when I was an undergraduate. An indispensable contribution from the earliest stages of research was made by Dr. Pauline Collins, Latin American bibliographer at the University of Massachusetts. Professor Peter J. Bakewell, of the University of New Mexico, has been an inspiration from the outset, read an earlier draft of this study and offered important comments, and graciously provided me with a draft of his own study of Potosí, recently published by the University of New Mexico Press.

While in Bolivia in 1979–80, I was encouraged and greatly assisted by Dr. Alberto Crespo R., director of the Archivo de La Paz and Biblioteca de la Universidad Mayor de San Andrés, the late Sr. Mario Chacón Torres, director of the Archivo Histórico de Potosí, Drs. Inge Marie Harman and Roger Neil Rasnake (then of Cornell University), Dr. Carlos J. Díaz Rementería of the Universidad de Sevilla, and especially Dr. Gunnar Mendoza L., director of the Archivo Nacional de Bolivia and Biblioteca Nacional de Bolivia, miracle worker and organizer of colonial documentation extraordinaire.

In Peru, Srta. Graciela Sánchez Cerro, directora of the Oficina de Investigaciones of the Biblioteca Nacional, and Sr. Mario Cárdenas, director of the Oficina del Archivo Histórico in the Archivo de la Nación, were both extremely kind during a brief stay in Lima. In Argentina, Dr. César A. García Belsunce, ex-director of the Archivo General de la Nación, and his staff were patient and exceedingly helpful, both in 1980 and during a return to the AGNA in 1982.

Back in the United States, Professors Jane M. [Loy] Rausch, Miriam U. Chrisman, and Donald A. Proulx of the University of Massachusetts endured the early drafts of the dissertation and made important contributions to its form and content. Professor Robert A. Potash, my chairman and mentor for five years, accepted my decision to write on colonial Alto Perú (rather than nineteenth-century Mexico or modern Argentina) and provided firm yet gentle direction thereafter. He made his greatest contribution earlier, however, by insisting that I meet his high standards of self-discipline and excellence.

Professor Brian M. Evans of the University of Winnipeg, a student of the 1683 *numeración general de indios*, has lent immeasurable aid. Thanks also go to Professor Kenneth J. Andrien of Ohio State University for comments on my work and overall encouragement; to the editors of *The Hispanic American Historical Review* and the *Latin American Research Review* for seeing fit to publish articles that were earlier versions of sections of this book; and to the unidentified readers for Stanford University Press, both the more recent, who caused its acceptance, and the initial, whose condemnation of the format and length of the dissertation prompted its thorough revision.

I owe my wife Marilyn the greatest thanks, however, for the year she spent away from the Greater Boston computer circuit to accompany me to South America; for her willingness to endure the plane, train, and especially bus trips, *panza*, *chuño*, the heat and humidity of Buenos Aires in February and March, and the thrills and chills of the November 1979 coup d'état in La Paz; for providing me with a word processing system; and for the understanding required to follow a tenuously employed academic from Concord to New Orleans, from New Orleans to Syracuse, and from Syracuse back to Massachusetts.

Leverett, Massachusetts   J.A.C.

Contents

Maps, Tables, and Figures

The Potosí Mita,
1573-1700

ONE

The Establishment of
the Potosí Mita

THE MITA was a draft Indian labor regimen designed by Viceroy
Francisco de Toledo in 1573 to meet the need for unskilled labor in the
revitalized silver industry at Potosí.* That revitalization was prompted
by the development of a new amalgamation refining method suitable
to the mining zone's high elevation, which held the promise that
Potosí might recapture the fabled production levels that had made it
famous during its first two decades of exploitation (1545–65). Once
Potosí had regained its old form, Toledo expected, the mita would no
longer be necessary, for Indian laborers would once again flock to the
mines as they had earlier.[1] The production boom that Toledo en-
visioned did indeed come to pass, but though silver production
reached many times its earlier levels, the mita did not soon fade away.
Instead it continued, with fundamental modifications, for more than
two centuries, until it was finally abolished by Simón Bolívar in
1825. The key to the mita's persistence lay precisely in those modifications, for it changed form over the course of 250 years in response
to changing needs at Potosí and changing conditions in Alto Perú.
This study concerns the metamorphosis of the mita during the seventeenth century, when Potosí was a crown jewel of the Spanish
Hapsburgs.

Toledo arrived in Peru in 1569 with the twin responsibilities of re-
storing royal dominion in a viceroyalty wracked by civil strife and

---

*The word "mita" is derived from the Quechua "mit'a," meaning a turn or period
of service. During the colonial period, the word "mita" was used in Peru to refer to a
variety of draft Indian labor systems in mining, textile, and other enterprises. When
used without qualification in this study, however, "mita" refers to the regimen for
Potosí.

organizing all aspects of royal revenue production. Central to his effort was the final legitimation of the Hapsburg claim to sovereignty in Peru.[2] In fact, the conquest of the Inca Empire was as yet incomplete, for Manco Inca and his successors held out at Vilcabamba until 1572. Concurrent with the consolidation of Spanish dominion was the replacement of the Indians' pre-Columbian life-style with a more Hispanized existence.[3] A general census, conducted by the viceroy himself during an extensive tour of the realm, recorded 1,077,697 Indians, belonging to 614 *ayllus* (large kin units, composed of one or more moieties).* The Indians were subsequently settled in new villages to facilitate their control, the collection of their tribute, and their religious instruction.[4] Members of one or more ayllus were settled in one of two *parcialidades*, and each parcialidad was placed under an Indian *gobernador* (governor) and other *kurakas* (Indian headmen, initially nobles, also called *caciques*†). The settlement of the Indians into aggregated villages had first been proposed in 1550 by President Pedro de la Gasca of the Audiencia of Lima, and was begun by 1567,[5] but it was only under Toledo that the program became extensive and effective. This was to be characteristic of his viceroyalty—the use of extant policies and practices in a larger, more organized manner.

Another of Toledo's missions was the harnessing of the *encomenderos*. The Crown was worried about the independence shown by the recipients of *encomiendas* throughout the Americas, and feared that it had created an ungovernable feudal nobility in its overseas dominions.‡ Toledo's approach centered on the direct administration of the far-flung provinces by *corregidores de indios*, who would thenceforth perform the administrative, judicial, and fiscal duties previously left to the encomenderos. The Viceroy Marqués de Cañete (1556–59) had been the first to attempt to introduce corregidores, but the encomenderos had forced him to recall all but those for Chucuito and Chincha. In 1565, President Lope García del Castro revived the idea and, despite making little headway, his program was under way when Toledo arrived. Under the new viceroy's leadership,

*These figures do not include the regions of the Río de la Plata, Chile, Quito, or Tucumán.
†I have used "kuraka" throughout this study, despite the fact that many times the sources refer to a "cacique," for the sake of clarity.
‡The rights and responsibilities of encomenderos are discussed briefly on p. 65 below.

corregidores were again sent to every corner of the realm; Toledo was able to overcome the opposition of the encomenderos by naming prominent *soldados* (conquistadores who had not received a grant of encomienda) to the magistracies.[6]

The viceroy understood that the generation of augmented royal revenues in Peru would depend upon a stable population base and an effective administration. The most promising sector of the colonial economy was mining, but the Crown's desire to profit by the exploitation of Peru's vast mineral wealth was tempered by lessons it had learned earlier, during the colonization of the Caribbean. The Indians there had been decimated by their forced application to mining ventures by Spanish colonists, obliging Charles V to promulgate the New Laws of 1542, which specifically banned the use of forced Indian labor in mineral exploitation.[7] The Crown's concern for the well-being of the Indians was in part a recognition that Indian labor was itself a precious natural resource.

In the case of Potosí, the need to force the Indians to work in the mines did not arise until the 1560's. Prior to that time, Indian and Spanish miners alike had crossed the *altiplano* and worked in the mining zone of their own volition, drawn by the prospects of immense profits. A year after the vast silver lode at Potosí was discovered, the boomtown at the base of the mountain (*cerro*) held some 170 Spaniards and 3,000 Indians. By 1547, when the settlement— later to be entitled the "Villa Imperial de Potosí"—was officially founded, its residents numbered 14,000.[8]

In those early years, the Indians dominated every phase of silver production. The Spaniards' efforts at smelting failed (their European methods were frustrated by the altitude); by contrast, Indian technicians using the pre-Hispanic *guayra* (wind oven) skillfully coaxed molten silver from the rich *tacana* ore.[9] At one point, there were as many as 15,000 guayras in use.[10] Many of the Indians who came to Potosí were *yanaconas*—artisans, former Inca retainers, and others who were not affiliated with an ayllu—men who had been displaced by the conquest. They worked individually, under contracts with Spanish mine owners, and were often called *indios varas* because they were assigned a specified length of vein (measured in *varas**) to work. This was the skilled component of a two-tier division of labor at Potosí; the unskilled component consisted of Indians brought

---

*A vara is approximately 33 inches, but in some usages it can be greater than a meter.

by their kurakas to earn the money with which to pay their ayllus' tribute. These worked in shifts of a few months to a year, performing the more physical task of carrying ore out of the mines, after which they would return to their home pueblos.[11]

The Spaniards' contribution to silver production was limited to their ownership of the mines and their determination to profit by them. Legal title was no small factor, however, for in practice only the Spaniards were able to fend off legal challenges and so protect their claims against interlopers.[12] The silver produced was shared by the mine owners and indios varas under terms prescribed by their contracts; the ayllu Indians were paid a fixed wage for their labor.[13]

In the 1560's, however, the high-grade ore began to run out. Attempts to introduce the new amalgamation refining process, developed in Mexico in 1554, failed for reasons unknown but probably having to do with the cold and oxygen-starved atmosphere of Potosí.[14] As the mines ran deeper, the extraction of ore became more demanding and the ore itself yielded less when it was refined. The profits of the indios varas and the wages paid to the ayllu Indians fell as a result, while their labor became more strenuous. Many left Potosí to work elsewhere; others remained but occupied themselves in other endeavors. Of the 20,000 Indians living in the Villa Imperial in 1561, only 300 were working in the mines (down from nearly 5,000 the decade before).[15] The Spanish mine owners thus found themselves confronted by a labor shortage that had very little to do with the number of Indians living in their midst. Rather, the shortage had been caused by economic pressures on the Indian laborers, who had decided that their profits simply were no longer worth the toil required.

Labor shortages were met elsewhere in the Americas with the importation of black slaves. In the Caribbean, Brazil, and lowland Peru, blacks filled a labor vacuum in activities from sugar refining to gold mining. At Potosí, however, they were not a viable alternative: first, the cost of their importation would have to be borne by the mine owners, who were not prepared financially to do so; second, if the cost of their introduction were to be minimized, they would come directly from Brazil via the Río de la Plata and Tucumán, an illegal channel of trade that the Crown was not anxious to encourage; and third, they were thought to be unprepared physically to withstand the rigors of Potosí's elevation and cold climate, let alone the task of carrying ore out of the mines.[16]

Royal officials in Peru were quick to see that something had to be done if the Potosí silver mines were to be saved, and most of them agreed that some form of compulsory Indian labor was going to be necessary.[17] Philip II, however, held fast to his father's prohibition of forced Indian labor in mining. Toledo's instructions in this regard were clear:

> Given that the mines of Peru cannot be exploited using Spanish laborers, since those who are there will not work in them, and as it is said that slaves cannot withstand the work, owing to the nature and coldness of the land, it appears necessary to employ the Indians. Though these are not to be forced or compelled, as has already been ordered, they must be attracted with all just and reasonable means, so that there will be the required number of laborers for the mines. To this end, it seems that great care must be given to the settlement of large numbers of Indians in nearby towns and estates, so that they might more easily apply themselves to the work involved.[18]

The king's instructions continued with injunctions that the Indians be well paid and treated, work reasonable hours, and not be detained once their shifts had been completed. Good working conditions and ample wages would thus attract the required number of Indian laborers without the need for recourse to force, which was expressly forbidden. It was left to Toledo to formulate a specific program that satisfied these criteria.[19]

Toledo was a skilled administrator, extremely efficient and adept at playing opposing groups against one another to the advantage of his sovereign. Efficiency was the hallmark of his resettlement program, and the "divide and conquer" gambit proved immensely useful in the distribution of corregidores. These skills were of little use to him, however, in confronting the issue of a labor force for Potosí. The viceroy was faced with a dilemma: the king wanted the Indians to work voluntarily for wages, but they were unwilling to hire themselves out for the compensation they would receive.[20] Subtle means of persuasion had been tried at Potosí since their exodus began in the 1560's, but without success. The suggestion that Indian settlements be founded nearby was not feasible, moreover, because of the area's geography: situated 4,000 meters above sea level, without significant vegetation for 25 kilometers in any direction, parched for nine months of the year and inundated by torrential rains the remaining three, Potosí had an environment so inhospitable that it would have been a desert had it not been for the discovery of silver there.[21] (See Photo 1.) In-

PHOTO I. The city of Potosí today from the entrance to the COMIBOL (Bolivian Mining Company) mines.

deed, the Villa Imperial was dependent upon distant valley regions, such as Chuquisaca (the environs of La Plata), for its sustenance. Food and other products brought in from 150 kilometers away commanded astronomical prices, but the profits in the early years had made them affordable.[22] Those profits, however, were now past.

For lack of realistic alternatives to some form of forced Indian labor, the viceroy called a *junta consultiva* (advisory council) in Lima to consider the pros and cons of a draft labor system for Potosí in October 1570. This body concluded that "legitimately, and without injury to the Indians, His Majesty, and in his name his viceroy, may compel the Indians, in a determined number, to work in the mines at Potosí and elsewhere in Peru, given certain provisions for their good treatment, adequate and assured compensation, and moderate work."[23] The decision reached by the junta was not as significant a break with royal policy as it may at first seem. A 1552 *cédula* (royal edict) had permitted forced Indian labor in activities that were in the common interest, with the exception of mining enterprises. Guided by the persuasive arguments of an *oidor* (judge) from the Audiencia of La Plata, Juan de Matienzo, the junta took note that the Indians were already working in any number of legal and illegal activities under the direction of Spanish colonists, and concluded that their labor would be better employed in service to the Crown, which received one-fifth of mineral production in its dominions.[24]

Despite the junta consultiva's endorsement, Toledo set forth (on October 24, 1570) on a five-year inspection (visita) of Peru uncertain about the merits of forced Indian labor in the mines of Potosí.[25] At Huamanga he witnessed the workings of a system designed by Juan Polo de Ondegardo in 1562, whereby local kurakas were required to deliver 700 Indians per week for employment in local mining operations. Impressed by that system's success in mobilizing a reluctant Indian work force, the viceroy consented to its continuation, but he insisted on the incorporation of ordinances for the good treatment, adequate payment, and religious instruction of the Indian laborers, as well as on the exaction of the royal fifth (quinto real) of production, thus bringing it into line with the junta's resolution.[26] By the time he left Huamanga, therefore, Toledo had seen a possible prototype for a draft labor regimen for Potosí at work.

In 1572, while the viceroy was in Cuzco, he learned that one Pedro Fernández de Velasco, recently arrived from the viceroyalty of New Spain, had perfected an amalgamation refining process that promised to be employable even at Potosí. Toledo summoned Fernández to Cuzco to demonstrate his technique and, encouraged by the results of the experiments, pushed on to Potosí confident that the revival of the mining center was at hand. Indeed, he had also received reports while in Cuzco that immense piles of discarded rock (desmontes, or tailings) produced during the previous 27 years of mining at Potosí held sufficient ore to last for a hundred years.[27] This ore had eluded the capabilities of the guayra but was suitable for amalgamation processing.*

Toledo set forth for the Villa Imperial on October 22, 1572. Having already concluded that the introduction of amalgamation refining would spark the regeneration of the Potosí silver mines, the viceroy stopped en route to meet with the kurakas of ayllus who had sent Indians to the mining zone in earlier years and insisted that they do so again. The total required from Canas y Canches, just south of Cuzco, was one-seventh of the tributary population (males between the ages of 18 and 50; apparently the total determined by his census

---

* Indeed, it seems that the richest ore consumed so much mercury during processing as to be unprofitable.

takers, though some sources suggest that the pre-Columbian figures were used initially), and from communities closer to Potosí slightly more. The kurakas were assured by Toledo that the profits they had known in the first epoch of Potosí would be repeated, but despite this effort to win their cooperation, there is no doubt that the viceroy required their compliance with his request.[28] By the time he arrived in Potosí late in 1572, therefore, the viceroy had already taken the first steps toward the establishment of a draft labor regimen for the mining center. But it also seemed possible that coercion might not be needed for very long.

Once at Potosí, however, Toledo was dismayed to find that the tailings, though substantial, were far less extensive than he had been led to believe, and that the Spaniards still working the cerro were unenthusiastic about the future. Nevertheless, the viceroy believed that the introduction of amalgamation processing, the reserves of easily refinable ore, and the huge influx ("*un buen golpe*") of Indian laborers who would soon arrive would ensure the prompt revitalization of production. Before the Spanish mine owners would cooperate with the viceroy, however, they required specific guarantees. The shift to the new refining process would require a significant investment in the construction of the requisite mills, and the new technology and tailings themselves would be of little value in the long run, they told Toledo, unless they were assured sufficient numbers of Indians to work in the mines and mills, for wages that they could afford to pay.[29]

The viceroy accordingly entered into an agreement with the mine owners under which they would build the mills at their expense and he would provide them with mercury and Indian labor, both at reasonable cost. The Crown would receive the royal fifth of silver produced, a profit on the mercury sold at Potosí, and other tax revenues. The mill and mine owners (hereafter referred to as *azogueros*, as they came to be called—after *azogue*, mercury) would keep four-fifths of gross production less costs.[30]

The viceroy preserved for the Crown some leverage over the azogueros through the royal monopoly on mercury. He considered the possibility of claiming exclusive rights to the tailings, but opted instead for control of mercury because he believed that it could be more easily monitored and would provide a means for tracking output. It would also prove to be more enduring.[31] Royal orders to locate mercury deposits in the Americas that followed the development of the amalgamation refining method in New Spain had led to the discovery and exploitation of the mercury mines at Huancavelica in 1566. Even before leaving Cuzco in 1572, Toledo had ordered that the private holdings there be expropriated—in anticipation of the conversion of Potosí silver production to Fernández's process—and prohibited the shipment of mercury to New Spain.[32] Huancavelica's proximity to Lima also gave Toledo reason to believe that he would be able to make a royal monopoly on mercury effective.

Toledo's guarantee to the azogueros of laborers for their new mills meant the formal establishment of the Potosí mita. Toledo neither created a new system nor resurrected an Inca one; though there is an undeniable connection between the Inca *mit'a* and the Toledan mita, the viceroy simply marshaled the ideas and practices he had encountered either on his arrival or during his progress through Peru. His draft labor system followed the guidelines provided by the 1569 junta consultiva and closely resembled the institution that Toledo observed at Huamanga on his way to Alto Perú.[33]

The Potosí mita was inaugurated in the first months of 1573. The Indians whom the viceroy had called upon to resume their periods of service in the mines began to arrive: 1,300 were drafted from the regions surrounding La Paz, 500 from the province of Chucuito (to join an equally large complement already at Potosí), and various others from provinces as far away as Canas y Canches and as close as Porco (see Maps 1 and 2).[34] The obligated regions all shared Potosí's high elevation and cold climate, and were also those that were closest to the mining center and under Crown control. Areas on the frontier with unconquered Indians (such as the Chiriguanaes southeast of La Plata) or of lower elevation were exempted. Cities were also left untouched, for their Indian residents were needed for municipal labor drafts.[35]

A total of 4,300 Indians were called to Potosí under the terms of the 1573 draft, to swell the ranks of 4,200 ayllu Indians who had remained there to raise their communities' tribute and 900 or so yanaconas. Of the draftees (*mitayos*), 3,738 were assigned to work in the mines and mills (1,430 and 2,308, respectively), in three roughly equal weekly shifts.[36] During the two weeks when their shift was not working, the mitayos could, if they wished, engage in other enterprises or hire themselves out for wages. Nonetheless, the corregidor of Potosí was empowered by Toledo to assign up to 1,000 mitayos from among the two resting groups to those miners who required

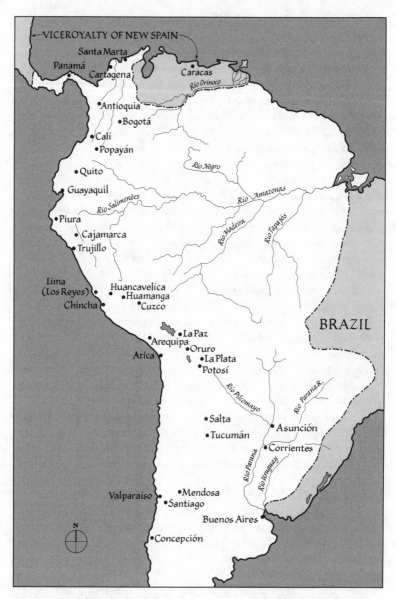

MAP I. *Hapsburg Peru.* Adapted from Cathryn L. Lombardi and John V. Lombardi, *Latin American History: A Teaching Atlas* (Madison: Univ. of Wisc. Press, 1984), p. 29.

MAP 2. *The Provinces of Alto Perú.* Adapted from Evans, p. 26; and Crespo, "Reclutamiento," p. 481. Province boundaries are approximate.

their assistance, on the premise that the profits generated by the renaissance of Potosí would soon cause these mitayos to work gladly.[37]

Toledo then departed for La Plata, where he drew together and published his ordinances for Potosí in 1574. When he returned to the Villa Imperial the following year, he was confronted by kurakas complaining that the corregidor was assigning more than the 1,000 Indians whom he was permitted, and that he had not drawn them on a prorated basis. The azogueros, it seemed, preferred some Indians to others, so that some ayllus found themselves working constantly, whereas others were left idle; the kurakas argued that the one-third fraction should be strictly enforced and the corregidor's powers be curtailed.[38]

In response to the increased demand for mitayos and the problems identified by the kurakas, Toledo devised a second mita charter (*repartimiento de la mita*) in October 1575, while in Arequipa. This time he drew varying percentages of Indians from various altiplano provinces, based on the number of tributaries documented by his census and on distance from Potosí: 17 percent from the region around La Plata; 16 percent from around La Paz; 15 percent from the environs of Cuzco; and 13 percent from Canas y Canches. Uros Indians, who lived throughout Alto Perú but primarily in the province of Chucuito, were considered less civilized and trustworthy than the Aymara majority, and were obliged to send two men for every mitayo drafted. Within each of the three weekly drafts (*mitas ordinarias*), 615 mitayos were assigned to the mines and 2,498 to the mills (either for their construction or for use in refining); others, assigned to support activities, brought the total to roughly 4,000 per week. The right of the corregidor to assign more was repealed.[39]

The viceroy's first priority was to provide sufficient numbers of Indians to work at Potosí, but since he was also concerned that the mita be attractive to the Indians and comply with the terms of the junta's ruling, he issued a series of orders for their good treatment and adequate compensation.[40] The mitayos were to serve one year, after which they were to return home. While in the mining zone, a given mitayo was to work one week and have the following two weeks to rest. Each Monday morning, those who were included in the weekly draft were to present themselves at Guayna—a smaller mound at the base of the cerro—for distribution to the azogueros and *soldados mineros* (miners who did not have a mill of their own). That afternoon, they would ascend to the mines or go to the mills, either in Potosí itself or in nearby Tarapaya.* (See Photo 2.) Work would then continue until Saturday evening, when the mitayos were to be paid their wages for the week.[41] Indians in the mines would earn three and

---

*Tarapaya is a valley region just northwest of Potosí, which enjoyed the benefit of a river, and thus a source of water for the refining mills. Eventually, the number of mills in operation there declined to a mere handful, because of the construction of reservoirs around the Villa Imperial and the difficulties involved in transporting ore from the cerro to Tarapaya.

PHOTO 2. The cerro of Potosí, with Guayna (topped by a small church) in the foreground.

one-half *reales* per day; those in the mills would receive two and three-quarter reales.[42] * No quotas were permitted.[43] Half-wages were to be paid for every day of travel from the home province to Potosí, based on a fixed number of leagues to be traveled each day.[44] While complying with their mita obligation, the Indians were to live in *rancherías* (small settlements) corresponding to their provinces of origin—a segregation meant to protect them from the designs of Spaniards, *criollos* (Hispano-Americans), mestizos, and others.[45] Two *veedores* (monitors) and an *alcalde mayor de minas* (chief magistrate for mining matters) were to assist a *protector de naturales* (natives' advocate) and six of the *capitanes enteradores* (kurakas who delivered the mitayos) in supervising the work in the mines and mills, and ensuring that the mitayos were not mistreated.[46]

The Indians were provided other incentives as well. They were to be taught the amalgamation refining process and one-third of the ore that was suitable for smelting in their guayras was to be distributed to them, so that the art would not be lost and the Indians' own profits would be augmented.[47] Their right to *kapcha*, moreover, permitted the mitayos to work in the mines for their own benefit from Saturday evening to Monday morning. The ore that they produced (plus what they secreted out of the mines during the week) was traded in the *ghatu* plaza of Potosí. This traffic in raw silver came to be known as *rescates*, and was originally the exclusive domain of the Indians.[48]

As one might expect, the degree to which these ordinances were obeyed was considerably less than that provided for by the viceregal orders. Nonetheless, Toledo clearly intended to restore the monetary incentives that had drawn the Indians to Potosí in its early period, while simultaneously justifying the establishment of the draft labor regimen. Mitayos from Cuzco or Chucuito may have had to travel for a month or two, covering up to a thousand kilometers to reach Potosí, but they had willingly done so in the 1540's and 1550's, when great profits awaited them at the end of their trek. Wages, travel allowances, the right to kapcha, and rescates were all meant to restore the economic incentive for the Indians to come and work at Potosí once again.[49] If the viceroy had given up hope that the need for compulsion might vanish altogether, at least the Indians' mita obligations would not rest too heavily on their shoulders, and the terms of the junta consultiva's accord would thereby be met.

---

*There were eight reales to a peso corriente; all monetary amounts in this study, unless otherwise noted, are expressed in pesos of eight reales.

The responsibility for delivering complete contingents of mitayos lay, according to Toledo's design, with the provincial corregidores. The corregidor of Potosí, meanwhile, was put in charge of directing the overall delivery (*entero*) of mitayos. In practice, however, the provincial officials depended upon the kurakas, for whereas the former had little real power over the Indians, the latter were quite effective. Under both Inca and Spanish dominion, the kurakas were able to muster the men and materials necessary to satisfy the demands made of their ayllus because in exchange they protected their communities from unreasonable exactions, organized the collection of surpluses in good years and their distribution in bad years, and maintained peace and harmony within their communities, always striving to ensure that the benefits of living within their pueblos outweighed the obligations. The importance of the kurakas to the delivery of the mitayos also stemmed from the communal nature of the mita, which was an obligation of the parcialidades (i.e., of the ayllus) and pueblos, not of individual Indians. This was in keeping with Andean tradition, for the Indians had contributed their labor to the Inca Empire in much the same manner. The kurakas therefore served as brokers between the Hapsburg Crown and the Indian community; as such, they were the crucial link in the mita's delivery mechanism.[50]

THROUGHOUT the 1570's, but especially after 1575, the combination of tailings, mercury, and mitayos met all of Toledo's expectations, and the Potosí silver industry enjoyed a spectacular renaissance (see Figure 1). When Juan de Matienzo conducted an inspection of the Villa Imperial in 1577, he marveled at the transformation that had taken place. The Spanish residents of Potosí had come to number 2,000—a tenfold increase over the previous decade—and the number of Indians living in the mining center had again reached 20,000. The azogueros, the Indians, and the Crown were all making handsome profits, Matienzo reported, because of the miraculous Toledan revitalization program.[51]

Three years after the 1575 repartimiento de la mita, most of the new amalgamation mills had been completed, a few had been abandoned, and some of the azogueros required more mitayos while others no longer deserved any. Another mita charter was drafted, this time in Lima, with Toledo basing the new distribution of mitayos on information supplied by government officials and private individuals in Potosí, including the results of Matienzo's inspection.[52] The

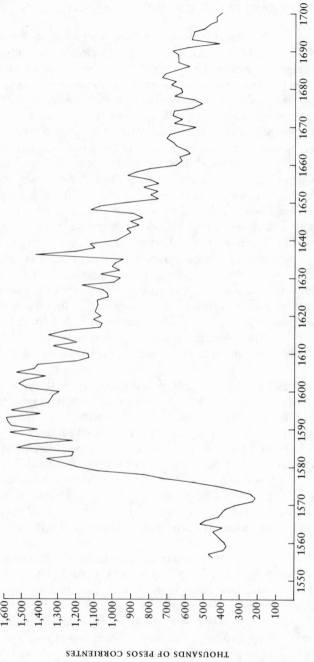

FIGURE 1. The Royal Share of Silver Marked at Potosí, 1556–1700 (factored in thousands of pesos corrientes). The royal share represents one-fifth of official silver production.

Source: Baquíjano y Carrillo, pp. 50–54.

annual draft (*mita gruesa*) grew to 14,296 Indians, with three weekly shifts of 4,426: 1,119 mitayos were assigned to work in the mines, 3,073 to the mills, and 234 to refine the tailings of the amalgamation process; the remainder of the annual draft—over 1,000 Indians—was reserved for allocation to deserving individuals, many of whom were engaged in mining at Porco. In addition, 200 mitayos were to be provided each month for employment in support activities; these came to be known as *indios meses* because the term of their service was one month. The Uros, meanwhile, had proven just as reliable as the Aymaras and were now obliged to send only 11 percent of their tributary population to Potosí each year.[53] A total of seventeen provinces were obligated: Chichas, Porco, Chayanta, Cochabamba, Paria, Carangas, Sicasica, Pacajes, Omasuyos, Chucuito, Paucarcolla, Lampa, Asangaro, Canas y Canches (counts as two; also known separately as Canas and Tintacanches), Quispicanches, and Condesuyos.[54] The 1578 repartimiento was itself revised in 1580, after irregularities in the distribution of mitayos had come to the attention of the viceroy, but Toledo left for Spain before implementing his fourth mita charter.[55] Nevertheless, the mita was clearly not established by the viceroy once and expected to function efficiently thereafter. Toledo had implemented three separate repartimientos (including the original), each time refining the system in the light of recent developments at Potosí.

The question arises of whether the mita was necessary at all. Given the profits generated by the introduction of amalgamation processing and the availability of tailings, would not enough volunteer laborers (*mingas*) have gravitated to Potosí without the mita, as they had before? It seems clear that the mita was necessary at its inception for three main reasons. First, it served as an incentive and a guarantee for the mine owners to build the new mills and commit themselves to silver production on a long-term basis. Second, it provided the labor necessary to build the new amalgamation refining mills. Third, it created a pool of unskilled ore carriers (*apiris*) to work in the mines, producing silver ore to supplement the tailings; mingas generally refused to do that sort of work or required hefty wages for it.[56] The mita also proved to be a source of additional mingas, at least at the start, from among Indians who stayed on after their year of service was complete, either to reap personal profits or to pay off debts they had incurred while mitayos.[57] Since the mitayos also brought products from their home provinces to sell or trade at Potosí, the mita was also a stimulus to commerce in the Villa Imperial.[58]

As the pace of work at Potosí increased, the need for draft labor did not evaporate, as Toledo had originally expected, largely because the mingas could choose the less onerous jobs in the mining zone—the demand for their services growing with rising production—and mitayos had to be pressed into service in the harder, more dangerous work within the mines and mills (in the mills, they were used primarily in the grinding of the ore). Indeed, with the 1578 repartimiento, Toledo virtually admitted that the mita would continue to be an integral part of the silver production formula.

Before moving on, mention needs to be made of the fact that similar draft Indian labor systems were introduced in New Spain at roughly the same time. As we have seen, too, in Peru such systems in nonmining activities predated the Potosí mita. Toledo had not created any sort of monster in the Potosí mita, nor had he damned the native population of Alto Perú. The tasks assigned to the Indians who served in the mita were not unlike those performed by vassals of the Hapsburgs elsewhere, including Iberia and Austria. Whatever the mita later became, it was not especially unusual at its inception.

Ten years after Toledo had first set foot in Peru, Potosí was a prosperous industrial center, with everything from the extraction of ore to the minting of coins performed there.[59] The industrialization of Potosí silver production involved substantial changes, however, that would later prove extremely important. The first was the center's new dependency on adequate supplies of mercury, which arrived via a lifeline extending from Huancavelica to Chincha, by sea to Arica, and overland again to Potosí.[60] The second change was the commitment on the part of the azogueros to Potosí silver production on an extended basis. By virtue of their 3-million-peso investment in the construction of 132 refining mills, they had evolved from low-investment, low-risk mine owners into industrial businessmen with property and interests to protect.[61] Third, silver production now required considerable supplies of water, which in a climate notorious for its all-or-nothing rainfall meant the construction of expensive reservoirs. Some 300,000 pesos were spent on the Cari Cari and San Pablo *lagunas* alone, and 280,000 pesos on five others. These costs, like those for constructing the mills, were borne entirely by the azogueros; the labor was provided by the mitayos.[62]

The fourth and most significant change, however, especially in terms of its eventual impact on Potosí, was that control of silver production had been removed from the Indians. In the earlier period, the

Indians had mined the ore and refined it in their guayras. Despite all the perquisites that Toledo had included in his mita, the Indians in the post-1573 period were merely wage earners, whether they were mitayos or mingas. Silver production was now controlled jointly by the viceregal administration (with its direction of the mita and monopoly on the provisioning of mercury) and the azogueros (with their ownership of the mills and supervision of the refining process).[63]

Removed as controlling interests, the Indians were nevertheless vital to the continued production of silver at Potosí. The government and the azogueros relied upon the kurakas to deliver the mitayos, thereby making the kurakas the linchpins of the entire system. The Indians, however, would cooperate with their kurakas only as long as their wages, right to kapcha, and rescates were sufficient compensation for their hard work; and they would remain in their pueblos only as long as the benefits of residence there outweighed the obligations. Indeed, when the Indians' own profits at Potosí again fell below an acceptable level, the Crown, the azogueros, and even the kurakas discovered just how difficult it was to make them work against their will.

Finally, we must note that Francisco de Toledo returned to Spain in 1581 without ever receiving royal confirmation of the mita. Philip II gave his hesitant consent to the establishment of draft Indian labor systems in other, nonmining sectors of the Peruvian economy in 1584, but he withheld his support for that at Potosí.[64] Despite the key role of the mita in the resurrection of Potosí silver production, the Crown's historical opposition to the system was reinforced by reports it received from nonmining interests, who competed with the azogueros for access to Indian labor, led by the Audiencias of Lima and of La Plata (the latter also known as the Audiencia of Charcas). The Lima tribunal was infuriated by Toledo's expropriation of the Huancavelica mercury mines, for its members were interested parties there. The judges in La Plata were similarly involved in agricultural enterprises in Chuquisaca and had been prohibited any stake in mining by the viceroy. The Audiencias voiced their opposition to the mita in official correspondence not by stating their true objections but by exaggerating the evils of the system to play upon the royal concern for the Indians' conservation.[65] The judges' charges were sufficiently convincing to keep Philip II from responding favorably to Toledo's repeated requests for confirmation. The viceroy wrote to the Council of the Indies in 1576, after it had undertaken an investigation of the system, that without the mita there would be no Potosí, and without Potosí there would be no Peru. In 1578, he challenged the king to consider whether he was prepared to do without his share of the silver produced by the mitayos.[66] Philip II never countermanded the viceroy, but he steadfastly refused him royal approval for the Potosí mita.

Indeed, the Crown's acceptance of the mita did not come until 1589, fully sixteen years after its inauguration. The Viceroy Conde del Villar (1585–90) was then instructed to follow Toledo's program for drafting Indians to work in the mines of Potosí. Philip II's decision to relinquish his implacable opposition to the mita was prompted by the high cost of his diverse foreign campaigns—the annexation of Portugal and its empire in 1580; his determination to subjugate the Netherlands and to protect them from Calvinism; his support for the Stuarts in their struggle with Elizabeth I of England, resulting in the naval disaster in the Channel in 1588; and his ill-fated support for the Catholic Guise family in France—and the degree to which these adventures depended upon silver shipments from the Indies.[67] The king's consent was predicated officially upon the lack of alternative labor sources and the therapeutic value of work for the otherwise lazy and frivolous Indians, and it was contingent upon their good treatment, religious instruction, and general conservation.[68] Nonetheless, the issue of the mita's justness was thereby inexorably linked to the need for revenue in Spain; and that relationship was destined to condition the government's approach to the mita during the next 125 years.

THOUGH THE METAMORPHOSIS of the mita during its first century and a quarter of existence is the principal focus of this study, the Hapsburg administration's efforts to keep pace with the changing situation at Potosí are also considered at length. The latter subject has important implications for the portrait of Hapsburg government first offered by John Leddy Phelan in his article "Authority and Flexibility in the Spanish Imperial Bureaucracy"[69] and developed in his subsequent publications. Central to Phelan's thesis was the contention that the Crown employed contradictory and mutually exclusive orders to maintain its authority over the colonial bureaucracy. Phelan argued, using the Indian labor question in late-sixteenth-century New Spain as a case in point, that the Crown's orders both for the preservation of the Indians and for the promotion of mineral production were typical of this phenomenon. The officials who received the orders were compelled, he said, to determine their sovereign's true intentions and to enforce them to the fullest extent possible given local reality.

Local officials were able to apply the mutually exclusive royal edicts selectively, Phelan maintained, because of the flexibility afforded them by the "*obedezco pero no cumplo*" ("I obey but do not comply") formula. Loyalty to the Crown was defined in Castilian law in terms not of blind obedience but of service to one's sovereign both as his eyes and ears and as his arms. Indeed, officials in the field were expected to provide the detailed information on which future royal cédulas would be based, and they could suspend any order that they deemed likely to create an injustice or undesirable social conflict on the grounds that the Crown had been deprived of adequate and/or accurate information. The suspension remained in effect until the Crown reviewed the matter in the light of the new data provided by the local officials. It could then reissue the edict in its original form or dispatch some modified version, but the officials retained the right to suspend any new directive under the same criteria.

The extent to which local officials might exploit the flexibility inherent in this system (i.e., the possibility of their burying an unwanted edict in bureaucratic processes) was limited by their being monitored by other government officials whose jurisdictions overlapped their own (including churchmen), by *visitadores* (inspectors), and ultimately by the *residencias* (reviews) conducted at the end of their terms in office. Furthermore, because local officials were unable to comply simultaneously with all of their instructions, they were ever vulnerable to reprimand or dismissal and thus attentive to the Crown's wishes. According to Phelan, the royal cédulas were Hegelian theses and the officials' responses antitheses, with the resulting government actions being syntheses. The continual interplay of theses and antitheses did indeed preserve the Crown's authority and the fealty of its officials, he argued, but it also created a bureaucracy that was very conservative and unreceptive to new ideas, and thus one that was unable to adapt to changing conditions.

The 125 years of Hapsburg administration of the mita described in this study yield many examples of the bureaucratic processes noted by Phelan. Indeed, we have already seen them at work during the viceroyalty of Francisco de Toledo. But Phelan's thesis cannot explain all of the bureaucratic gambits involved in the direction of the Potosí mita. We shall see, for example, that the Crown's mutually exclusive cédulas had another purpose beyond, but not necessarily inconsistent with, the goal of managing its bureaucracy: to advance the Crown's position vis-à-vis local elites.

In *The Kingdom of Quito in the Seventeenth Century*, Phelan subsequently argued that the bureaucracy in America was the only local elite, that there was no equivalent to the medieval nobility with which the Crown had been forced to contend in Iberia.[70] In Alto Perú that was not so, for the encomenderos (whom he dismissed in the case of Quito) and the azogueros of Potosí were both very much like the independent-minded nobility of medieval Iberia, and their independence was enhanced by their geographic isolation from the centers of royal authority, Madrid and Lima.

As we have seen, the Crown created a privileged class at Potosí, the azogueros, by confirming the creation of the mita. The azogueros received access to forced Indian labor and other guarantees from Viceroy Francisco de Toledo in exchange for their capital investment in the construction of new amalgamation refining mills and long-term commitment to the Potosí silver industry. But unlike the conquistadores who became encomenderos, the government had to grant the mine owners concessions before they would consent to become azogueros. More importantly, the mita, unlike the encomienda, was also part of an agreement between the Crown and the azogueros to share thereafter the profits of the Potosí silver industry; the Crown would contribute mercury and the administration of the mita, the azogueros would build and operate the mines and mills.

Not only had the Crown created a privileged class, it had also indicated that its first priority was the production of royal revenue. The conservation of the Indians remained an important concern, but it was clearly secondary. Once the Crown had confirmed the creation of the mita, however, it began to learn that the azogueros were abusing the terms of their agreement. Indeed, the struggle that developed between the government and the azogueros in the seventeenth century was to be a dispute between partners over control of the silver industry. The Crown was at a distinct disadvantage, for it was isolated by distance and time from the Villa Imperial, and had to rely on its colonial bureaucracy. The azogueros were much more effective, but they would come to have problems in controlling the Indians similar to those the Crown would have with them.

TWO

The Metamorphosis of the Mita, 1580-1680

JUST AS in its first decade, the form of the Potosí mita continued to change during the remainder of its 250-year existence. And just as Francisco de Toledo had been compelled periodically to adapt the system to the changing needs of the silver industry and the kurakas, so too did the mita require viceregal adjustment following his departure for Spain. However, subsequent viceroys proved less able, or less willing, than Toledo to keep pace with the changing reality in the mining zone, and thus the distance between official policy regarding the mita and the actual regimen widened throughout most of the Hapsburg period.

The first major transformation of the mita took place as a result of the exhaustion of the tailings in the late 1570's. Juan de Matienzo noted that the stockpiles of easily refinable ore had already been consumed at the time of his inspection of the Villa Imperial in 1577, and he reported that the apiris were extracting slag from within the mines for refining in the mills. That solution was clearly an interim one; the mills soon came to depend entirely on freshly mined ore. As a result, more and more mitayos were forced to work within the cerro, and the one-third fraction of the weekly draft assigned to that task by Toledo swelled to three-quarters and more.[1] The mitayos became an even more critical element in the silver production formula, but their increased importance was not accompanied by an improvement in their working conditions.

As the mines plunged deeper into the cerro, the work grew harder and accidents became more common. Mitayos were buried in cave-ins, suffered broken limbs in falls, and succumbed to respiratory disease—pneumoconiocis.[2] Father José de Acosta, an observer of the 1590's, described the apiris' life within the mines:

> They labor in these mines in perpetual darkness, not knowing day from night. And since the sun never penetrates to these places, they are not only always dark but very cold, and the air is very thick and alien to the nature of men; so that those who enter for the first time get as sick as at sea—which happened to me in one of these mines, where I felt a pain at the heart and a churning in the stomach. The [apiris] always carry candles to light their way, and they divide their labor in such a way that some work by day and rest by night, and others work by night and rest by day. The ore is generally hard as flint, and they break it up with iron bars. They carry the ore on their backs up ladders made of three cords of twisted rawhide joined by pieces of wood that serve as rungs, so that one man may climb up and another down at the same time. These ladders are twenty meters long, and at the top and bottom of each is a wooden platform where the men may rest, because there are so many ladders to climb. Each man usually carries on his back a load of twenty-five kilograms of silver ore tied in a cloth, knapsack fashion; thus they ascend, three at a time. The one who goes first carries a candle tied to his thumb, . . . thus, holding on with both hands, they climb that great distance, often more than 300 meters—a fearful thing, the mere thought of which inspires dread.[3]

Toledo had ordered a maximum of two trips per day for the apiris, but as early as the 1580's as many as 25 were made. During the 1590's, the common daily quota (*tarea*) was nineteen loads (*montones*)—this despite the fact that quotas themselves had been prohibited by the viceroy.[4] To complicate matters further, springs within the mountain flooded many of the richer mines. Some of these had to be abandoned, but others were worked by mitayos in knee-deep water. This practice too was illegal, but it continued nonetheless, and pneumonia regularly struck the mitayos who worked under such conditions.[5]

The mitayos' lot was made still worse by their treatment at the hands of *mayordomos* and *pongos* (white and Indian foremen, respectively). The Indians were whipped, beaten, struck with rocks, made to carry heavy loads on their backs, and forced to work both day and night and on Sunday—all to fill their weekly quotas.[6] By 1590, the mitayos no longer received two weeks of rest for every one they worked, and of those who were supposedly "resting," 200 continued to be obliged to serve as indios meses under Viceroy Martín

Enríquez's 1582 repartimiento de la mita and subsequent mita charters.[7] By the seventeenth century, the three-to-one relationship between the weekly draft and the annual draft had collapsed completely.

Ill treatment and the increased pressure on the mitayos to produce more silver ore were the product of the azogueros' efforts to
maintain the substantial profits of the late 1570's and early 1580's
without the benefit of the tailings. Many of the azogueros found
themselves squeezed between increasing production costs and de-
creasing amounts and quality of ore. Others had overextended themselves by pouring their initial profits into further construction, or had
otherwise spent the money made during the boom period.

The availability of mercury was a perennial problem. The price per
quintal (hundredweight) did not change appreciably (in fact, it fell
gradually from 85 to about 65 pesos), but more was needed to refine
the poorer ore, and the early practice of distribution on credit was
halted in the light of unpaid debts. Other production elements—
transport, wood, salt, copper, iron, etc.—also cost more by 1600.
Labor costs climbed as the azogueros sent most of their mitayos into
the mines to work as apiris and hired mingas to take their places
in the mills, as well as to work as *barreteros* (pickmen; probably former indios varas) within the cerro; mingas demanded substantially
higher wages than those paid to the mitayos. The azogueros petitioned the government to assign them more mitayos, to provide them
with mercury at a lower price and on credit, and to reduce the royal
share of production from a fifth to a tenth (the *diezmo*), but their
requests went unfulfilled.[8]

The total level of silver production at Potosí did not fall substantially until the early years of the seventeenth century, but to maintain
a high level of production, the resourcefulness of the azogueros and
the endurance and patience of the mitayos were sorely tested. Travel
allowances were not paid to the mitayos, and their wages were withheld in part or in their entirety.[9] Many of the day-to-day expenses of
mining, such as the cost of candles for the apiris, were pushed onto
the Indians themselves.[10] The right to kapcha and the trade in rescates
were attacked by the azogueros, who charged the Indians with steal-
ing the richest ore, either by sneaking it out of the mines during the
week or by stockpiling it until Sunday, when they could take it for
themselves.[11] Some of the azogueros also balanced their higher costs
by selling or renting a portion of their mitayos. The best of the lot
were kept, but those who were older, feeble, or uncooperative were

sent to other mining camps, farms, textile mills, and other enter-prises. The demand for Indian labor in Alto Perú was such that these "loaners" brought the azogueros 150 pesos apiece annually and more. The money was used to fund abridged yet lucrative operations (i.e., to ensure substantial profit margins). Indeed, some of the azogueros found it best not to produce any silver at all, but lived instead off the income generated by the sale and rental of their mitayos.[12]

The deterioration of the mitayos' condition at Potosí did not bring about their wholesale destruction, despite the assertions of a few well-publicized contemporary treatises on the subject.* The Indians did not permit the mita to exterminate them; to suggest that it did is to attribute more control over them to the azogueros or the kurakas than either in fact exercised. Rather, the Indians responded to the worsening situation in the mines by using every available means to evade the mita. Some avoided further periods of service, ironically enough, by staying in Potosí once their year's service had been ful-filled, for the Villa Imperial was exempt from mita recruitment. Still more escaped to other cities or mining zones, or to farms, ranches, and distant valleys. Those few mitayos who did return to their homes after a year in Potosí often discovered that their lands and homes had been sold by their kurakas during their absence, and were forced to look elsewhere for employment.[13]

Most of the Indians would not return to their original pueblos, however, because they suffered an oppression there that was simi-

---

* Cañete y Domínguez, pp. 115–16, dismisses exaggerated contemporary estimates of population loss caused by the mita. The cream of the crop is Friar Antonio de la Calancha's *Crónica moralizada . . . de la provincia del Perú* [1638 or 1639]; Calancha argued that ten Indians died for every peso of silver produced at Potosí. Ayanz's "Breve relación . . ." is one of many more responsible antimita treatises. Unfortunately, the wild charges of Calancha and others are those that the popular press continues to re-peat (e.g., Simon et al., "The Man-eating Mountain"). In the 1580's, Luis Capoche estimated that 50 mitayos died each year (Zavala, *Servicio personal*, vol. 1, p. 165). A century later, Corregidor Pedro Luis Enríquez investigated Potosí's parish registers for deaths and births and found that between 1677 and 1681, some 1,534 men had died (of all causes) while 3,545 boys had been born; and that 1,226 women had died while 2,938 girls had been born. He noted that women did not serve in the mita, and so concluded that death in the mines was not a significant cause of mortality among the men (Enríquez to the Crown, Potosí, Jan. 24, 1682, AGI, Charcas, leg. 270, no. 5). The most significant demographic impact of the mita was the promotion of Indian mi-gration, as Alberto Crespo has argued since 1955; in addition to his articles, see Sánchez-Albornoz, "Migraciones internas" (comparing the 1645 census of the Viceroy Marqués de Mancera to the figures derived under Toledo) and "Mita, migraciones, y pueblos" (incorporating the results of the 1680's *numeración general de indios*—see Chap. 6 below for a discussion of this census); see also Evans.

lar to that at Potosí. They were forced to work for their kurakas, corregidores, and priests in transport, agricultural activities, animal husbandry, and small industry. They had to buy goods that they did not need and pay tribute to boot. And they faced the prospect of future service in the mines at Potosí. In exchange, they received continued access to their own and community lands, and the security and psychological support offered by their ayllu. In the pull between their identity—defined in terms of their ayllu—and the demands foisted on them within their pueblos and at Potosí, most of the Indians opted to sacrifice the former and leave home. Some migrants left the colonized zone altogether and joined the ranks of the unconquered "infidels," but most simply made their way to cities or to rural agricultural enterprises, the owners of which offered them security and land in exchange for their labor. The Spanish *estancieros* (ranchers) and *chacareros* (farm owners) became the migrants' new patrons, therefore, because they could protect the Indians from the mita, unlike the kurakas.[14]

Indian migration was the mita's principal legacy,[15] and it was unwittingly encouraged by Toledan ordinances that had been meant to make the mita more acceptable to the Indians. For example, the mitayos were given two months' notice before their departure for Potosí, so that they might put their affairs in order and provide for their families; the warning actually gave them time to escape.[16] Once absent from their home pueblos, the Indians became *forasteros*—nonlandowning outsiders whose lack of property freed them from the mita and full tribute payments—even if they only moved from one pueblo within the mita provinces to another.[17] Outsider status, moreover, was hereditary, so that Indians born away from their ancestors' original pueblo were also forasteros. Designed to lessen the weight of the mita on the Indians, these provisions hampered its effectiveness. As some Indians fled from their pueblos and others failed to return from Potosí, those who remained were obliged to meet the lion's share of their pueblos' responsibilities (in some cases, absent Indians or their employers contributed money in partial compensation for their lost services). The increased pressure on the remaining original residents (*originarios*) encouraged them, in turn, to join the exodus.[18]

As fewer mitayos arrived in Potosí from the obligated pueblos, which no longer housed sufficient numbers of originarios to fill the required levies, the Indians already in the Villa Imperial were forced by their kurakas to serve longer, prompting them to flee. The kurakas also denied the mitayos the prescribed rest periods, and delivered younger and older men than the Toledan ordinances permitted.[19] The kurakas abused the system in these ways to keep the mitayo-craving azogueros from punishing them, but the result was even greater pressure on the mitayos in Potosí and on the originarios in the obligated provinces, and thus the acceleration of Indian flight in an increasingly more vicious circle.

The product of this massive migration away from the Toledan pueblos was the evident "depopulation" that many contemporary observers described. Of course, other factors contributed to the decline of the Indian population of those settlements, most notably epidemics of smallpox, measles, influenza, and typhus. Many pueblos were consumed by a series of epidemics in the late 1580's and early 1590's, and even Potosí—usually spared the ravages of epidemic disease, despite dense settlement, because of its cold climate—was hit hard.[20] Moreover, the psychological impact of the conquest affected the Indian population through lowered rates of reproduction. We must remember also that the influx of Spaniards and blacks into the viceroyalty resulted in widespread miscegenation, and with each new mestizo or mulatto, a potential addition to the Indian community was lost.

The relationship between the mita and the depopulation of the Indian pueblos of Alto Perú is therefore a complicated matter. The mita was not the only factor contributing to Indian migration, and migration was not the only reason for the loss of tributaries within the pueblos. Nonetheless, the lower number of originarios in the obligated provinces and the deteriorating conditions in the mines at Potosí certainly caused the original and intended form of the mita to break down entirely. Travel allowances were not paid, quotas were common, and wages were withheld. Indians and their kurakas were beaten, whipped, and otherwise intimidated. The fractions employed by Toledo—one-seventh of the originarios from a province, one-third of the annual draft for the weekly draft, and one-third of the weekly draft for the mines—all crumbled under the pressure. Every provision for the good treatment of the mitayos was routinely disobeyed. At the same time, the conditions in the mines were worse and the obligated provinces were less able to support mita recruitment.

THOUGH THE CHANGES in the mita between 1580 and 1600 were dramatic, those in the seventeenth century were so great as to create

TABLE 1

Indian Workers in the Potosí Silver Industry, 1603

Type and Activity	Number
Mitayos working in the mines	4,000
Mingas working in the mines	600
Mingas involved in cleaning the ore (young men earning one peso per day)	400+
Indians (men and women) sorting the ore at the mine entrances	1,000
Mitayos working in the mills	600
Mingas working in the mills (for seven reales per day)	4,000
Indians (men and women) refining *lamas* (the mixture of mercury and ground ore) for one peso per day	3,000
Indians working with llamas, carrying the ore from the mines to the mills	320
Indians bringing salt to Potosí	180
Mingas bringing salt to Potosí	1,000
Indian merchants bringing wood	1,000
Indians bringing firewood	1,000
Indians bringing llama dung for fuel	500
Indians bringing llama dung for fuel in melting the lamas	200
Indians making and bringing charcoal	1,000
Indians making candles	200
TOTAL	19,000+

SOURCE: "Descripción (1603)," p. 377.

a system totally different from anything that Toledo could have imagined. A source that illustrates just how much had changed even by 1603, and that incidentally lays the foundation for the mita's evolution in the 1600's, is an anonymous description of the Indian work force in the Potosí silver industry.[21] Table 1 provides a breakdown of the various categories of Indians said by that source to be employed in the Potosí silver industry. To the total of 19,000+ found in the table, however, should be added the 10,000 who were engaged in transporting food from Tomina, Cochabamba, Petantora, Chuquisaca, and elsewhere, plus the families of workers and enough other Indian residents to arrive at the more than 60,000 Indians we know to have lived in the Villa Imperial (a 1611 census documented 76,000).[22] Less than one-third, therefore, were involved in any way with mining itself, and only one-twelfth were mitayos.

As Bakewell points out, a resident Indian population sufficient to meet the silver industry's need for labor—the goal advocated by the Audiencia of La Plata and Philip II in the 1570's—existed at Potosí by the early seventeenth century, for the rancherías in aggregate held many more Indians than were needed to work the mines and mills.[23] A free, resident Indian labor force had been promoted as an alternative to compulsory labor, but the 1603 description verifies that the need for the mita sprang not from a lack of available manpower but from the Indians' unwillingness to perform the tasks assigned to them, especially those within the mines. Of the 4,600 mitayos included in Table 1, 4,000 worked in the cerro as apiris, producing the ore upon which the well-being of everyone else at Potosí depended. The mitayos were therefore more important to the silver industry than their relative numbers might suggest, and given the huge numbers of Indians involved in sustaining the city at the beginning of the seventeenth century, the mitayos were also the core of a regional economy involving most of Alto Perú.

While the mitayos were busy carrying ore, mingas performed the skilled tasks in the Potosí silver industry. Not all mingas were skilled workers, to be sure, for many mitayos hired themselves out as mingas during their infrequent weeks of rest. Nevertheless, as Bakewell has ably demonstrated, the two-tier division of labor characteristic of the first Potosí mining enterprises survived the introduction of the mita: the draft laborers provided the unskilled labor and resident volunteers performed those tasks that were less taxing physically and more profitable.[24] Again, the shortage was not of Indians at Potosí, but rather of Indians who would willingly enter the mines to work as apiris. The 600 mingas who served in that capacity—probably "resting" mitayos for the most part—demanded as much as a peso and a half (twelve reales) per day in wages, and the barreteros commanded twice that amount. The mitayos, meanwhile, received less in a week than a barretero did in a day—a mere two and one-half pesos (twenty reales)—and they had to contribute a half-peso per week to pay the veedores and alcalde mayor de minas.[25] Thus, the mita was not only central to the extraction of ore, it was also an important subsidy, saving the azogueros five pesos per week per apiri.

For the Indians who served as apiris during the seventeenth century, life was very harsh indeed. The mitayos would assemble each Monday at Guayna, where they would sit about, segregated into corrals according to their provinces of origin, while the corregidor, veedores, azogueros, and kurakas went about the business of dividing up the available manpower. As they awaited their assignments, the Indians drank *chicha* (maize beer) and wine, and chewed coca. Finally, sometime after noon, the alcohol-pacified mitayos were taken to the mines or mills to which they had been assigned for the week.[26]

Once inside the cerro, the apiris rarely saw the light of day, except for their brief appearances at the mouths of the mine shafts with their loads of ore. They were divided into three groups, with one working while the other two rested (the shifts were marked by the time required to consume one candle). Halfway through the week, at Thursday noon, the wives of the mitayos appeared with warm meals for them. For the rest of the week they were dependent upon the rations provided by their mayordomos and pongos, and, for lack of adequate provisions, on coca. The Indians were forced, as they had been in the sixteenth century, to produce quotas of ore or suffer whippings, other physical abuse, extended periods of service, or lost wages.[27] A case in point was Alonso Pucho, whose bag of ore sprang a leak while he was carrying it from a mine to a mill; he was punished with blows to his head and legs. Another apiri, Juan Azero, was forced to work in an unbuttressed tunnel, and a cave-in smashed his leg; he later died in the hospital. Finally, on Saturday evening, the apiris returned down the side of the cerro to the rancherías below. The following morning, after mass, they received their wages for the week. The next day, the entire process began anew.[28]

Indians who were injured while serving in the mita were supposed to be paid two reales per day while they were recuperating. In fact, however, they were forced to hire mingas to take their places, even after the Audiencia of La Plata ruled, in 1615, that injured and dead mitayos were not to be replaced under any circumstances. If a mitayo died in the hospital, moreover, his wife and children were forced to hire a minga substitute or to serve in his stead. Hospitalized mitayos and their families were further preyed upon by priests, who charged exorbitant sums for religious services and demanded devastating compensation for funerals.[29]

The mitayos' meager wages were not enough to meet their needs. The trade in rescates was illegal and suppressed by 1600, and those Indians who did involve themselves in it had to compete with Spaniards, criollos, and others. Only by working as mingas during their occasional off-weeks could they hope to feed themselves and their families. But as the number of rest weeks fell, the mitayos' opportunities to keep pace with their expenses also fell; hence their wives

and children often came to work alongside them, to aid in the fulfill-
ment of their quotas. The *protectores de naturales* of Potosí sent numerous petitions to Lima asking the viceroys to lower the cost of
necessities in the Villa Imperial, and especially the price of food, but
their efforts were fruitless. Desperate for food, the Indians at times
resorted to eating their own llamas.[30]

Under these circumstances, it is hardly surprising that the Indians continued to evade mita service by every conceivable means.
Their principal way of doing so continued to be flight from Potosí
and from their "original" pueblos. The number of Indians living in
those pueblos, moreover, continued to be affected during the seventeenth century by diseases and by the attraction of a growing number
of competing enterprises.[31] The ever falling number of originarios in
the villages and the deteriorating working conditions at Potosí soon
made it impossible for the kurakas to satisfy the azogueros' demands
for mitayos. This is not to say that the kurakas were negligent, for
they often went to extraordinary lengths to regain the services of just
a few Indians. Their efforts were foiled, however, by the ability of the
Indians and their new patrons to protect them from reincorporation
into their original ayllus. The difficulties faced by the kurakas can
best be described with a number of examples.

In 1608, the *kuraka principal* of Puna, Francisco Michaca, complained to the Audiencia of La Plata that a Spaniard named Pedro
Andrada Sotomayor was holding four Indians from his pueblo on a
farm with the intention of renting them at Potosí. A local judge
ordered Andrada to return the Indians to the kuraka's custody,
but Andrada countered with evidence that the four had lived on his
farm for 30 years, thus invoking viceregal orders by Luis de Velasco
(1596–1604) and the Conde de Monterrey (1604–6) that any Indian who was resident in one place for ten years could not be returned to his original pueblo against his will. Andrada denied, moreover, that he had any intention of renting the Indians in the Villa
Imperial. The Audiencia apparently settled the matter, though its decision in the case is lost to us; what is important for us to note is the
ability of a Spanish landowner to protect the Indians who had come
into his employ.[32]

The position of Indians working on agricultural estates was complicated by the fact that Francisco de Toledo had assigned many
yanaconas to those enterprises. In compensation, they and their descendants—*yanaconaje*, like forastero status, was hereditary—were

exempted from mita service. Cognizant of the advantages of being a yanacona, Indian refugees who worked for estancieros or chacareros assumed the title, with the consent and collaboration of their employers. By the early seventeenth century, it was virtually impossible to verify which Indians on agricultural estates were legitimate yanaconas and which were imposters.[33] The Jesuit colleges at Juli and Arequipa enjoyed the services of yanaconas on their estates. They had obtained the rights to those Indians when the lands to which they were assigned were acquired from the private grantees. Throughout the seventeenth century, the Jesuits skillfully foiled the efforts of kurakas who attempted to include their Indians in mita contingents.[34]

Landowners were not the only ones to protect their Indians. In a case from 1682–83, the capitán enterador for Caquiaviri, Francisco Quispi, vied with the San Francisco convent at Potosí for the services of an Indian named Pascual Huanca. The Franciscans objected to Quispi's efforts to make Huanca serve in the mita on the grounds that because Huanca had married the daughter of a yanacona, and as Toledo had ordered that husbands should live with their wives' ayllus, then he too must be considered a yanacona (and exempt from the mita). Pascual Huanca was jailed for a time, but he was released after his father-in-law pledged to produce him when a decision was reached in the dispute. Corregidor Pedro Luis Enríquez then ruled that Huanca would have to serve in the mita until the Audiencia of La Plata made a definitive ruling in the case, for Quispi was obliged to hire a minga for every week that Huanca did not serve. Huanca was nowhere to be found, however, and the efforts to force his father-in-law to pay for the minga dragged on. Again, the final resolution of the case is not included with its documentation, but the frustrations that the kuraka suffered are testimony to the ability of other interests to protect Indians from the mita.[35]

The Audiencia's traditional opposition to the Potosí mita no doubt contributed to its willingness to hear the cases of Indians who were attempting to evade service in the Villa Imperial. But kurakas also had difficulties with provincial and city-based corregidores. In 1634, the capitán enterador for Pacajes, Gabriel Fernández Guarachi, was frustrated in his attempt to deliver the province's mita contingent for 1634 by the corregidor of La Paz. Fernández Guarachi spent most of 1633 rounding up Indians with the assistance of other kurakas. To ensure that the captured Indians would be on hand when the contingent was dispatched, Fernández kept them locked up in a La Paz

jail. The kuraka's task was nearly complete when the corregidor, re-
fusing to honor the commission that Fernández had obtained from
the Audiencia of La Plata to conduct the *reducción* (aggregation), set
the captives free. Once loose, the Indians fled to parts unknown, and
Fernández Guarachi could do little else but ask the viceroy to allow
him to resign as capitán enterador.[36]

If the capitanes enteradores found it difficult to deliver originarios
to Potosí, they were not shy about including forasteros whenever
possible. In 1680, the corregidor of Porco ordered the kurakas of
Puna to leave Pedro Mamani alone after he complained that he was
being forced to serve in the mita despite being a forastero. The
corregidor's ruling did not end the dispute, however, for Mamani
had to petition the Audiencia of La Plata later to obtain a reinforcement of the earlier decision.[37]

The capitanes enteradores also had their problems with their fel-
low kurakas. The capitán for Puna, Juan Bautista Catari, complained
to the Audiencia of La Plata in 1684 that Gobernador Pedro Anava
was diverting some mitayos for his own use, and that he was commit-
ting other abuses as well.[38] Bautista Catari was not alone. In 1690,
on orders from the Viceroy Conde de la Monclova (1689–1705),
Corregidor of Potosí Pedro Luis Enríquez questioned the capitanes
enteradores about the problems they faced in delivering mitayos to
Potosí. To a man, they charged that other kurakas prevented them
from bringing as many as they might otherwise produce. The kurakas used some of the reserved Indians in their own enterprises, the
capitanes noted, but they also rented some to local estancieros and
chacareros.[39]

Finally, in addition to the opposition of landowners, church officials, the Audiencia of La Plata, corregidores, and other kurakas, the
capitanes enteradores had to contend with the Indians themselves,
and they proved extraordinarily inventive in the means they devised
to avoid mita service. For example, when the Viceroy Príncipe de Esquilache (1615–21) looked into the cause of an unusually high female
birthrate in the obligated provinces, he discovered that boys were
being baptized as girls to save them from future mita obligations.[40]

The gobernador and capitán enterador of Santiago de Yanaoca,
Fernando Surco, accused Pedro Alata Arusi of changing his name to
Pedro Gualpa and his professed place of origin from Santiago de
Yanaoca to Oruro in an effort to evade mita service. Surco had tracked
Pedro "X" down after he fled Potosí following only a few days work-

ing inside the cerro, and had jailed him pending a decision in the matter by the Audiencia of La Plata. Pedro said that he had been born in Oruro and later moved to a Spaniard's ranch at the age of seven, after his parents died. Evidence from both sides of the case showed that he had then been entrusted to Domingo Arusi and raised with Arusi's own sons. Arusi was originally from Santiago de Yanaoca, and he had served in the mita from the ranch; when his sons came of age, they too traveled to Potosí as part of the mita contingent from their original pueblo (in this instance, clearly, the kuraka and the rancher had reached an agreement that served both their interests). Pedro had gone as well, but he had fled after his first taste of the mita. Only after being captured by Surco did Pedro challenge the legal basis of his obligation. Despite serious questions concerning his true place of origin—he changed his professed place of origin to Arequipa during the course of the litigation—the Audiencia ruled that his adoption by Domingo Arusi did not oblige him to serve in the mita and voted to set him free.[41]

Antonio and Agustín Carrillo won exemption from the mita in 1603 with the claim that they were mestizos and therefore exempt from mita service. The two lived in an obligated pueblo, Potobamba, and their father was an originario of the village, but their mother was a mestiza. The Audiencia of La Plata ruled in favor of the Carrillos despite the objections of its *fiscal* (royal advocate), who counseled the tribunal that a ruling in favor of the brothers would open a Pandora's box of problems for the mita, for the judicial system would soon be clogged with petitions from Indians claiming some degree of Spanish ancestry. He noted that the two defendants looked, dressed, and lived like Indians. The Audiencia rejected the *fiscal*'s ethnological definition of "Indian-ness," as well as his logistical concerns, and voted to prevent the kurakas of Potobamba from including the Carrillos in future mita contingents. This did not end the matter, however, for the brothers had to return to the Audiencia in 1615 and 1638 to obtain reinforcements of the 1603 ruling.[42]

When legal means were insufficient to ward off a kuraka, violence could be used. In 1679, the capitán enterador for the pueblos of Toropalca, Yura, Potobamba, and Chaqui—Bartolomé González— asked the Audiencia of La Plata for permission to carry a sword and dagger while performing his official duties. González provided the tribunal with testimony concerning the difficulties he had faced the last time he had served as capitán enterador (in 1668): four Indians had vehemently refused to serve in the mita; they had beaten him up on one occasion and pelted him with sticks and stones on another. The Audiencia granted González permission to carry the arms.[43]

The most compelling case involving the mita during the seventeenth century is that of Francisco Sonco Cari. Sonco Cari appeared before the Audiencia of La Plata in 1673, claimed to be the kuraka principal of Asillo, and charged that the corregidor of Asangaro, Francisco de Castro, was guilty of a number of abuses, including misuse of mita labor. Sonco Cari brought a series of witnesses before the Audiencia to corroborate his charges and the tribunal was sufficiently impressed with the case against the corregidor that it sent a judge to Asangaro to investigate the matter further.[44]

Testimony gathered by the judge in the province, however, was completely at odds with Sonco Cari's claims. Indeed, the kurakas and other Indians of Asillo said that Sonco Cari was not a kuraka and had never been one, but was instead a common Indian who had been sent to Potosí in the mita four years earlier despite his ardent objections to serving. The other witnesses involved in the preliminary hearings were all unknown to the residents of the pueblo. The judge therefore ruled that the charges against the corregidor had been fabricated and the Audiencia confirmed his decision. If Sonco Cari was in fact a disgruntled mitayo, then the judicial process had been manipulated—if not in the long run successfully—by a common Indian at the expense of a provincial corregidor.[45]

THE DIFFICULTIES that the kurakas faced in the delivery of mitayos had led them, as early as the late sixteenth century, to evade or infringe on the Toledan mita ordinances. By the early 1600's, however, even such abuses were unable to fill the quotas for which the kurakas were held responsible. When they could no longer meet their obligations, the corregidores of Potosí began to fine the kurakas nine, and later seven and one-half pesos for every mitayo they failed to deliver—ostensibly so that a minga might be hired in his place. The kurakas were also forced to pay when the azogueros rejected as unfit for service the Indians they had delivered. From these two exactions came an entirely new transformation: the *entero en plata*, or "delivery in silver." The payments were collected each Tuesday, after Monday's distribution of "mitayos in person" at Guayna was complete and the kurakas' remaining obligations were compiled.[46]

President Alonso Maldonado de Torres of the Audiencia of La Plata noted that the azogueros were already accustomed to receiving mita deliveries in silver in 1606, and two years later he estimated that 20 percent of the annual draft was satisfied in that fashion.[47] In 1629, Licenciado Pedro Ramírez del Aguila (a curate) reported that his village of Tacobamba routinely "served in silver," and he claimed that the kurakas spent most of their time chasing Indians to collect the money with which to pay the amount required. Corregidor of Potosí Rafael Ortiz de Sotomayor had lowered the sum from nine to seven and one-half pesos, Ramírez noted, because some of the azogueros had begun to reject Indians who appeared in person simply because the azogueros saved the two and one-half pesos per week that the mitayos were paid (the azogueros would ostensibly have had to make up the remainder of the nine-peso minga wage, but the arithmetic is a bit askew).[48]

The fraction of the mita that arrived in Potosí in the form of silver grew quickly to significant proportions. A source from the second decade of the seventeenth century broke the various provinces' mita deliveries into their component parts (see Table 2). On the basis of this information, which was probably produced by Corregidor Ortiz de Sotomayor, Silvio Zavala has estimated that half of the effective mita was delivered in silver and half in person, with an eighth or ninth of the annual draft not delivered at all.[49] A royal cédula of 1620, which responded to figures submitted by Controller Alonso Martínez de Pastrana, also claimed that over one-third of the mita appeared in Potosí in the form of money.[50] In 1626, moreover, the Crown asked the Viceroy Marqués de Guadalcázar (1622–29) whether a report that only 800 of 4,000 mitayos served in person was true.[51]

And how did the kurakas come up with the money to meet their mita obligations in silver? Whatever the actual fraction of the mita that was satisfied in money, the sums involved were enormous. A kuraka who was responsible for as few as twenty Indians and could only come up with ten would have to pay 75 pesos per week in compensation. Gabriel Fernández Guarachi was responsible for the mita delivery from the entire province of Pacajes ten times from the 1630's to the 1660's. The quota for just two of the obligated villages came to 16,408 pesos per year, and the total for the province was just under 50,000 pesos.[52] The kurakas from the province of Porco contributed between 65,000 and 70,000 pesos per year by midcentury.[53] Superin-

TABLE 2

Mita Deliveries in Person, in Silver, and Not at All, ca. 1615
(*Percent*)

Province/Pueblo	In Person	In Silver	Not at All
Chichas	–	–	–
Porco			
Puna	*some*	*most*	–
Chayanta			
Chayanta	*100%*	–	–
Machacopoata	*50*	*50%*	–
Aymaya	*50*	*50*	–
others in Charcas[a]	*50*	*50*	–
Sacaca	*100*	–	–
Cochabamba			
Santiago del Paso	–	*50*	*50%*
Tinquipaya	–	*50*	*50*
Cochabamba	–	*100*	–
Tapacari	–	*50*	*50*
Casaya [?]	–	*100*	–
Capinota	–	*100*	–
Sipesipe	–	*50*	*50*
Paria			
Quillacas	–	*67*	*33*
Asanaque	–	*100*	–
Uruquillas	–	*33*	*67*
Toledo	–	*100*	–
Aullagas	–	*100*	–
Carangas	*a few*	*primarily*	–
Sicasica	83–86	14–17	–
Pacajes	86–88	12–14	–
Omasuyos	14–17	83–86	–
Pucarani	–	–	67
Copacabana	83–86	14–17	–
Chucuito	86–88	12–14	–
Paucarcolla (most)	50	50	–
Capachica	–	–	83–90
Puno	33	33	33
Lampa	–	*mostly*	–
Cavana, Cavanilla, and Nicasio	–	–	83–90
Orurillo and Nuñoa	67	33	–
four other pueblos	80–83	17–20	–
Asangaro (most)	83–86	14–17	–
Arapa	–	–	100
Canas y Canches	83–86	14–17	–
Quispicanches	80–83	17–20	–

SOURCE: Zavala, *Servicio personal*, vol. 2, pp. 68–69; see n. 46, Chap. 2, for the manuscript from which the data are taken.

[a]This may include the province of Chichas.

tendent of the Mita Francisco de la Cruz reported that 50,000 pesos per year for a province was quite common by the late 1650's, and given the figures for Porco and Pacajes, his estimated total of 587,000 pesos per year in mita deliveries in silver by 1660 is quite credible.[54]

The money that the kurakas used to meet these astronomical sums came from a variety of sources. Some, as already noted, was garnered from absent Indians or their employers. The miners in recently discovered mining zones, for example, were often willing to pay an Indian's mita obligation in silver in return for his services, such were the levels of profit and demand for labor in the newer mining camps.[55] Fernández Guarachi's province had a similar means of raising money: *indios maharaques*. When the Indians from Pacajes came together at Topoco each year for dispatch to Potosí, they were first offered for hire to anyone who needed Indian labor. The kurakas, and often the Indians themselves, would contract out their services in exchange for 150 pesos to cover the mita obligation and payment of their tribute. The indios maharaques also received two reales per day in wages during the course of the one-year contract. The chaplain of Caquiaviri estimated that there were as many as 500 indios maharaques working in the Merenguela mining zone alone in 1662. The testimony of the capitanes enteradores before the corregidor of Potosí in 1690 revealed the existence of similar arrangements in most of the obligated provinces: would-be mitayos were rented to ranchers and farm owners in exchange for the satisfaction of their mita obligation in silver and payment of their tribute.[56]

Indios maharaques served, however, only to convert into silver those mitayos who otherwise would have gone to Potosí in person. Other sources of money had to be found to make up the difference between the mitayos—in person and in silver—that the kurakas could raise in their pueblos and the mita quotas for which they were responsible. The means used in the province of Paucarcolla, although not completely successful, are instructive. In his preparation for the dispatch of the mitayos from that province in 1669, Corregidor Josef Ordóñez del Aguila ordered the local kurakas to prepare lists of those who would serve and make ready for their departure. The kurakas of Puno and Icho responded that they could not deliver the number of Indians required of them in person and that their personal resources— with which they had satisfied those demands in silver in the past— were no longer sufficient to make up the difference. They asked that they be allowed to resign their posts. The corregidor investigated their claims, found them to be valid, and accepted their resignations.[57]

Four years later, Ordóñez began to prepare for the dispatch of the mita much sooner. In April 1673, he jailed the kuraka principal of Macari, Gerónimo Cajíamarca, for a number of offenses, including his failure to comply with his mita responsibilities. Cajíamarca, the corregidor charged, had run a series of illegal enterprises and conducted unlawful collections of money from the residents of his pueblo—including women, old men, and forasteros—ostensibly to meet the village's tribute and mita obligations (the latter in silver). He had then kept the money for himself.[58] The details of the dispatch of the mitayos from Puno the following November are even more enlightening. The gobernador of the pueblo of Paucarcolla provided Ordóñez with five Indians; a sixth was to be picked up in Oruro en route to Potosí. The kuraka of Capachica sent ten Indians in person, but the new kurakas of Puno and Icho could only entrust the corregidor with 450 and 400 pesos, respectively. They said that they had collected that money through the rental of land to forasteros and yanaconas, and the sale of their own property and livestock. The gobernador of San Francisco de Tiquillaca provided Ordóñez with two Indians in person and 300 pesos in lieu of the usual third (the province of Paucarcolla had the unusual custom of sending contingents to Potosí for two years rather than one). He too had raised the money through collections among the forasteros and others.[59]

The case of Paucarcolla makes it clear that legally exempted classes of Indians, including forasteros and yanaconas, were not entirely free of mita or tribute responsibilities. The rent these groups paid for their lands and their contributions to extraordinary collections were used to pay communal tribute and satisfy mita obligations in silver. In addition, the kurakas' own funds and property were often used to make up any remaining shortcomings. From other, more fragmentary source materials, it is clear that kurakas in other provinces also raised the funds to meet their obligations in these ways. Despite this newly developed means for meeting mita responsibilities, however, the overall delivery of "mitayos"—in person and in silver—in the seventeenth century fell continually (see Figure 2). In 1640, for example, the corregidor of Potosí and the president of the Audiencia of La Plata were forced to send an envoy to oversee the delivery of mitayos from Canas y Canches, Carabaya (Quispicanches?), Chu-

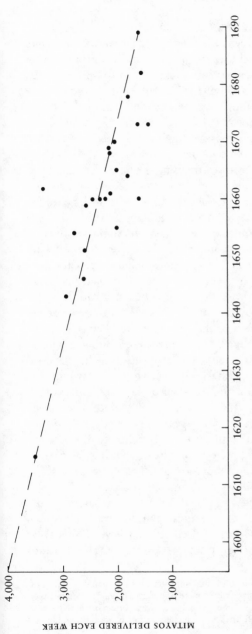

FIGURE 2. The Effective Weekly Draft (Mita Ordinaria), 1600–1689.

Sources: 1615, Zavala, *Servicio personal*, vol. 2, pp. 68–69; 1643, Corregidor Blas Robles de Salzedo to the Viceroy Marqués de Mancera, Potosí, May 30, 1643, described in Castillo, f. 15; 1646, Azogueros Guild to the Marqués de Mancera, Potosí, July 29, 1646, AGNA, Sala 9, leg. 6.2.5; 1651, "Testimonio de los Yndios que enteraban siendo Correg.ʳ d. fran.ᶜᵒ sarmiento que eran 2600," AGI, Charcas, leg. 266, no. 19A; 1654, "Resumen de la Vissita de minas y ingenios hecho por d. fran.ᶜᵒ Sarmiento Oydor de la Ciudad de los Reyes Y Correg.ʳ de Potosí," July 4, 1654, AGI, Charcas, leg. 266, no. 19D; 1655, Relación of the Viceroy Conde de Salvatierra, in Hanke and Rodríguez, eds., *Virreyes* (Perú), vol. 4, p. 40; 1659, President Bartolomé de Salazar to the Viceroy Conde de Alba, Potosí, Nov. 30, 1660, AGI, Charcas, leg. 266, no. 60B (before the arrival of Cruz there had been 2,580); 1660, *Ibid.* (after Cruz there were only 1,603); 1660, Archbishop of Lima to the Crown, Lima, Dec. 30, 1661, AGI, Charcas, leg. 267, no. 16 (in 1660, there had been 2,447); 1660 (approx.), Acarete du Biscay, pp. 137–38; 1661, AGI, Charcas, leg. 267, no. 16; 1662, President Bartolomé de Salazar to the Crown, Potosí, May 23, 1662, AGI, Charcas, leg. 267, no. 29; 1664, Procurador Francisco de Arracola y Diaguez to the Crown, Potosí, Apr. 18, 1664, AGI, Charcas, leg. 267, no. 36; 1665, Corregidor Gabriel Guerrero de Luna to the Crown, Potosí, May 6, 1665, AGI, Charcas, leg. 267, no. 46; 1668, Corregidor Luis Antonio de Oviedo to the Crown, Potosí, Oct. 8, 1668, AGI, Charcas, leg. 267, nos. 56C and 56D; 1669, Testimonio of Oviedo's activities as corregidor, AGI, Charcas, leg. 268, no. 58B (sent with a letter to the Crown, Potosí, Mar. 25, 1678, AGI, Charcas, leg. 268, no. 58); 1670, *Ibid.;* 1673, Copy of a letter from Oviedo to the viceregal government in Lima, Potosí, May 26, 1673, AGI, Charcas, leg. 268, no. 38A; 1673, Oviedo to the Crown, Potosí, Nov. 22, 1673, AGI, Charcas, leg. 268, no. 44; 1678, AGI, Charcas, leg. 268, no. 58B; 1682, Corregidor Pedro Luis Enríquez to the Crown, Potosí, Jan. 24, 1682, AGI, Charcas, leg. 270, no. 5; 1689, Duque de la Palata to the Crown, Lima, Feb. 19, 1689, AGI, Charcas, leg. 270, no. 32.

cuito, Larecaja (Asangaro or Sicasica?), Omasuyos, Pacajes, Paria, and Paucarcolla.[60]* The Viceroy Conde de Chinchón (1629–39) had earlier ordered that each pueblo in the province of Chucuito be represented by its own capitán enterador, in the hope of improving that province's abysmal record of compliance with the mita; it did not.[61]

A more persuasive indication that the kurakas were unable to deliver their full contingents of mitayos—in person or in silver—was included in a report to the Viceroy Marqués de Mancera (1639–48) by the Azogueros Guild (gremio de azogueros) in 1646. After commenting on a series of proposals for revising the mita, the azogueros expressed their hope that the revamped mita system would require all the mitayos to serve in person; the kurakas, they argued, no longer brought the money they collected from the Indians for the purpose of meeting their mita obligations in silver.[62] The situation did not soon improve, however, for in that same year, the corregidores of Colquemarca (Carangas), Desaguadero (Pacajes), Chayanta, Chucuito, and Paria all reported that the mita contingents from their provinces would not be arriving in Potosí, because the kurakas had fled with the Indians they were supposed to deliver.[63] In fact, the corregidor of Potosí, Juan de Velarde, wrote to the viceroy in October 1646 to report that only half of the obligated provinces were sending any mitayos in person at all: Canas y Canches, Collao (Quispicanches?), Asangaro, Paucarcolla, Chucuito, Omasuyos, Pacajes, and Chayanta.[64]

The inability of the kurakas to meet their obligations, either in silver or in person, caused the mita to change form once again. One aspect of this transformation was the appearance of rezagos de mita—the demand that a kuraka's failure to deliver his complete complement of mitayos in some previous year be met during the current year in silver, and thus the accumulation of debts on the part of the kurakas for their past inabilities as capitanes enteradores. The corregidores of Potosí sent judges to prosecute the errant kurakas, and to collect the rezagos.[65] Lack of faith in the kurakas was also shown in the employment of sacadores (collectors, themselves Indians) by the azogueros to gather money from the kurakas.[66] The methods

*Province lines and names changed throughout the Hapsburg period. In addition, corregimientos (magistracies) and provinces were not identical, and the names were often different. Thus, some pueblos in the region of Larecaja, for example, might have sent mitayos to Potosí even though it was not officially included among the obligated provinces.

used by the sacadores and their abuses of their contracts with the azogueros can only be surmised, but it is clear that the kurakas were no longer a dependable vehicle for the delivery of the mita—at least as far as the azogueros were concerned.

The worst manifestation of the mita's continuing metamorphosis, however, was the use of torture and extortion by the azogueros to squeeze as much silver from the kurakas as possible. Some of the most serious charges were lodged by the kurakas of Pacajes in a 1657 complaint to the Crown, and they were joined by the capitanes enteradores of the other mita provinces in a common petition of January 1660.[67] Superintendent Francisco de la Cruz reported, also in 1660, that the azogueros were hanging the kurakas by their hair and beating them to within an inch of their lives.[68] Four years later, the *protector de naturales* provided the Crown with a pair of examples: the kuraka principal of Calcha had been whipped and his wife and children jailed because he was unable to meet his mita quota in silver; another kuraka had sold everything he owned to raise 1,100 pesos of a 2,000-peso debt for rezagos de mita, but because he could not come up with the remaining 900 pesos, his wife and children had been jailed for three years.[69]

A more subtle form of pressure was applied by the *capitán mayor de la mita*, a subordinate of the corregidor of Potosí. The man who occupied that post in 1677, Joseph Fernández de Valencia, employed a combination of financial, corporal, and psychological means to force the kurakas to deliver as many mitayos as humanly possible. According to a joint complaint lodged against Fernández by the kurakas, he exacted an illegal delivery tax, imprisoned newly arrived capitanes enteradores until they could be bonded by other kurakas, forced them to bring him presents from their home provinces, required that they provide him with mules and building materials for his own enterprises, and demanded that they supply decorations for his parties.[70]

The corregidor of Potosí suspended Fernández de Valencia for one year, largely because of his use of illegal bonding to control the kurakas, but the capitanes enteradores were not satisfied with that sentence. Fearful that the capitán mayor would return after a year and take revenge, they appealed the corregidor's decision to the Audiencia of La Plata and submitted a second complaint charging that the capitán mayor forcibly sold wine and chicha to the Indians at

Guayna each Monday; that he forced the kurakas to come to his home and bid him good day; that he used physical and verbal abuse that was not appropriate to their noble status; that he forced them to grind silver ore by hand while in his jail; and that he prevented them from hearing mass while they were imprisoned. The second complaint was sent to La Plata even before the corregidor could rule on it (a shrewd ploy), and in combination with the first prompted the Audiencia to order a perpetual suspension from office for Fernández de Valencia, as well as a hefty fine.[71]

The increasing pressure on the kurakas to deliver the mita—and particularly in silver—reflects a fundamental change in the character of the mita. Originally a labor imposition on the obligated pueblos, with the kurakas as the means for tapping that resource, the mita had also been transformed by 1680 into a money tax on the kurakas themselves. The azogueros had come to view the capitanes enteradores as a source of wealth in their own right—over and above what might be dug out of the cerro of Potosí—and they used sacadores, torture, and local government officials in their efforts to exploit that wealth. The inability of the kurakas to satisfy the azogueros' cravings was caused, meanwhile, by the deterioration of the Indian pueblos, itself a product (in part) of Indian flight from the mita. The originarios left their villages to take up residence elsewhere as forasteros or to work on Spanish agricultural estates as "yanaconas." At times they were replaced by forasteros, but the influx of migrants was never able to match the impact of out-migration and epidemic disease and thus the Indian population of the pueblos fell to a level far below that required to meet their mita and tribute obligations. We will return to this topic in Chapter 6.

The Hapsburg administration of Peru failed to prevent the transformation of the Potosí mita into a money tax for the benefit of the azogueros and it was unable to protect the kurakas from the abuses that characterized the collection of that tax. Before the issue of the government's direction of the mita may be considered, however, the role of the mita in the battle for Indian labor on the altiplano must be discussed, because the information upon which the Crown and its Council of the Indies based their policy toward the mita was derived from three sources: (a) the Azogueros Guild; (b) the enemies of the mita, the owners of enterprises that competed with the Villa Imperial for access to and control of Indian labor; and (c) official correspondence from royal officials throughout Peru. Since the government officials generally repeated, for personal or philosophical reasons, the arguments of one or the other of the first two groups, the descriptions of the mita (as well as the fundamental issues at the root of those depictions) emanating from the azogueros and their competitors are essential to explore.

THREE

The Mita and the Azogueros, 1580-1680

WE HAVE SEEN how the azogueros sought to exploit the mitayos more efficiently once the tailings were exhausted, and how they limited the Indians' share of the cerro's silver through the imposition of quotas, night-and-day work, and an attack on the right to kapcha and other mitayo perquisites. Indeed, the azogueros' accelerating demands on the mitayos were largely responsible for driving the Indians from Potosí and the pueblos that were subject to mita recruitment. Some azogueros, moreover, found it more profitable to rent or sell the Indians allotted to them than to continue producing silver. Nevertheless, of the 132 mills (*cabezas de ingenio**) built during the initial construction phase, both at Potosí and at Tarapaya, as many as 124 were still in operation during the first decades of the seventeenth century.[1]

From the turn of the century on, however, the azogueros watched their fantastic levels of profits fall irrevocably, and they slowly but surely lost their once dominant position within the Potosí economic community to silver merchants and moneylenders. As early as 1602, for example, many azogueros were unable to repay the loans they had contracted in order to purchase mercury upon its arrival from Huancavelica (in this, the azogueros were much like farmers, who must borrow to pay for seed months before their harvests come in). Although they were protected by Toledan and royal *provisiones* against imprisonment for debts—another part of the initial pact be-

---

*I must distinguish here between *cabezas de ingenio* (mill heads) and *ingenios* (mills). A cabeza de ingenio was a collection of stamping mechanisms (*mazos*), usually four in number. At times, an ingenio would have two cabezas, that is, two sets of mazos. For simplicity's sake, I have employed "mills" in this study rather than "mill heads."

tween that viceroy and the first azogueros—many had been forced to renounce their right to secure an agreement with a silver merchant or moneylender. As more and more of the azogueros were jailed, the guild petitioned Viceroy Luis de Velasco to extend their immunity to cases where the right had been waived. After considerable vacillation, and interim decisions by the corregidor of Potosí and his lieutenants, Velasco agreed to the extension, but he refused to make his order retroactive. Soon thereafter, he sought to solve the azogueros' predicament by permitting the royal treasury officials of Potosí to rent any given azoguero's mill to raise the money to pay his creditors. The viceroy even permitted the inclusion of the respective mitayos in such rentals, despite his own earlier prohibition of such arrangements.[2]

There are other indications that the azogueros were in considerable financial difficulty. In 1603, when the Crown raised anew the idea of importing black slaves to take the mitayos' places in the mines, Father Alonso Mesía Venegas counseled Velasco that only a few of the azogueros had sufficient funds to buy slaves.[3] And when the guild voted to construct new reservoirs and aqueducts in 1609, following a crippling drought the previous year, many of the azogueros failed to make their pledged contributions, and the subsequent attempt by the association's officers to collect those donations gave rise to an extremely bitter intraguild squabble.[4]

The situation of the azogueros, as a group, did not improve during the remainder of the Hapsburg era. One of the clearest indications of their worsening condition is the gradual decline in the number of silver mills in operation at Potosí and its environs. The number of mills that received mitayos—a figure nearly identical to the number in use—dropped from the 132 included in the sixteenth-century repartimientos to 124 in 1624, 99 in 1633, 60 in 1689, and 34 in 1692.[5] In part the fall in the number of mills—in 1689 and 1692 especially—was the product of lower official annual drafts of mitayos, but generally the officials who were responsible for the new charters denied mitayos only to those mills that were already abandoned (vacos).

The causes of the falling silver production levels and the declining number of mills are many and related. The azogueros were able to compensate only temporarily for the exhaustion of the tailings by demanding more of their mitayos. Their financial difficulties during the seventeenth century were caused by a shortage of apiris (i.e., mitayos in person), problematical supplies and financing of mercury, lower-quality and less-accessible ore, and water crises.

Supplies of mercury were insufficient at times because of production ebbs at Huancavelica, as was the case in 1608–9, but more often because a shipment had been delayed, stolen, or lost. The mercury was transported from Arica to Potosí over some of the most treacherous terrain in the viceroyalty, and could only be moved using mule trains—a slow and expensive means of conveyance.[6] More importantly, the distribution of mercury to the azogueros was complicated by restrictions resulting from its earlier distribution on credit. That practice had led to immense debts to the royal treasury (a total of 2.5 million pesos by 1608) and was halted.[7] The azogueros therefore had to borrow from local creditors to pay for the mercury when it arrived, sacrificing a portion of their allocation to pay the financing charge. As though this were not enough, the government aggressively sought to collect the sums owed it for mercury later in the century, applying further pressure on the azogueros.[8] These difficulties were compounded as the ore mined from the cerro dropped in quality, requiring more mercury for each mark of silver produced.

Water was another crucial production ingredient, for it was required to power the stamping mechanisms of most mills (others used horses) and to wash the ore and the mixture of mercury and ground ore, called *lamas*. Just as the azogueros were dependent upon the arrival of mercury shipments from Huancavelica, they were similarly dependent upon their reservoirs for ample supplies of water and their aqueducts to deliver that water to the mills. Once the new reservoirs and channels were built in 1609, the azogueros were able to survive periods of short-term drought with few problems.[9] But on March 15, 1626, they were faced with a water crisis of a different sort when the largest of the reservoirs, Cari Cari, collapsed, sending water cascading down on the mills and the city below, causing catastrophic destruction. With the help of government loans of mercury (which of course increased their debt) and the assignment of the mitayos who had been working for miners at Porco to the reconstruction of the mills, however, most of the azogueros were able to rebuild their enterprises.[10]

The decline in the number of mitayos arriving in Potosí during the seventeenth century, documented in the preceding chapter, caused a further strain on the azogueros. The apiris were almost wholly mitayos, and the apiris produced the ore upon which the entire silver industry depended. To replace a mitayo with a minga represented a cost to an azoguero of five pesos per week, the difference in the two workers' salaries. The drop in the number of mitayos—especially of those who were willing to serve at Potosí in person—to a mere fraction of the Toledan levels was caused, as we have noted, by the deterioration of working conditions at Potosí and the growth of attractive alternative sources of employment. One of the first serious competitors to appear was the mining zone of Oruro, established in 1606. The discovery of easily accessible deposits of rich ore there caused Indians to flock to the newly founded "villa" of San Phelipe de Austria (so named in the hope of winning royal support from Philip III) much as they had to Potosí in the 1540's and 1550's. Many of those Indians were mitayos who were already in Potosí or en route to the Villa Imperial from the provinces north of San Phelipe.[11]

The azogueros were quick to recognize the threat represented by the Oruro mining zone and they demanded of the Viceroy Marqués de Montesclaros that he enforce their guild's exclusive rights to both mitayos and mercury. The viceroy complied by denying the miners of San Phelipe access to mercury in 1608 and by preventing the establishment of an Oruro mita in 1612. The quality of the ore at Oruro fell soon thereafter, but it remained an important mining zone throughout the century and so continued to attract mingas, many of them from Potosí.[12] And Oruro was only one of many competing mining zones by the end of the 1600's; Potosí also had to contend with Salinas, Aullagas, Puno, Porco, Nuevo Potosí, Merenguela, and a host of others. None was ever able to match Potosí in terms of production, but each employed a significant number of Indian laborers.

Agricultural, transport, textile, and other enterprises—many of them dependent upon the Potosí market, ironically enough—also competed with the Azogueros Guild for access to and control of Indian labor. The viniculturalists of Pilaya y Paspaya, the coca industry of Cochabamba, the cattle ranches and farms of Tucumán and elsewhere, the *obrajes* (textile mills) in the cities—in short, a wide variety of enterprises both within and outside the mita provinces—all needed Indian labor if they were to survive and prosper. With the influx of Spanish entrepreneurs throughout the colonial period and the decline in the Indian population on the altiplano, the demand for labor increased while the attraction that Potosí once held for the Indians turned to utter revulsion. As a result, the Indians migrated toward those enterprises that offered them the most, in terms of land, profits, and security.[13]

The combined impact of problems with regard to mercury, mitayos, and water caused the azogueros gradually to lose control over capital in the Villa Imperial. By 1643, only a handful of azogueros had managed to avoid becoming dependent on loans from silver merchants and moneylenders to finance their purchases of mercury.[14] This is not to say that silver production at Potosí was no longer profitable, however, for the survival of the silver industry into the eighteenth century confirms that profits were still to be had. The reconstruction of the refining mills in the wake of the 1626 collapse of Cari Cari is a clear indication of the azogueros' belief in the prospects for future gain.

Furthermore, the azogueros fought what amounted to a protracted civil war with other factions during the mid-1620's over control of the silver mining industry. The conflict pitted the predominantly Basque azogueros against an alliance of other Spaniards and criollos, known collectively as the "Vicuñas" because they wore vicuña-skin hats. Eighty of the 132 mills in the 1580's had been owned by Basques, who transferred the mining heritage of their homeland to the Villa Imperial; Castilians, Andalusians, and other Spaniards tended instead toward those enterprises that did not require a significant effort or capital investment on their part. As their own fortunes waned in the early seventeenth century, the Basques moved to monopolize their control of the most profitable mines and Potosí's Cabildo (municipal council) at the expense of the other Spaniards and criollos. The Vicuñas tried to block that gambit through a formal challenge before the Cabildo and other legal means, but when those efforts were ineffective, they resorted to arms. Hostilities occurred from 1615 on, with a particularly bloody episode beginning in 1622. After three years of intermittent warfare, a fragile peace was finally achieved only through mutual exhaustion, but because neither side could claim victory, the prospects for violence in the Villa Imperial remained close at hand.[15] The battle between the Basques and the Vicuñas would not have been waged had there been nothing for which to fight. Clearly, however, mining would only remain profitable if the number of participants were trimmed (i.e., if the available mercury, labor, and ore were split fewer ways), and the battle for control of the ebbing Potosí silver industry had therefore begun.

Contributing to the shakeout was the long wait, from 1633 to 1689, that the azogueros had to endure before a new repartimiento de la mita was implemented. During that period, the Toledan production formula fell into a shambles: the provisioning of mercury by the government and the direction of production by the azogueros were both problematical, and the kurakas proved totally incapable of delivering sufficient numbers of mitayos. To remedy that situation, the azogueros called upon the government to execute a wide-ranging program for the revitalization of the Potosí silver industry. The declining quality of the ore and the problems with water were beyond the abilities of the Hapsburg administration to rectify; the azogueros simply built their reservoirs and aqueducts, and prayed for divine assistance. But the shortages of apiris and mercury were both matters for which the government could be held accountable, for those ingredients in the Toledan production formula were its responsibilities.

The Azogueros Guild began its call for further government assistance during the first decade of the seventeenth century. In 1608, the association asked the Viceroy Marqués de Montesclaros for permission to send a representative to Madrid to argue its case directly before the Crown. The viceroy turned down the guild's request, arguing that he could resolve the azogueros' difficulties without bothering the king, and had the azogueros draft a synopsis of their current situation and needs.[16]

> Their financial difficulties stemmed, they said, from production costs that outstripped profits, and from the burden of their past debts. The latter, they argued, should be waived.
>
> There were not enough mitayos, for the corregidores and priests in the provinces conspired to strangle the mita, so that the Indians would be free to work in their enterprises.
>
> The Indians were spread far and wide, moreover, because the corregidores had failed to keep them in their original pueblos.
>
> The viceroy's order that Oruro was not to divert mitayos from Potosí was not being enforced and the result was the endangerment of future silver production at Potosí.
>
> Mercury was absolutely crucial and had to be readily available in the Villa Imperial; the azogueros argued, therefore, for the creation of a strategic reserve of mercury at Potosí.
>
> In recognition of the azogueros' previous service to the Crown, the royal share of production should be lowered, they said, to 10 percent, as it had been in New Spain. Mercury should be distributed, furthermore, at cost.
>
> The mitayos should work on feast days, the guild maintained, because the priests wasted a great deal of the Indians' money on their festivals, which regularly ended in drunken spectacles. It was better, the azogueros added, that the Indians work than get drunk.

Lest the viceroy or the Crown take their situation lightly, the azogueros warned that silver production at Potosí would soon come to an end unless their condition improved. They even threatened, for good measure, that the industry might fall into the hands of the Protestants.

The threat that the Potosí silver industry would collapse without further assistance from the Crown was to be a key element in the azogueros' various petitions. They were, to some extent, holding the cerro hostage; it was about the only thing they still controlled. The azogueros sent a veritable stream of petitions to Lima and Madrid thereafter, in which their message changed only slightly. In 1610, for example, they again asked the Crown to lower its share of silver production to a tenth and to sell mercury at Potosí at cost. The azogueros now called for the mitayos to work on Mondays rather than on feast days, however, and added a request that the *alcabala* (sales tax) be abolished in the Villa Imperial.[17] Later, in 1617, the guild insisted that something be done to ensure that the designated numbers of mitayos arrived from the provinces, and it asked the Viceroy Príncipe de Esquilache to assist the azogueros in their efforts to restore the mita, and the Toledan production formula in general, to its earlier glory. None of the guild's petitions, however, had the desired effect.[18]

IN LIGHT OF the failure to secure further government assistance through correspondence, the Cabildo of Potosí underwrote the expenses of a procurador, Sebastián Sandoval y Guzmán, to argue its case directly before the Council of the Indies in the early 1630's. His arguments were published in Madrid in 1634 under the title *Pretensiones de la Villa Imperial de Potosí*.[19] The first part of the work proposed a series of means for improving silver production at Potosí; the second part dealt with the pursuit of viniculture in nearby valleys and other matters of interest to the residents of the Villa Imperial.[20] In the section on mining, Sandoval contended that the azogueros deserved to receive their mitayos because of their guild's record of service to the Crown. That sentiment was also expressed in his opening letter to the president of the Council: "[Potosí], which until recently has supported the full weight of the Monarchy with its great riches, now places itself humbly at the feet of Your Excellency, needing your protection and asking for justice."[21] This line of argument—that the Potosí silver industry deserved royal consideration because of its past service to the Crown, and that it required justice if it were to continue to serve its sovereign—had been employed earlier in the guild's synopsis for the Marqués de Montesclaros. The azogueros were clearly aware that their value to the Crown was fading with their overall production level, and that their monopoly on draft labor was threatened by the growing number of mining centers in Alto Perú. Sandoval's mission, therefore, was to convince the Council of the Indies that Potosí could once again become the financial anchor of the Spanish world.

The procurador proposed four innovations to revive the silver industry at Potosí. They were, first, the reduction of the royal share of production from 20 to 10 percent; second, the execution of a *reducción general* (to return the now-dispersed Indians to their original pueblos and thus rebuild the population base upon which the mita depended); third, the distribution of mercury at cost and on credit to the azogueros; and fourth, the formation of a *consulado de azogueros* (azogueros consulate), with authority to serve as a court of first instance in mining disputes, relegating the Audiencia of La Plata to a purely appellate role.[22] The first and third proposals were not new, for the azogueros had requested such measures with regularity. Both would lower the azogueros' costs, but they would also reduce the level of royal income from Potosí; Sandoval maintained that the lost revenue would quickly be recouped through expanded production. The halving of the royal share of production, for example, would permit the refining of recently produced tailings, and thus every available stone that contained silver would be processed. New exploration would also take place, he said, and the Indians would return to Potosí to work voluntarily. The temporary shortfall would be a mere 335,000 pesos per year, moreover, whereas the alternative was the irreversible demise of the entire industry.[23]

Sandoval's second request, for a reducción general, reflected the demographic problems affecting the mita provinces. The Crown did not need to be convinced of the desirability of a resettlement program, for it had in fact been pressing for one since the late sixteenth century. Successive viceroys had countered, however, that they did not have the officials to undertake such a massive campaign, and that should the reducción be completed badly, then the mita and tribute quotas would have to be lowered proportionately. More telling, perhaps, was the viceroys' belief that Spanish and criollo landowners would oppose the process, to protect the Indians who worked on their estates, and that food production in the realm would suffer if the Indians were removed from their agricultural pursuits. Finally, the viceroys had argued that the pueblos held little or no attraction for the Indians, and that without their cooperation the resettlement program would inevitably be a disaster.[24]

Sandoval admitted the validity of the arguments advanced by the viceroys, but he argued that a reducción general was nonetheless imperative if Peru were to recapture its former prosperity. It was not the mita or the Indians' other responsibilities that had caused them to flee their pueblos, he claimed, but rather the attractions of life on a farm or ranch. Thus the solution was to make life in the pueblos more attractive than it was elsewhere: the Indians' debts should be pardoned, their tribute should be waived while they were serving in the mita, and their lands should be returned to them, even if they were now legally held by Spaniards. Once the pueblos were repopulated, the weight of the Indians' obligations would again fall on many shoulders and hence would no longer be excessive. The azogueros called for the resettlement program because they were confident that the number of Indians in Alto Perú had not fallen overall, but rather that Indian migration away from the obligated regions had caused an apparent depopulation. Kurakas and corregidores also called for the reducción general, Sandoval noted, to prove just the opposite—that their jurisdictions were and would continue to be devoid of Indians. This was the Crown's opportunity, he concluded, to demonstrate who was right.[25]

It is clear from the procurador's comments that the agricultural interests, in combination with the kurakas and corregidores in the provinces, had come to be a serious source of opposition to the continued perquisites of the Azogueros Guild. Another of the guild's enemies, this one of longer standing, was the Audiencia of La Plata. It was against this enemy that the fourth proposal, for a consulado de azogueros, was aimed, for it would award the guild a degree of self-government in mining matters and free it from the continual meddling of the nearby Audiencia. The tribunal's judges, Sandoval argued, did not understand the complexities of mining and therefore were unqualified to adjudicate disputes among the various elements of the silver industry. Once free of the Audiencia's constant interference, the azogueros would be able to concentrate on producing silver. Perhaps that last phrase should have been "able to concentrate on their profits," for had the second and fourth proposals been accepted by the Crown, the azogueros might well have regained the primacy at Potosí they had enjoyed in better times.[26]

Each of Sandoval's proposals was supported with legal and prag-
matic reasons why it should be adopted. Each was drafted, moreover,
in such a way that it could be accepted individually, without affecting
the others. The Crown was assured at all turns that it would not lose
any revenue by granting the new concessions, but that it would surely
lose Potosí if it failed to act. Despite that warning, however, and
the best efforts of the procurador, none of the four proposals was
successful.

Why was the Crown not convinced? To answer that question, one
must first remember that Toledo had decided to establish the mita
only when it seemed that silver production in Potosí might rise like a
phoenix, fueled as well by the tailings and the introduction of amalgamation technology. The role of the mita in convincing the miners
to make the requisite capital investment must also be recalled. The
Crown, moreover, had consented to the creation of the mita only
after the silver boom of the late 1570's and 1580's (matched with
Philip II's rising need for American silver) caused a reordering of its
priorities. The prospects for Potosí 60 years later were far less promising. Despite numerous efforts to develop a significantly better refining method, the amalgamation process continued to be standard;
there was no technological revolution to compare with its introduction.[27] Tailings existed, but they were composed of ore cast aside
since 1573 because it would require excessive amounts of mercury
and other refining ingredients to process. The mills were already
constructed; indeed, more of them existed than were needed. The
azogueros no longer controlled capital in the mining center, and
Potosí was no longer the sole economic support of the Peruvian viceroyalty. Thus, there was very little that the azogueros could exchange
for a government program on their behalf, and they were hardly in a
position to demand anything; all they could do now was to warn the
Crown that the collapse of Potosí was at hand and remind it of
the Villa Imperial's importance as a strategic administrative and com-
mercial center. As long as reports from Peru did not suggest the immediate collapse of the Potosí silver industry, however, the Crown
had little cause to implement a thorough revitalization program; the
expected benefits simply did not justify the expense.

Another problem for the azogueros was their ongoing debate with
the government over their debts for mercury. The azogueros' failure
to pay off those debts hampered their effort to portray themselves as
loyal and deserving subjects. This cloud had a silver lining, however,

for the immense sums that the azogueros owed caused the government to take a greater interest in their solvency than it otherwise
might have; for should they go out of business, the Crown would
never collect on the debts.[28]

The Crown also asked why the Potosí silver industry had not already collapsed for lack of new concessions, if the azogueros' earlier
warnings were accurate. If matters were so serious, how had they
managed to survive thus far? The azogueros were able to continue,
albeit in smaller numbers, because of the emergence of mita deliveries
in silver and the uses to which they put the money they collected
from the kurakas. Indeed, the appearance and growth of mita deliveries in silver owed as much to the needs of the azogueros as it did
to the depopulation of the pueblos and the other reasons why the
kurakas were unable to deliver mitayos in person. The azogueros
found these sums of money to be a new source of operating capital,
without interest to be paid or other restraints, which provided them a
degree of flexibility in an increasingly unfavorable and uncontrollable
economic situation. By diverting some of the money to cover a portion of their mercury and other material costs, their minga labor
costs, and their other expenses, the azogueros were able to run
smaller, less productive, but still profitable enterprises.[29]

Within those smaller mining operations, the balance between
minga and mita labor seems to have been maintained. In 1603, the
relationship was roughly 55 percent mingas to 45 percent mitayos.
A source from 1639 documents 3,450 mingas and 2,800 mitayos, or
approximately the same ratio.[30] In 1668, Corregidor of Potosí Luis
Antonio de Oviedo reported that each week on average there were
1,424 mitayos serving in person, some 700 delivered in silver, and
900 mingas; the following year, his figures were 1,777 mitayos in
person, 374 in silver, and 1,282 mingas.[31] If we assume that some of
the mita deliveries in silver were used to hire mingas, then a slight
shift in favor of mitayos had taken place, but the roughly one-to-one
balance of free and forced laborers had been preserved.

The azogueros' reallocation of mita deliveries in silver permitted
more of them to remain in business than otherwise would have been
possible, despite the production crises of the early 1600's and their
ongoing inability to secure new concessions from the Crown. The appearance of moneylenders and silver merchants as important figures
by the 1640's suggests, however, that most of the azogueros were unable to regain control of their enterprises despite their *indios de*

faltriquera ("pocketed Indians"—mita deliveries in silver that were not used to hire minga replacements). The development of ever more violent means to deal with the capitanes enteradores in the 1650's and 1660's is another clear indication that even this transformation of the mita was unable to offset entirely the difficulties that the azogueros faced in other production areas.

Indios de faltriquera were patently illegal, for even mita deliveries in silver were considered by the government to be an abuse of the mita ordinances. The precise uses to which the deliveries in silver were put cannot be documented fully because they were not divulged, just as the amount of silver that left the Villa Imperial as unmarked contraband is subject to varying speculation (some contemporary estimates placed that sum at as much as two-thirds of total production). It is because of the existence of illegal sources of income that the issue of azoguero profits, and the relationship of the mita to their profits, cannot be discussed—in the seventeenth century*—on any but the most general level.[32] Indeed, we shall see in the following chapters that even the official production figures were regularly manipulated.

It is interesting that the mita had been transformed, in part, into a means of attracting those laborers whom the azogueros of Potosí needed almost as much as apiris and ore grinders: skilled laborers. To help pay the higher wages the mingas demanded, the azogueros used mita deliveries in silver. The tax funds produced by the kurakas, collected in the native communities or from other employers, therefore subsidized the hiring of free laborers at Potosí. Though it was attacked as an abuse of the mita, the practice of mita deliveries in silver actually represented the partial realization of Philip II's earlier quest for a means of attracting the necessary laborers to the Potosí silver industry. Bakewell notes that debt peonage was not widespread at Potosí, in contrast to contemporary New Spain (where it helped to eliminate the need for draft Indian labor),[33] and it may well be that the mita deliveries in silver were part of the reason: they provided higher wages for skilled labor, subsidized by the native communities and other enterprises of Alto Perú.

The azogueros' indulgence in indios de faltriquera was an impor-

---

*Enrique Tandeter has been able to ascertain the relationship between the mita and azoguero profits in the latter half of the eighteenth century, because by that time many mills were rented and financing was provided by the Real Banco de San Carlos, providing reliable data for such computations; see Tandeter, "Forced and Free Labour."

tant reason why they were unable to win further assistance from the Crown. Not only did the practice undermine their contention that they needed royal favors to survive, it fueled the Crown's suspicion that the azogueros did not deserve new concessions. The mita's enemies—who now helped to subsidize the very institution they opposed—made sure that the Crown was well informed of the azogueros' abuses of the mita, as well as of their mistreatment of mitayos and kurakas. Indeed, as they had in the sixteenth century, the mita's enemies focused the Crown's attention on the horrors of the system for the Indians involved. The mines at Potosí were said virtually to devour the poor souls who were dragged off in the mita, often in chains or tied to the tails of horses.[34] Other Indians, the enemies reported, had committed suicide by casting themselves off cliffs or into rivers, and women had maimed or killed their male babies to prevent them from ever serving in the mita.[35] Such accounts would later become the stuff of the Black Legend, but they were produced with the purpose of pricking the royal conscience and thereby winning the abolition of the mita—so that the Indians would be free to work in other enterprises. Though they were unable to bring about the eradication of the mita, these negative reports did serve to undercut the azogueros' argument that they deserved mitayos in recognition of their many years of faithful service to the Crown.

The azogueros and their competitors were engaged in ritualized, rhetorical combat. They could not argue for royal intervention on their behalf on the basis that such aid would improve their own condition, but rather had to cloak their true purposes behind the betterment of the common good and the royal welfare. Nevertheless, they simultaneously had to convince the Crown that they were worthy of royal assistance, whereas their competitors were not. Despite the rhetoric employed on both sides, we must not lose sight of the real object of their struggle: access to and control of Indian labor.

This also explains why the azogueros continued to submit petitions despite their ineffectiveness. The guild persisted specifically to offset the impact of the antimita treatises produced by its enemies. The azogueros were constantly aware that the Crown might legitimately, at any moment, revoke their right to receive mita labor or institute some sort of reform that would seriously threaten their interests. Sandoval y Guzmán's *Pretensiones de la Villa Imperial* of 1634 may not have resulted in the implementation of any of the requested programs, but it did serve to remind the Crown of the impor-

tance of Potosí to the well-being of the Spanish Empire and to iden-
tify as the underlying reason for the antimita reports the competition
for Indian labor on the altiplano.

The azogueros' next comprehensive effort to ward off their enemies came 38 years later, when their representative, Nicolás Matías
del Campo y de la Rynaga, issued a tome entitled *Memorial apologético, histórico, jurídico y político* to counter the Viceroy Conde de
Lemos's 1670 proposal to the Crown that the mita be abolished.[36]
Campo likened Peru to a sick patient whom the doctors had failed to
cure because they had applied mere half-measures. Some of those
physicians (Lemos et al.) had recently deduced, moreover, that the
disease was incurable and that the infected organ (the mita) would
have to be removed (abolished). From a list of fifteen offenses that
they blamed on the mita, they had arrived at these four conclusions:
(1) that the assignment of the Indians to labor at Potosí was unjust,
and that it was counter to their natural liberty; (2) that the Crown
had aggrieved its royal conscience with the assignment of the Indians
to the mines of Potosí; (3) that the mita and the offenses of the
azogueros had destroyed and depopulated the subjected provinces;
and (4) that the Crown should, and in defense of its royal conscience
must, abolish and revoke the assignment of the Indians to Potosí, or
at least (in case that course was rejected) assign them to other mining
centers, leaving Potosí to be worked by resident mingas.[37]

To combat these four conclusions, Campo sought to ally the interests of the Crown with those of the azogueros, and to demonstrate
that those who would see the mita abolished had not the Crown's
interests but rather their own private interests at heart. Article 1 of
the *Memorial* maintained that the king had an unquestionable right
to order his vassals to work for him and so defended the justness of
the mita. The offenses that were currently plaguing the system, Campo
argued, were not the fault of the Crown or inherent in the mita,
but rather the product of individual azogueros' malice. He agreed
that those who were guilty of wrongdoing should be punished; but
abolition would unjustly penalize the Crown and the meritorious
azogueros as well.[38]

Article 2 responded to the charge that the Potosí mita had depopulated the provinces. On the contrary, Campo claimed, the priests,
kurakas, and corregidores in the provinces had advanced that notion
to protect themselves, when they were equally to blame for driving
the Indians from their original pueblos. He admitted that the mis-

treatment suffered by the mitayos at the hands of some azogueros had contributed to Indian flight, but he again assured the Crown that the system could be reformed, that the elements of the mita that gave rise to Indian migration could be purged without destroying the regimen altogether.[39]

Campo argued for the continued assignment of mitayos to the azogueros in Article 3, on the basis of the Villa Imperial's earlier service to the Crown, the azogueros' current needs, and the ill effects that could be expected should the Indians be dispatched to other mining centers. He reiterated, therefore, all the tenets of the azogueros' long-standing position in defense of the mita save one: that the current members of the guild deserved to receive mitayos because of their own hard work and sacrifices. Perhaps Campo realized that the usefulness of that argument had been eroded by the lower levels of Potosí silver production and the extent to which the mita had changed—both phenomena having been documented in the Conde de Lemos's proposal. Campo chose to compensate by stressing the continued importance of the Potosí silver industry to the Hapsburgs. Without the mita, he said, Potosí would fall; when Potosí fell, then Peru would fall; when Peru fell, then Spain would fall; when Spain fell, then the Catholic Church would fall; and when the Catholic Church fell, the world would be left to the mercy of the Protestants. If Potosí could no longer be portrayed as the backbone of the Spanish Empire, Campo did his best to make it appear as Catholicism's Achilles' heel.[40]

Campo took on all fifteen of the abuses that the mita's enemies had claimed were the product of the system in his fourth and final article. In summing up his arguments, he called for a new repartimiento de la mita to replace that of 1633, the new charter to be based not on a reducción general (as Sandoval had suggested) but a general census, with new pueblos and provinces added to the obligated territory if necessary. This proposal was in keeping with the azogueros' traditional position that the Indians in the mita provinces had not been decimated by mita service, but had fled from their obligations and were now living in the exempted sectors of Alto Perú. It also was an acknowledgment of the impossibility of undertaking a comprehensive resettlement program after a century of Indian migration.[41]

The Campo Memorial not only helped to defeat the Conde de Lemos's bid to abolish the Potosí mita, it also identified the means that would soon be used in an extensive revitalization effort directed by the Viceroy Duque de la Palata (1681–92).[42] Now that the respective positions of the azogueros and their competitors have been traced—now that the battle lines have been drawn in the struggle for Indian labor in seventeenth-century Alto Perú—we may turn to the government's inability to cope with the metamorphosis of the mita and the negative ramifications of that evolution.

FOUR

Administering the Mita, 1580-1650

FRANCISCO DE TOLEDO'S immediate successors in the viceregal office were less than enchanted with his creation. Viceroy Martín Enríquez (1581–83) felt that his predecessor had overstepped the bounds of his instructions and disobeyed royal cédulas by establishing the mita.[1] The Viceroy Conde del Villar (1585–90) and second Viceroy Marqués de Cañete (1590–96) bemoaned Toledo's lack of foresight.[2] Yet despite their feelings that the mita was an unfortunate legacy, these viceroys did not question its importance, for they understood that the future of Peru depended upon Potosí silver production, and that the silver mines and refining mills of the Villa Imperial depended upon the mita. Each therefore devised his own repartimiento de la mita with the hope of correcting the difficulties presented by that of his predecessor; each sought to repair or replace those parts of the system he believed responsible for the appearance of abuses, and thus in essence to keep pace with the changing reality in Alto Perú.[3]

These viceroys understood that the evolution of the mita was tied to dislocations in the Toledan production formula, caused initially by the exhaustion of the tailings. The Conde del Villar counseled the Crown, for example, to halve the royal fifth of silver production and lower the price for mercury, to compensate the azogueros for their falling profits—proposals that would later come from the guild itself. At the same time, Villar and a junta he convened in May 1586 to consider the problems at Potosí moved to reinforce the incentives that Toledo had hoped would attract and keep Indian laborers at Potosí. Despite the many difficulties surrounding the right to kapcha and rescates, the viceroy and junta voted to preserve those incentives, even though they clearly gave rise to illegal activities. Just as the mita was a necessary evil, Villar reasoned, so too was the theft of rich ore by the Indians for sale in the ghatu plaza.[4]

By 1592, just three years after the mita was finally endorsed by Philip II, the system required comprehensive repairs. The Viceroy Marqués de Cañete wrote to his sovereign that Indian flight from the Toledan pueblos was already so extensive that the population base of the mita was badly eroded.[5] The effects of migration, moreover, had been worsened by the ravages of epidemic disease in 1589 and 1590.[6] Cañete sent Juan Díaz de Lopidana, an oidor of the Audiencia of La Plata, to Potosí to conduct a thorough inspection and to implement 55 new ordinances that the viceroy hoped would ensure that the azogueros would have sufficient numbers of mitayos and that the mitayos would be well treated and well paid. The Marqués prohibited the sale or rental of mitayos, their diversion to other activities than those to which they were assigned, and the other practices by which the azogueros currently adapted the mita to their individual needs. He also banned the extraction of ore from the cerro on weekends, thereby outlawing (but not halting) the practice of kapcha. Other means were provided to compensate both the azogueros and the Indians for any revenue lost as a result of these orders.[7]

Cañete's orders are impressive in their number and scope, and for the understanding of the dynamics of Potosí silver production that they demonstrate, but they had very little effect on the status quo in Alto Perú. Indeed, by 1595 the viceroy had given up on the Villa Imperial. He wrote to the Crown that the mines were now so deep and the ore so poor that the government would do better to subsidize other mining centers. The azogueros were forcing the Indians to work beyond their physical limits, he reported, in a desperate effort to cover their production costs. Moreover, the administration could not prevent the azogueros' abuse of the mitayos, and in fact the more one tried to govern Potosí, the more ungovernable the place became.[8] Those words would prove to be prophetic.

Having only recently agreed to bless the foundation of the mita, Philip II was not ready to dispose of it so quickly, especially in the light of the vast royal income generated by the Potosí silver industry. In his instructions for Viceroy Luis de Velasco, therefore, the king spoke of mining as the "nervio principal" of Peru and exhorted the viceroy to make its regeneration his primary concern. With regard to Potosí per se, Velasco was ordered to reduce the price of mercury (from 85) to 60 pesos per hundredweight, with its distribution to the azogueros on credit if necessary, and to include more Indians in the mita.[9] Velasco complied with the latter order in his repartimiento de la mita of 1599, providing a weekly draft of 4,634 Indians, and by issuing 26 new ordinances for Potosí, designed—as had been Cañete's—both to reinforce the government's opposition to the various illegal changes in the mita and to make those modifications unnecessary.[10] Carrots were offered by these viceroys, in the form of more mitayos and cheaper mercury, at the same time that the stick was wielded, because the azogueros' abuses of the mita were understood to stem from the deteriorating Toledan production formula.

Despite the tenor of his short-term orders, Velasco's instructions called for the eventual eradication of the mita. The Crown clung to the concept of a resident labor force for Potosí, an idea championed by the Audiencia of La Plata, and encouraged the viceroy to begin settling Indians in the vicinity of the Villa Imperial. The transition to a free resident labor force was to be gradual, owing to the difficulty of the task, and was to be directed by the corregidor of Potosí.[11] The concept had no more viability in 1599 than it had had thirty years earlier, when Francisco de Toledo received similar instructions,* but it served two important purposes. First, it reminded the viceroy that the Crown considered the mita a temporary expedient, justifiable only for lack of alternatives; second, it kept the preferred means of providing Indian labor for Potosí close at hand, ready to be implemented should the prospects for its adoption improve.

These same desires were held by Philip III, who ascended the throne in 1598. The possibility that Velasco might transform the royal position on the mita into effective policy was strengthened by the young monarch's 1601 cédula on Indian personal service. The king was troubled by reports from Cañete and Velasco, as well as from other officials in the Indies, about the plight of the Indians and the inability of the government to control the most prominent colonists—especially the encomenderos, but also the azogueros and other elites.[12] Because the metropolis was entering a period of relative calm following the more adventuresome reign of Philip II, free from the threats posed earlier by Elizabeth I of England and Henry IV of

---

* As we noted in Chap. 2 above, the inviability of the concept had less to do with the settling Indians in and around Potosí (as the 1603 description of the Villa Imperial attests) than with persuading the Indians to serve in the mines and refining mills for economic compensation that they found insufficient.

France,[13] Philip III was able to turn his attention toward the well-being of his Indian vassals and the unruliness of his Spanish subjects in the Americas.

The similarities between the encomenderos and the azogueros are instructive, for in many respects the privileges granted to the azogueros by Toledo were reminiscent of those awarded the encomenderos by the Crown. The latter were entrusted with newly conquered Indians in a given geographical area and were made responsible for their religious instruction and protection, as well as for the administration of justice. In return, the encomenderos were granted the right to a portion of the tribute owed the Crown by the Indians. In similar fashion, the azogueros were granted access to draft Indian labor from a determined geographical region, and other privileges, in exchange for their construction of the new amalgamation mills at their own expense and the oversight of the silver production process thereafter. In both cases, the privileges were granted by the government because it could not realize its goals alone: the conquests would not have been possible had the conquistadores not been willing to forgo remuneration until after the battles were won; the revitalization of Potosí in the 1570's would not have been possible without the participation of the mine owners. Over time, however, the grantees and their descendants came to consider their privileges to be their rights and they overstepped the limitations to their delegated powers. The Crown then found itself unable to restrain them; an effort to revoke grants of encomienda in Peru in the late 1540's, for example, had led to a bloody civil war between Gonzalo Pizarro and the vice-regal authorities in Lima.[14] With no other force than his ultimate legal authority and unquestioned right to revoke at any time the privileges his ancestors had granted, Philip III now found it necessary to threaten to abolish the encomienda and the mita in order to impel the encomenderos and azogueros to adopt more responsible postures.

Thus, although the 1601 cédula called for the abolition of all Indian personal service, the Crown's intent was in fact to keep its colonists from subjugating the Indians for their own purposes. The official responsible for pursuing that goal in Peru was Viceroy Luis de Velasco. The final chapter of the cédula instructed him to consult with experienced and knowledgeable persons, and to make any modifications that he deemed necessary.[15] The cédula was therefore less an edict than a list of suggestions that Velasco was supposed to edit into effective policy; put another way, it was an arsenal from which

the viceroy could choose those weapons necessary to restrain the colonial elites and simultaneously protect the vital interests of the
Crown.

Velasco understood the motivations behind the 1601 cédula and
he appreciated the need to keep the colonists from drawing their own
ultimate weapon—armed insurrection. The viceroy's task was to
fashion a synthesis that advanced the Crown's cause as far as possible
without provoking a violent backlash, not to present the antithesis
to the Crown's thesis, as Phelan argued. Indeed, the edict had been
drafted with the implementation process in mind, for the demands
expressed in the 1601 order were purposely exaggerated, in part, so
that the king's original goals might survive the modification procedure.

The first step in that procedure was the suspension of Philip III's
cédula in 1602, upon its arrival from Spain. A junta of notables was
then convened to debate the best course of action to pursue.[16] The
positions adopted on the mita by Friar Miguel de Agia and Father
Alonso Mesía Venegas on the one hand, and Dean Pedro Muñiz of
Lima on the other, represent the poles of opinion among the con-
ferees. Agia and Mesía Venegas both defended the mita on the
grounds that Potosí silver production was indispensable to the war
against Protestant heresy and that no other labor procurement system
could take its place (they claimed that black slaves would be too costly,
that mingas required prohibitive wages, and that a resident labor force
could not be settled in the inhospitable environs of Potosí*).[17] Muñiz,
to the contrary, was totally opposed to the continuation of the mita
and argued for its prompt eradication. He admitted that Potosí silver
was important to the Crown and that the mita was not the great
killer of Indians that many claimed it to be, but he considered the
system reprehensible and unnecessary. Spain had carried on its holy
war against heresy long before the cerro of Potosí was discovered, he
noted, and would continue to do so long after production there had
come to an end.[18]

Mesía Venegas and Agia argued that the final chapter of the 1601
cédula provided Velasco with carte blanche to solve the problems
then afflicting the mita without undermining the economic foundation of the Catholic world. That, of course, was the intent of the
edict; and thus the viceroy followed their advice and issued a series of
reform orders for the mita, most of them taken directly from selected

* Again we must note the fallacy of this statement, given a resident Indian population at Potosí of 76,000 in the early 1600's.

chapters of the Crown's cédula. Velasco decreed that the Indians' travel allowances were to be paid; he reinforced Toledo's order that only the eldest legitimate son of each kuraka principal be exempted from both the mita and tribute (his other legitimate sons were exempted only from the mita); he decreed that the Indians were not to be treated as beasts of burden; and he reinforced the second Viceroy Marqués de Cañete's orders against the sale or rental of mitayos. Velasco also extended to other provinces a 1596 plan for improving mita deliveries from Chucuito. All the mitayos from a province were henceforth to be dispatched in a group, leaving from a designated place on an appointed day; a list of those included in the contingent was to be prepared in triplicate, with the names, ages, and ayllu affiliations of the Indians denoted; a copy was to be carried to Potosí by the capitán enterador, who was to be selected each year from among the kurakas by the corregidor; and the entire mitayo squadron was to return to its province of origin at the end of one year, again led by its capitán enterador.[19]

Each of Luis de Velasco's orders was meant to make the mita more efficient and less burdensome for the Indians and kurakas involved. There was little more that the viceroy could do at the time, given the dependence of the Peruvian viceroyalty on Potosí silver and the possibility of open conflict with the azogueros should he try to enforce the 1601 cédula more vigorously. Philip III conceded his relative weakness with regard to the azogueros in 1609, in a second cédula on Indian personal service. All the goals of the 1601 edict with regard to the mita were preserved, but the king instructed the Viceroy Marqués de Montesclaros to delay their enforcement until the prospects for their implementation were more promising.[20]

Montesclaros and other viceroys of Peru in the early seventeenth century were well aware of the limitations on their power. The Príncipe de Esquilache was ordered in 1619 to establish a resident work force at Potosí, but he suspended the execution of the edict because he recognized that it was inoperable.[21] In 1621, the Marqués de Guadalcázar was instructed to abolish mita deliveries in silver, but given the extent to which the practice had grown and the violence then pervading the Villa Imperial, he chose instead to try to increase the percentage of the mita delivered in person. As had Esquilache before him, Guadalcázar empowered the corregidor of Potosí to suspend and replace any provincial corregidor who failed to meet his quota.[22]

The limitations on the viceroys' power and influence made them only minimally effective as brokers between the Crown and the azogueros, at least from the Crown's perspective. Because they were stationed in Lima, the viceroys were isolated from the everyday realities of silver production at Potosí and dependent upon officials stationed in Alto Perú—and hence on the same governing techniques employed by the Crown. There were, in Phelan's terms, two flexible linkages in the administration of the mita. An order issued by the king was modified once in Lima to conform to the viceroy's view of its appropriateness and chances for implementation; it was then subjected to a second modification by government officials in the Villa Imperial or La Plata. Not only were the Crown's directives subject to wider interpretations as to their intent and the extent to which they could be executed, but the entire procedure could literally take years, even decades, to complete. In addition, of course, the viceroys' own decrees were themselves vulnerable to modification by officials in Alto Perú, who served, in turn, as brokers between regional interests and the viceregal administration.

The Hapsburg government's administration of the mita was complicated still further by the fact that no single official in Alto Perú was its representative for mita matters. Instead, the Audiencia of La Plata was assigned the task of protecting the Indians from physical abuse—but only by reporting incidents of mistreatment to the viceroy—and the corregidores of Potosí were assigned the daily administration of the mita, including supervision of the provinces' compliance with their mita obligations. The presidents of the Audiencia, however, were responsible for directing the shipment of refined silver from the Villa Imperial, for distributing mercury from the royal warehouses, and for drafting new repartimientos de la mita. This division of responsibilities was considered necessary to ensure that the Crown and its viceroys would receive information from more than one source, and to prevent the azogueros from co-opting or intimidating the officials who were sent to oversee the silver production industry. It was also meant to generate healthy competition and mutual oversight among the officials, prompting them to perform their assigned duties to the fullest extent possible.

The assignment of mita responsibilities to various officials in Alto Perú was not complemented, however, by a distribution of authority over the mita. Instead, the viceroys insisted that they remained the supreme authority where the mita was concerned, and they defended that stance by citing the Toledan junta consultiva's resolution that only the viceroy, in the name of the Crown, could rightfully require the Indians to work in the mines against their will.[23] The principal opposition to that argument came from the Audiencia of La Plata, which had to be reminded a number of times in the seventeenth century to refrain from interfering in the daily administration of the mita.[24] The fatal flaw in this arrangement was the viceroys' inability to exercise the authority they so ardently protected, in part because of their physical distance from Potosí—and thus dependence on local officials—and in part because of the demands of their own duties. The Marqués de Guadalcázar, for example, also had to contend with the "civil war" in the Villa Imperial, Dutch attacks on the port of Callao, Indian wars, drought, and famine.[25]

A more important reason why the viceroys were unable to bring their authority over the mita to bear was the fact that ultimate authority lay not with them in Lima, but with the Crown in Madrid. There were two centers of authority within the Hapsburg administration of Peru, the one—delegated and more immediate—in Lima, and the other—ultimate but distant—in Madrid. This arrangement was necessary to provide for the prompt resolution of critical matters in a faraway realm, but the result was an administrative nightmare. A party to any dispute could appeal to whichever of the centers seemed more likely to side with his cause: an official who disagreed with a viceroy could complain to the Crown; one who disapproved of a royal cédula could argue for its legitimate suspension by the viceroy. No decision was ever final and there was little incentive for competing sectors of the government to come to an accommodation with one another.

As the situation in Potosí and in the obligated provinces of Alto Perú deteriorated during the seventeenth century, professional jealousies and the protection of personal interests by officials combined to foment intragovernmental conflicts that went beyond healthy and productive competition. Those conflicts completely overwhelmed the mechanisms by which the Crown and its viceregal brokers hoped to administer the Potosí mita, for the flexibility in the bureaucratic design proved to be more than the authority inherent in the system could handle.

Feelings were especially bitter between government officials in Lima and the Audiencia of La Plata. Their traditional antagonism

was heightened when Velasco decreed that the corregidor of Potosí—
an official subordinate to the Audiencia within the judicial hierarchy—would henceforth be the viceroy's sole representative in administering the mita's delivery. The Audiencia responded that it would
continue to protect the legal rights of the Indians serving in the Villa
Imperial, as the Crown had instructed it to do. La Plata, the tribunal
argued, was much closer to Potosí than was Lima, and the Audiencia's proximity to the mining center guaranteed the quick resolution
of disputes and an ongoing concern for the mitayos. Government officials in Lima and Potosí, the Audiencia added, cared only about the
amount of silver they were able to dispatch to Spain.[26]

When the Conde de Monterrey died in 1606, the Audiencia of
Lima claimed the right, under the terms of a 1550 cédula, to govern
the viceroyalty until the arrival of his successor. The Audiencias of
Quito and La Plata responded that they were the equals of the Lima
tribunal and would therefore attend to their respective jurisdictions.
Both were dismayed when the Crown backed the Audiencia of Lima
in an edict of November 20, 1606. The silver deposit at Oruro was
discovered that same year, and by the time the Crown's directive
reached Peru, Oruro and Potosí had become pawns in the struggle
between La Plata and Lima. The Audiencia of La Plata backed the
new mining center's request for mercury and mitayos; the Audiencia
of Lima argued that only Potosí should receive government assistance. When the Marqués de Montesclaros finally arrived in 1607, he
ordered the altoperuano tribunal to abandon its championship of the
Oruro miners' requests and banned the delivery of mitayos or mercury to San Phelipe.[27] Stung by yet another rebuff of its contention
that it was the Crown's best representative in Alto Perú, the Audiencia of La Plata simply redoubled its efforts to defend the region from
misguided viceregal interference.

Relations between the corregidor of Potosí and the Audiencia of La
Plata deteriorated as a result of the battle over Oruro as well, for the
corregidor's support of the Azogueros Guild brought him into an alliance with the Audiencia of Lima. In retaliation for this act of "treason," the Audiencia of La Plata suspended the commissions both of
the judges the corregidor had sent to San Phelipe to retrieve Indians
who had gone there from the Villa Imperial and of judges he had sent
to the provinces to oversee the dispatch of mitayos.[28] The Audiencia's
right to intercede in these matters was hotly contested by officials in
Lima, Potosí, La Plata, Oruro, and Madrid, but the most important

effect of the suspensions was to provide the provincial corregidores and competing economic interests with an important ally in their efforts to keep their Indian employees from being packed off to Potosí.

As government officials in Lima and Alto Perú squared off against one another, their squabbling blocked nearly every attempt to administer the mita from the viceregal capital. The clearest indication of the viceroys' ineffectiveness was the constant stream of their reiterated yet disobeyed orders. In 1616, for example, the Príncipe de Esquilache reissued Luis de Velasco's 1603 provisión for the orderly delivery of mitayos, since it was being ignored.[29] The Marqués de Guadalcázar was compelled to repeat Velasco's and Cañete's provisiones (as well as royal cédulas) that the mitayos were to work only at those activities to which they had been assigned.[30] All the viceroys ordered the azogueros to pay the Indians their travel allowances, but rarely were they paid. Indeed, it sometimes seemed that the only impact a viceregal order could have was the opposite of that intended: the Príncipe de Esquilache found it necessary to revoke Velasco's order empowering the royal treasury officials to rent indebted azogueros' mills when he discovered that other creditors than the Crown were always paid first and that some azogueros were purposely indebting themselves so that their mills (and hence the mitayos assigned to them) could be rented.[31]

If the viceregal orders were ineffective, why were they reissued? In part they were repeated to remind local officials of the goals toward which they were supposed to be striving. In part, too, like royal cédulas, they were designed to increase the ability of local officials to perform their assigned duties. And as with the 1601 cédula calling for the abolition of the mita, they were purposely exaggerated in their official demands in the hope that their true goals might survive modification at the local level. One of the keystones of the viceroys' official position on the mita was their insistence that any departure from the Toledan ordinances was an inexcusable abuse, punishable by the loss of one's mitayos; the implication was that the Toledan system was still viable, though as we have seen, the late-sixteenth-century and early-seventeenth-century viceroys understood very well that it was not.

This official stance on the mita was used with limited success. Each time a new repartimiento de la mita was implemented—and this occurred regularly through 1633—some azogueros were denied access

TABLE 3
Official Weekly Draft (Mita Ordinaria) Totals, 1578–1633

Year	Viceroy	Draft	Source
1578	Francisco de Toledo	4,426	Castillo, ff. 7–7v.
1582	Martín Enríquez	4,453	Capoche, pp. 141–44.
1588	Conde del Villar	4,143	Cañete y Domínguez, p. 102.
1599	Luis de Velasco	4,634 ⎱	
1610	Marqués de Montesclaros	4,413 ⎰	Valera, p. 8; Angulo, ff. 2–2v.
1618	Príncipe de Esquilache	4,294	
1624	Marqués de Guadalcázar	4,175	AHP, CR 201, last item.
1633	Conde de Chinchón	4,115	Hanke and Rodríguez, eds., *Virreyes* (Perú), vol. 4, pp. 38–40.

to mitayos because of their past misuse or mistreatment of Indians.[32] The allocation of mitayos to azogueros thereby acquired a greater resemblance to the encomienda, for the grantees now received draft Indian labor in recognition not only of their production capacity, but also of their past performance. The azogueros did not immediately protest this attack on their contention that mita labor was their right by virtue of their pact with Toledo, because they had gone to great lengths to describe themselves as meritorious vassals in their petitions to the Crown, because those who lost their mitayos were few in number, and because the remaining azogueros received more mitayos as a result.

Two side effects of the viceroys' adoption of their official position with regard to the mita were to have great repercussions in the future. First, the repartimientos de la mita showed very little change in terms of the total weekly draft or the number of Indians required from most pueblos (see Tables 3 and 4), despite the diminution of the tributary populations of those villages. Second, the distinction between the official viceregal stance on the mita and the government's perception of reality blurred over time, for later viceroys and other royal officials came to believe that the Toledan system was indeed recoverable— with dire consequences.

The mita charters of the first third of the seventeenth century also gave little indication that mita deliveries in silver existed, and for the most part they ignored the difficulties that the provinces were having in meeting their quotas. The 1624 repartimiento, prepared by President Diego de Portugal of the Audiencia of La Plata, did make some allowances for the falling originario population in the subject prov-

TABLE 4
Official Weekly Draft (Mita Ordinaria)
Quotas, 1578, 1624, and 1633

Province/Pueblo	1578	1624	1633
Chichas	–	35	23
Talina	6.7	–	–
Cotagaita	–	–	–
Calcha	–	–	–
Chichas Total	6.7	35	23
Porco			
Chaqui	35.7	35	35
Caiza	51.3	–	–
Tacobamba	32.7	18	18
Colocaquina y Picachuri	28.7	17	18
Puna	65.3	54	65
Porco Total	213.7	124	136
Chayanta			
Macha y S. Marcos	118	118	118
Chayanta Micani	122.7	71	122
Sacaca y Acasio	59.3	41	59
Caracara	9.7	9	9
Chayanta Total	309.7	239	308
Cochabamba			
Tapacari	66.3	59	64
Sipesipe	46.3	10	16
Santiago del Paso	38.7	21	21
Tinquipaya	28.3	18	28
Cochabamba Total	179.7	108	129
Paria			
Toledo	215	–	–
Quillacas y Asanaque	136.7	126	137
Aullagas y Uruquillas	66	66	66
Paria	–	–	143
Uros de Paria	–	61	–
Paria Total	417.7	253	346
Carangas			
Urinoca	14	14	14
Andamarca			
(y Colquemarca)	123.3	123	123
Chuquicota (y Sabaya)	120	116	128
Totora	74	75	74
Carangas Total	331.3	328	339
Sicasica			
Sicasica	30.3	25	30
Ayoayo	24.3	19	24

TABLE 4
(continued)

Province/Pueblo	1578	1624	1633
Calamarca	21	21	21
Caracollo	43.3	43	43
Sicasica Total	119	108	108
Pacajes			
Callapa	65.3	65	–
Caquiaviri	81	81	94
Caquingora	86	86	86
Jesús de Machaca	68	68	68
S. Andrés de Machaca	40.7	41	41
Viacha	45.3	45	45
Guaqui	58	58	58
Tiahuanaco	43	43	43
Julloma	–	–	65
Pacajes Total	487.3	487	500
Omasuyos			
Laxa	40	40	40
Copacabana	54	47	54
Ancoraimes	7	7	7
Carabuco (Saman y)	28	28	28
Guaicho	24.3	24	24
Achacache	34.7	34	34
Guarina	58.3	58	58
Pucarani	54.7	54	54
Omasuyos Total	301	292	299
Chucuito			
Chucuito	136	116	116
Juli	142	105	105
Pomata	106	93	93
Zepita	80	76	70
Ilave	96	83	83
Acora	104	80	90
Yunguyo	70	61	61
Uros [?]	–	104	–
Chucuito Total	734	718	618
Paucarcolla			
Puno e Icho	50	46	46
Moho y Conima	14	14	14
Capachica	60.7	60	61
Paucarcolla	49.3	48	48
Tiquillaca	–	–	–
Paucarcolla Total	174	168	169
Lampa			
Caracoto	20.3	20	20
Juliaca	22.3	22	22

TABLE 4
(continued)

Province/Pueblo	1578	1624	1633
Nicasio	12	12	12
Ayaviri y Cupi	33.3	60	29
Lampa	35.3	–	29
Llalli	10	10	10
Macari	8	8	8
Cavanilla	33	17	17
Cavana	27	23	27
Atuncolla	26.3	26	26
Manoso	33.3	33	33
Orurillo	42	42	42
Nuñoa	30	30	30
Umachiri	12	9	9
Lampa Total	345	312	314
Asangaro			
Asillo	45.3	21	27
Arapa	65.3	42	56
Saman y Carabuco (see Omasuyos)			
Taraco	34	24	34
Asangaro	54.7	51	55
Caquijana	16.3	16	16
Chupa	17.3	17	17
Caminaca	6	6	6
Achaya	11.3	–	11
Alpaya (Achaya?)	–	11	–
Asangaro Total	250.3	188	222
Canas y Canches			
Sicuani	12.3	19	19
Senca y Lurucache	11.7	15	15
Marangani	5.3	5	5
Coparaque	12	–	11
Corapa (Coparaque?)	–	11	–
Ancocaba	1	1	1
Yauri	31	–	31
Checasupa	15	21	15
Layosupa	11	11	11
Languisupa	12	18	12
Pichigua	43	31	43
Checacupi	21	–	21
Cangalla	5	5	5
Cacha	17	17	17
Charrachape	2.3	2	2
Tinta y Pampamarca	26.7	24	24
Combapata	12	12	12
Yanaoca	27	16	29
Canas y Canches Total	265.3	208	273

(continued overleaf)

TABLE 4
(continued)

Province/Pueblo	1578	1624	1633
Quispicanches			
Cullopata	8.3	8	8
Acopia	7.3	7	7
Pomacanche	25	25	25
Quispicanches Total	40.7	40	40
Condesuyos	–	189	–
Pomatambo y Condes	40	–	–
Cotaguasi	10	–	–
Achampi	10	–	–
Achanquilla	6	–	–
Chumbivilcas-Caratopa	15	–	–
Chachas y Ucuchos	6	–	–
Andagua	6	–	–
Viraco y Machacuay	7	–	–
Pampacolca	15	–	–
Guaicota	20	–	–
Condesuyos Total	135	189	–
Unmatched 1624 Groups			
Siguanes	–	14	–
Uros de coata	–	7	–
Uros de checa	–	3	–
Yapalares	–	7	–
Total Unmatched Groups	–	31	–

SOURCES: 1578: Cook, ed., *Tasa de la visita*; 1624: AHP, CR 201, last item; 1633: from the unimplemented repartimiento de la mita of the Viceroy Marqués de Mancera (1646), AGNA, Sala 9, leg. 6.2.5 (it provides both the 1633 and proposed 1646 figures).

NOTE: The 1578 quotas are derived from the annual draft (mita gruesa) figures. The 1624 quotas were compiled from the individual assignments.

inces, but only by spreading the effects of a lower effective annual draft around: the Indians who habitually failed to arrive in Potosí were distributed among all the azogueros. Moreover, the indios meses, who had earlier been assigned to work in support activities, were now sent into the mines to work as apiris. For the most part, however, the repartimientos of the early 1600's simply ensured that the status quo would not be interrupted and thus that silver would continue to be sent from Potosí to Spain. A very large part of a viceroy's reputation, we should note, hinged on the production of royal revenue under his administration.[33] By issuing a new repartimiento, he could maintain the appearance of action and efficiency, while simultaneously reminding the azogueros of the form that the mita was "supposed" to take and without risking his professional career.*

To the list of reasons why the viceroys were unsuccessful in their efforts to exercise their authority over the mita, therefore, we must add their reticence to take any step that might make things worse than they already were. Given the fact that viceroys served terms of only a few years, and given the importance of mineral production to their reputations as officials, it is not difficult to see the relative attraction of appearance over action. This tendency would become particularly debilitating after 1650, but its role within the government's administration of the mita clearly grew in concert with the worsening situation in the Villa Imperial.

THE HAPSBURG GOVERNMENT of Peru was unable to halt the effects of Indian migration in Alto Perú, just as it was unable to prevent the evolution of the mita. Velasco, Monterrey, and Montesclaros were all instructed to return the forasteros to their original pueblos,[34] but none had the means to comply. The only officials who could conceivably execute such a program were the provincial corregidores, and they were among the interests who depended upon the forasteros for labor. Moreover, any effort to resettle the forasteros would surely have been opposed—with violence if need be—by the Indians' employers. Later, the Príncipe de Esquilache ordered all the forasteros in Potosí and La Plata to return to their original pueblos or serve in the mita, but since his decree was not enforced locally, most decided to stay where they were.[35] And in 1623 the Marqués de Guadalcázar told President Portugal to have each corregidor hold the forasteros who were living in his province or city until their own corregidores and kurakas could come to retrieve them.[36] Like the earlier edicts, this last order was thoroughly unenforceable and hence ineffective.

Guadalcázar was convinced, nonetheless, that the Indian population of the pueblos would not be able to support the mita at the cur-

* A curious aside from the present discussion, but one that bears mentioning, is that official silver production at Potosí rose in the year following any new repartimiento de la mita (see Figure 1). It also increased with the arrival of a new corregidor or other important official. Though I am unable to document the link between the implementation of a new mita charter and higher silver production in every instance, it is clear from the events documented in Chaps. 5–6 below that the production figures were regularly manipulated to demonstrate the administrative prowess of a viceroy or other official.

rent levels for very long. He wrote to the Crown to suggest that the number of mitayos required of each pueblo be reduced to one-seventh of its tributary population, no matter what the effect on Potosí silver production might be. He received Philip IV's permission to proceed, but because he feared that the azogueros might revolt if the downward revision were implemented all at once, the Marqués waited for the individual villages to request *revisitas* (reinspections) before adjusting their mita quotas. Seven revisitas were conducted during the last years of his viceroyalty, and the mita obligations of a few pueblos were lowered, but the official weekly draft fell by only 147 mitayos.[37]

By the early 1630's, the Crown was convinced that the effects of Indian migration in Alto Perú were irreversible. That realization came at a time when Spain's need for colonial revenues was heightened. The authoritarian foreign policy of Philip IV and his chief minister, the Conde Duque de Olivares, had led by 1628 to Spanish campaigns in Italy, Flanders, and Germany—wars that taxed heavily the already overextended royal treasury.[38] A period of relatively good relations with England had died with James I in 1625, and France was now rebuilding under the firm direction of Cardinal Richelieu. Worse still, the Austrian branch of the Hapsburgs was under attack, and its downfall before Protestant armies led by Gustavus Adolphus of Sweden appeared to be at hand. And Pope Urban VIII, who was in a position to save the Austrian court, seemed less than concerned about the demise of the defenders of the true faith.[39]

To pay for Philip IV's multiple military campaigns, the people of the Iberian peninsula were heavily taxed, and their young men were drafted to serve in armies throughout Europe. At the same time, the Indies were expected to contribute to the cause as well. With the mining sector of Alto Perú in decline, Olivares and the king looked to other elements of the Peruvian economy, including the Indian communities, to augment immediately the dispatches of royal revenue from the viceroyalty. New taxes were imposed on agricultural enterprises, forced donations were collected, and the lands abandoned by absent originarios were ordered sold. Kenneth J. Andrien has pointed out that this program threatened the interests of various elites in Peru,[40] but it may well have assisted some in Alto Perú to expand into the fertile lands of the underpopulated Indian pueblos. That process, combined with the sale of government offices to the highest bidders (another component of the wartime revenue program) and thus often to wealthy Peruvian notables, meant short-term financial gains for the Crown at the expense of the Indian communities and of its own position vis-à-vis the colonial elites.

The Viceroy Conde de Chinchón tried to persuade Philip IV that the sale of lands in Alto Perú would permanently eliminate any chance of returning the Indians to their original pueblos, but the king insisted and the viceroy reluctantly obeyed.[41] With the execution of a resettlement program no longer an option, Chinchón was faced with the need to develop some other means of reconciling Potosí's demand for mitayos with the depleted originario population in the obligated provinces. The solution that he settled upon was, very simply, an enforcement of the official viceregal position concerning the mita— that whatever few mitayos were available should be assigned to the azogueros solely on the basis of merit. The viceroy expected that the azogueros' widespread involvement with indios de faltriquera and other abuses would easily disqualify most of the guild, and that there would be plenty of mitayos for the few remaining meritorious azogueros. Chinchón's plan was born of viceregal powerlessness to control either the Indians or the azogueros. It was also selective abolition—the limited application of the government's ultimate weapon, which through the ever-growing gulf between the current form of the mita and the Toledan ordinances had actually grown more threatening. Had this new policy been implemented by the president of the Audiencia of La Plata or the corregidor of Potosí, its impact on Potosí might have been so modified as to be negligible. The viceroy decided, however, to circumvent those officials and send Visitador Juan de Carvajal y Sande to the Villa Imperial to formulate and implement the new mita charter.[42] Thus, the traditional administrative buffer between official viceregal policy and altoperuano practice provided by the local officials was removed, and policy and reality came face to face.

Carvajal chose not to reduce the weekly draft by any significant amount, because of the pressing financial needs of the metropolis, but he did deny mitayos to the owners of 29 of the 100 mills then extant. He also ordered that travel allowances be paid to the mitayos, and he terminated the traditional exaction of four reales from each mitayo's weekly wages to pay the veedores and the alcalde mayor de minas, ordering the azogueros to pay those officials instead.[43] The Azogueros Guild was infuriated. The changes that Carvajal demanded, in terms of the Toledan system, were not very great; and in truth the mills to which he denied mitayos had not been in production for some time. It was the functional effect of the visitador's repartimiento that provoked the shrill outcry from the azogueros. First of all, Carvajal assigned the mitayos in complete ayllus or pueblos, so that their service in person might be more tolerable for them. This meant that some azogueros received entire allocations of Indians who normally complied with their mita obligations, whereas others received only Indians who had not appeared in Potosí for decades.[44]

There were three even more important reasons for the azogueros' unhappiness with the new repartimiento. First, their acceptance of the terms of the charter would mean their official capitulation on the issue of whether mitayos could be denied them on the basis of misuse, and would represent an open confession that abuses were widespread. Second, the owners of the 29 mills also owned active enterprises, and were accustomed to using all their mitayos to sustain those mills, thereby compensating for the falling effective weekly draft.[45] And third, the assignment of the mitayos in complete ayllus disrupted the azogueros' arrangements with kurakas for mita deliveries in silver, as well as the mixture of mitayos in person and deliveries in silver that they had received under the 1624 charter. The azogueros could not condemn the Carvajal repartimiento for these reasons, however, lest they unveil the actual workings of the mita at the precise moment that Sebastián de Sandoval y Guzmán was attempting to win them new concessions by arguing that they deserved further royal assistance because of their years of sacrifice and meritorious service to the Crown.

The azogueros were reluctant to resort to violence, moreover, as long as there was reason to hope that they could win the recall of the Carvajal repartimiento by peaceful means. They complained to the Council of the Indies that Carvajal's innovations would lower silver production significantly and result, if his orders were not revoked promptly, in the demise of the industry—a line of argument consistent with their earlier claim that Potosí silver production would collapse without further concessions.[46] The visitador defended his actions in his own lengthy correspondence with the Council.[47] Needless to say, there was little in common in the two portrayals of the situation in the Villa Imperial; Carvajal characterized the azogueros as greedy and disloyal, whereas Sandoval y Guzmán described them as long-suffering, devoted subjects. The Council was perplexed by the lack of common ground in the two positions, so it ordered the

Conde de Chinchón to investigate the matter and act according to the findings of his inquiry. Philip IV signed a cédula to that effect on April 6, 1636; he strongly suggested, however, that another repartimiento be drawn up to replace that of Juan de Carvajal y Sande.[48]

The azogueros' gambit seemed to be working. They were fortunate to have as their ally the president of the Audiencia of La Plata, Juan de Lizarazu. The president was willing to lock horns with Carvajal because of his professional and personal dislike of the visitador. Lizarazu chafed under Carvajal's usurpation of his powers during the visitador's stay in La Plata (a standard practice), and he resented charges that he and the oidores were corrupt and incompetent. More importantly, the two officials clashed openly over various extralegal measures that Lizarazu had seen fit to allow—such as the distribution of mercury to the azogueros on credit—in his efforts to augment Potosí silver production. Indeed, the president believed that the industry should be administered by a single official—one with practical administrative experience and an adequate understanding of the production process (i.e., himself)—and he proposed to the Crown that he be permitted to do so. Lizarazu lost the battle over the distribution of mercury on credit, primarily because the royal treasury officials sided with Carvajal, and his suggestion that he be allowed to administer the Potosí silver industry unhindered was turned down as well, but he did manage to outlast Carvajal.[49] The Conde de Chinchón recalled his emissary in 1638, upon receipt of the April 1636 cédula; the president enjoyed only a brief respite, however, before having to contend with another visitador.[50]

Juan de Lizarazu provided Chinchón with a plan for a new repartimiento de la mita that, if implemented, would have benefited the azogueros greatly. The program called for (1) fixed quotas of mitayos for the mills based on the number of stamping mechanisms (*mazos*); (2) a total of 300 mitayos for the soldados mineros; and (3) a limitation of two mills (cabezas de ingenio) per azoguero. These parameters, the president argued, would ensure that the Indians were distributed fairly, to as many recipients as possible.[51] The Azogueros Guild supported Lizarazu's proposal because its adoption would mean the restoration of the status quo ante 1633, for merit would play no part in the proposed repartimiento. Indeed, the azogueros asked the Crown to reinstate the 1624 charter until the replacement was completed.[52]

The president's arguments in this regard won him the confidence of the viceroy, who eventually concluded that Carvajal's greatest talent was his ability to alienate everyone with whom he came into contact. Chinchón and Lizarazu corresponded throughout 1639 on a remedy for the problems that the visitador had left in his wake, and the viceroy even granted the president the power to adjust the 1633 repartimiento. Lizarazu responded, however, that mere adjustments would not be sufficient, that more fundamental changes were needed. Indeed, in explaining the need to replace the 1633 charter, he defended the current form of the mita—including deliveries in silver—as a natural and justifiable result of declining ore quality and rising production costs. The president maintained, moreover, that indios de faltriquera should not be considered an abuse punishable by elimination from the next mita charter.[53] This discussion of the relationship between the prescribed and actual forms of the mita was not included, interestingly enough, in Lizarazu's explanation to the Crown of his refusal to adjust the 1633 repartimiento.[54] He undoubtedly understood that such admissions would harm the azogueros' chances of winning new concessions from the Crown.

Chinchón never did comply with the April 1636 cédula and instead left it to be dealt with by his successor, the Marqués de Mancera. The Crown and the Council of the Indies also deferred to the judgment of the new viceroy, although their instructions for him showed a distinct preference for Lizarazu's program.[55] Mancera's efforts to draft a new repartimiento were to be the most significant of the 1633–80 period, but they illustrate further the weaknesses that prevented the Hapsburg government from effectively administering the mita.

DESPITE HIS WILLINGNESS to permit minor modifications of the silver production formula at Potosí—a temporary reduction of the royal fifth to a tenth,[56] for example—the Marqués de Mancera was in no hurry to replace the 1633 repartimiento. By 1642, the azogueros were frustrated by the new viceroy's inaction, besieged by another shortage of mercury, and plagued by Visitador Juan de Palacios.[57] One bright spot for the guild continued to be the assistance it received from the president of the Audiencia of La Plata, now Dionisio Pérez Manrique. The azogueros informed the viceroy in October 1642 that they were confident that Pérez Manrique could rectify all of their problems if he were afforded the opportunity.[58] Mancera responded that the president would indeed be empowered to adjust the 1633 mita charter to their satisfaction.[59]

The replacement of Carvajal's repartimiento was again within the azogueros' grasp. Unfortunately for them, by the time the vice-roy's answer arrived in the Villa Imperial, they and the president were locked in a struggle over indios de faltriquera. Though Pérez Manrique shared his predecessor's desire to assist the azogueros, he did not accept Lizarazu's contention that misuse of mita deliveries in silver was justifiable. He therefore empowered his brother Pedro, as his deputy, to remove 70 mitayos from three of the guiltier azogueros. For the guild, the president's action was a serious threat to current mita practice and hence to their livelihood. The azogueros countered by warning that Potosí would collapse; and to breathe new life into that old threat—as well as to ensure that the matter would be re-viewed by the Crown and/or the viceroy—they presented Corregidor Juan Vázquez de Acuña with the rights to their mitayos and chal-lenged him to distribute the Indians to anyone who could employ them better in service to the Crown. Why, they asked, should they continue to postpone the inevitable demise of Potosí?[60]

The azogueros' *dejación* (waiver) and the corregidor's subsequent refusal to accept the mitayos were a prearranged, concerted ploy to pressure the Marqués de Mancera to intervene on the azogueros' be-half. If future attacks on the mita were to be prevented, then a new repartimiento de la mita based on Lizarazu's nonmerit guidelines was imperative. The azogueros' gambit grew more problematical, how-ever, when the soldados mineros, led by Pedro Pérez Manrique, of-fered to assume responsibility for the Potosí silver industry in the azogueros' place. That brought a stern warning from the guild that such a move would lead to serious trouble. Indeed, its possibility alone brought about an armed confrontation between the soldados and the azogueros in the center of Potosí on the last day of Novem-ber 1642.[61]

Meanwhile, the Azogueros Guild dispatched deputies to Lima to present its case before Mancera, with an initial stop in La Plata to in-form the Audiencia of their mission. That caused the president to change his tune, for rather than assume the onus of having pre-cipitated the shutdown of the Potosí silver industry, Dionisio Pérez Manrique agreed not to carry out his anti-abuse program until he had received confirmation of his orders from the viceroy or the Crown. In return, the azogueros agreed to recall their deputies.[62] Once the issue of the waiver was settled—once the azogueros and the president had come to an understanding—nothing more was ever said about the events of November and December 1642. Indeed,

under the president's guidance, the azogueros drafted another petition to the viceroy reiterating the requests made ten years earlier by
Sandoval y Guzmán.[63]

The azogueros now faced an uphill battle in their quest for the replacement of the 1633 repartimiento, despite strong support for a
new charter from President Pérez Manrique and Corregidor Blas Robles de Salzedo.[64] The Marqués de Mancera's earlier inclination to assist the azogueros had given way to a growing distrust; he now accused them of greatly exaggerating their plight. The viceroy's review
of the documentation surrounding the waiver, of correspondence between Juan de Carvajal y Sande and the Conde de Chinchón, and of
the ongoing denunciations of one azoguero by another for misuse of
mita deliveries in silver was responsible for this change in attitude.[65]
The last cause is significant, for it points to the fact that not all the
azogueros stood to benefit from the drafting of a new mita charter,
and those who did not sought to protect their advantage by publiciz-
ing the degree to which others were engaged in abuses. Their charges
raised important questions about the azogueros' credibility at the
very moment that Mancera was weighing his response to the guild's
petition.

The Marqués drafted a new repartimiento de la mita, nevertheless,
but only because of the metropolis's need for silver to fund its war
with the Protestants.* The process took another two years to complete; the delay was caused by the need to conduct an enumeration in
the sixteen† mita provinces, for the viceroy doubted that there were
sufficient Indians to sustain Potosí's appetite for mitayos. The census
results showed, however, that there were enough Indians in the provinces, and the Marqués proceeded.[66] To increase the Indian labor
force beyond the totals provided by the 1633 repartimiento, moreover, Mancera added the 380 mitayos who had been assigned to the
mines at Porco and one-tenth of the yanaconas living in the obligated
region (or roughly 700 per week).[67]

Unsure about the feasibility of the innovations included in his
handiwork, the viceroy sent a draft of the repartimiento to Potosí for
comments. This gesture of renewed cooperation between the govern-

---

*Philip IV was now faced with insurrections in Catalonia and Portugal, as well as
the ongoing wars in the rest of Europe. Indeed, the definitive end of Spanish preemi-
nence—the Peace of Westphalia—was less than five years away (Domínguez Ortiz, pp.
99–103).

†The reduction to sixteen provinces reflects the loss of Condesuyos, exempted from
mita service following the 1624 repartimiento (see Table 4).

ment and the azogueros was undermined, however, by the variety of responses that Mancera received in return. Most of the azogueros met on July 29, 1646, under the direction of the corregidor, and responded as a group. They noted that the number of mitayos actually working at Potosí had fallen to 2,600 per week and that a mere 80 were then toiling at Porco—the addition of those Indians would be welcomed, but it would not have as great an impact as the viceroy expected. The azogueros were also concerned about the dependability of the yanaconas. They thanked the viceroy for his efforts on their behalf, nonetheless, and requested that whatever the total annual draft might be, the Indians be distributed on the basis of production capability (i.e., not on the basis of merit) and with the various ayllus' records of service in mind.[68]

Individual azogueros, the royal treasury officials, Corregidor Juan de Velarde, and others wrote separate responses to the new mita charter, and their suggestions were the opposite of those of the guild.[69] Velarde was concerned that Mancera's repartimiento favored many azogueros whose involvement with indios de faltriquera was extensive, and he cautioned the viceroy that a host of recriminations would engulf the Villa Imperial should the distribution not be altered to reward the more deserving azogueros. Hence, the corregidor insisted that merit be used as the basis of the new assignment of mitayos, whereas most of the azogueros demanded that production capacity be the determining criterion. Individual azogueros who had benefited by the 1633 repartimiento supported the corregidor's position. This inconsistent response to the drafted charter raised a new series of questions in Mancera's mind, and he sent back four more queries for the azogueros and officials to answer; one asked whether it was feasible to obligate the forasteros in the sixteen provinces to serve in the mita.[70]*

By the time the viceroy sat down to the final revision of the new repartimiento de la mita, he had the results of a visita of the cerro and mills conducted by Velarde and other officials, a request from the Azogueros Guild to push forward with the new charter despite the objections of a few in their midst, and the azogueros' answers to the four questions. Specifically, the guild agreed that the incorporation of the forasteros would be beneficial, for the viceroy's census had demonstrated that there were many of them and the gap between the cur-

---

*The three other questions asked about the status of the mills, which Indians were good and which bad, and why there were only 80 Indians working at Porco.

rent effective delivery of mitayos and the provincial quotas might, by their inclusion, be bridged.[71]

The Marqués de Mancera was correct to wonder about the feasibility of including the yanaconas or forasteros in the Potosí mita, for how were the kurakas supposed to deliver them? That question was not immediately put to the test, however, for the viceroy never completed work on the new repartimiento. He became discouraged by the lack of a consensus in the reports he received from Potosí and generally by the problems involved in running the mita from Lima. The royal treasury officials in the Villa Imperial did not help Mancera's resolve when they alleged that the azogueros' involvement in indios de faltriquera was the principal cause for the fall in the value of the royal fifth during his viceroyalty. In fact, they charged that the azogueros mistreated the mitayos who served in person by design, so that the Indians would flee from Potosí and the kurakas could be required to replace them with deliveries in silver. The officials' own inspection of the mines and mills, they reported, had shown that the azogueros were refining worthless tailings if anything at all, and that they did so only to provide the appearance of activity.[72]

By the end of 1646, Mancera was thoroughly frustrated. The royal fifth, the treasury officials announced, was down more than 43,000 pesos from the previous year's level, despite the viceroy's suspension of the collection of mercury debts and adoption of other pro-azoguero measures.[73] The Marqués was especially upset by the extent to which the azogueros were involved in indios de faltriquera and disheartened by a report from Velarde that the mita quotas for the upcoming year would not be met by most of the provinces.[74] The Crown was at war with heresy and needed money, the viceroy argued, and thus anyone who did not strive to raise that money was a traitor. The azogueros' misuse of mita deliveries in silver was no longer just an abuse; it was treason. Mancera informed the azogueros, in no uncertain terms, that only those who deserved assistance would receive it. "And for now," he told them, "the proof of who qualifies and who does not will be based on two factors. The first is the punctual payment for mercury, and the second is the improvement of the royal fifth. Not only must the fifth not go any lower, it must return to its earlier levels. Any of you who fails me in this regard, I assure you, will feel my response personally and in his pocketbook."[75] The viceroy had clearly rejected the azogueros' contention that the mitayos should be distributed on the basis of production capacity rather than merit. He had decided, in fact, that a new repartimiento would be a concession to the azogueros and that they as a group did not deserve government assistance.[76]

Thus, the azogueros did not get their new mita charter.[77] The intervention of Juan de Carvajal y Sande in 1633—the circumvention of the traditional administrative buffer between viceregal policy and altoperuano reality—had caused them great harm. The azogueros' opportunity to recover from that blow—an opportunity won through appeal to the Council of the Indies—fell victim to their brief struggle with Dionisio Pérez Manrique over indios de faltriquera and to Juan de Velarde's insistence that merit play some part in the distribution of mitayos. The local officials did not, in this instance, serve the interests of the azogueros, but rather prevented them from achieving their goal. The importance of the individuals occupying those posts must therefore be noted. Indeed, the azogueros had learned just how dependent they were on local government officials, and would not soon forget that lesson.

The azogueros did not give up the battle for a new repartimiento. To overcome the intransigence of the Marqués de Mancera, they again tried to bring the Council of the Indies into play on their behalf by exploiting the Crown's desperate need for revenue. Given the financial difficulties resulting from the stewardship of Olivares (which lasted long after his forced resignation in 1643),[78] the guild anticipated that the Crown would be receptive to suggestions that it could raise silver output significantly. The Council of the Indies did in fact prove to be more concerned with silver production than with the merit-versus-production-capacity debate. The guild then discovered, however, that the very weaknesses in the Hapsburg administration of Peru that had prevented viceroys from affecting the mita in the past could also be used by viceroys to keep the Crown from coming to the azogueros' rescue.

FIVE

Administering the Mita,
1650-1680

In response to the Marqués de Mancera's decision not to implement a new repartimiento de la mita and the subsequent complaints
from the Azogueros Guild, the Council of the Indies developed a
two-part program that it hoped would appease the legitimate demands of the azogueros, protect the Crown's economic and political
interests, and ensure that the Indians would not be mistreated. The
first step was taken on April 18, 1650, when Philip IV signed a
cédula ordering a new mita charter, to be preceded by a reducción
general in the sixteen obligated provinces. The Council considered
the cédula to be a concession to the azogueros because it acceded to
Sandoval y Guzmán's second proposal of 1634; moreover, the edict
was complemented by a simultaneous edict to suspend the collection
of their mercury debts until further notice.[1] The second step of the
program began with a May 6, 1651, cédula ordering the president of
the Audiencia of La Plata, Francisco Nestares Marín, to put an end
to the practice of indios de faltriquera. The concessions granted
the previous year, the councillors argued, had removed any cause
for the azogueros to engage in abuses of the mita.[2]

The balanced program developed by the Council of the Indies
in the early 1650's represented a break with the traditional pattern of
issuing exaggerated orders with the understanding that they would
be modified by officials stationed in Peru. The Crown was now trying
to serve as referee between the azogueros of Potosí and the viceregal
authorities in Lima. The two cédulas also indicate that the Council
had come to believe the official viceregal contention that the Toledan
mita was recoverable, if only the production formula were adjusted
to benefit the azogueros and the current abuses of the mita were

eliminated. By the mid-seventeenth century, that stance was wholly unrealistic.*

The conceptual foundation of the Council's program was not immediately put to the test in Peru, however, because the two cédulas were rendered completely ineffective by the ongoing struggle between the azogueros and the viceregal administration. The Conde de Salvatierra (1648–55) was the first viceroy to receive the 1650 order, and he chose not to implement it because he believed that a reducción general would be impossible to execute, and because he had been convinced by the Marqués de Mancera that the azogueros did not deserve further government assistance and that their abuses of the mita could not be prevented. Salvatierra was also concerned that any government intervention in the Potosí silver industry might bring on its collapse and thus cause a substantial drop in the amount of royal revenue produced in Peru during his viceroyalty. It was better to let Potosí fall of its own weight, he later told his successor, than to risk bringing on its sudden collapse through the introduction of innovations.[3] President Nestares Marín, meanwhile, complained that his ability to implement the 1651 cédula was curtailed by his lack of jurisdiction over the mita, which was the province of the corregidor of Potosí.[4]

Salvatierra's reluctance to act on the 1650 cédula did not close the matter, however, for the Crown then instructed Corregidor Francisco Sarmiento de Mendoza to direct the reducción general and to devise the subsequent repartimiento de la mita. The traditional division of responsibilities for the mita in Alto Perú was thereby observed, for Nestares Marín continued to be responsible for the elimination of the practice of indios de faltriquera.[5] The Council of the Indies was aware that there would be some antipathy between the president and the corregidor, but it believed that their rivalry would ensure that each would comply with his orders to the best of his abilities. That was not to be the case.[6] Once policy initiatives regarding the mita began coming from Madrid, moreover, the viceroys of Peru became active combatants in the intragovernmental struggle over the system's future.

Corregidor Sarmiento de Mendoza championed the azogueros' cause much as President Lizarazu had done, and his program for a

---

*It is possible that given the metropolis's desperation for funds, the councillors were prepared to pursue any avenue that might yield augmented revenues, whether realistic or not.

new repartimiento reflected the latter's design: first, no azoguero would be permitted to have more than two mills; second, the mitayos would be assigned to each azoguero solely on the basis of the number of stamping mechanisms he owned; and third, those mills that were owned by widows or children would be rented to worthy individuals for two years at a time. To augment the annual draft, the corregidor planned to include yanaconas and forasteros in the mita (the viability of this idea having gone unchallenged because Mancera had not implemented his 1646 repartimiento); moreover, mita deliveries in silver would be legalized, so that those who declined to serve in person might meet their obligations otherwise.[7] And, like Lizarazu, Sarmiento asked the Crown to award him sufficient authority to administer the Potosí silver industry free of interference from any other official (primarily Nestares Marín, but also the viceroy).[8]

Nestares Marín was a visitador as well as the president of the Audiencia of La Plata, and he had earlier been ordered to collect the azogueros' mercury debts. Thus, he was already the guild's enemy when he was instructed to extirpate the practice of indios de faltriquera. Nestares Marín was also very much opposed to Sarmiento's handling of the new mita charter, but his condemnation of the corregidor's activities in that regard had little immediate effect, for his complaint to the Crown went to the bottom of the sea with a shipwreck in 1654.[9] The president did not have to worry, however, for the viceroy had already moved to keep Sarmiento from completing a new mita charter: in May 1654, Salvatierra ordered the corregidor to suspend his work on the repartimiento until the new viceroy arrived.[10] The Conde's suspension of a royal order that had been meant to circumvent his opposition to the Council's program points to a glaring weakness in the administrative structure. Not only did Salvatierra bequeath the professional liability for the new repartimiento to his successor, he confused matters further by sending a last-minute directive to Nestares Marín to assume absolute control over the mita. This order heightened the tension between the president and the corregidor to such an extent that their squabbling rendered them absolutely ineffective as royal agents.[11]

If Salvatierra's reluctance to act was frustrating for the Council of the Indies and the azogueros, his successors' few moments of efficiency proved to be disastrous. One such moment came during the viceroyalty of the Conde de Alba (1655-61). Like his predecessor, Alba was reluctant to rush into any program that had anything to do with the mita, for he had been persuaded by Salvatierra's caution that innovation might bring on the prompt collapse of the silver industry. Thus, in response to an April 18, 1657, cédula to assume the direction of both halves of the Council's program, Alba feigned uncertainty about who was to be responsible for its implementation and requested clarification from Madrid.[12] That ensured him at least one year of grace, given the delays inherent in transatlantic correspondence.

While the Conde de Alba waited for the Council of the Indies to reply, however, he felt compelled to undertake an investigation into the issue of a new repartimiento—to offer the appearance of progress toward a resolution of that matter—by convening the Real Acuerdo (a meeting of the Audiencia of Lima to advise the viceroy) in August 1658. Under his direction, the Acuerdo decided to send an emissary to Potosí to report on the situation there, and to implement later the Council's program should approval for the use of a single, third-party administrator be forthcoming from Madrid (the appropriate request was then dispatched to the Crown). Alba's choice for the mission was the bishop-elect of Santa Marta, Friar Francisco de la Cruz.[13]

Francisco de la Cruz arrived in Potosí on May 20, 1659, armed with a commission appointing him "superintendent of the mita" and giving him authority and powers superior to those of the corregidor and the president, so that he might go about his investigation unhindered. His apparent omnipotence was circumscribed, however, by secret instructions from the viceroy to secure Alba's approval before taking any direct action.[14] Though the viceroy seemed to be postponing any action until he had irrefutable instructions from the Crown, he had virtually assured himself that those would not be forthcoming by sending his proposal that a superintendent implement the two cédulas on the heels of his earlier request for clarification, and was in fact trying to put off the matter until the arrival of his own successor.

Within a week or two of Cruz's arrival in Potosí, however, he broke with his secret instructions and sent three judges into the field to conduct a census in the sixteen obligated provinces and fourteen exempted corregimientos—cities and provinces—of Alto Perú.* He decided to take that step because he had seen very few Indians while en route to the Villa Imperial and so doubted that there were sufficient numbers to support a new repartimiento.[15] The superintendent also

_____

*The fourteen exempted corregimientos included the cities of Potosí, La Paz, La Plata, etc. Thus the word "corregimiento" will be used hereafter when referring to a combination of cities and provinces.

announced to the azogueros that the coming mita charter would include strict penalties for any abuse, and he began to collect information from silver merchants and others with which to judge the merits of each azoguero.[16]

Cruz's initial inquiries revealed that the sums collected by the azogueros for mita deliveries in silver came to some 587,000 pesos per year. The royal fifth, meanwhile, amounted to a mere 300,000 pesos. Why not, he asked, simply send the mita deliveries in silver directly to the Crown? More importantly, Cruz found that to extract the 11,000 pesos per week from the kurakas, the azogueros were using torture, including the hanging of kurakas by their hair, beatings, and whippings. He also learned of one kuraka who had killed himself upon hearing that he would have to serve as a capitán enterador—a story that may not have been typical, but one that troubled the superintendent greatly. He found, as well, that the azogueros were selling Indians to enterprises in Lipes for 250 pesos apiece, and that they were carrying on a thriving contraband trade with the Dutch—with whom Philip IV was at war—via Buenos Aires.[17]

These revelations caused the superintendent to turn against the azogueros with a vengeance. In June 1659, Cruz ordered all mita deliveries in silver halted and instructed the kurakas to hire mingas themselves with any money remitted to Potosí for the purpose of meeting mita obligations.[18] Cruz also banned rezagos de mita (the kurakas' debts for their prior failures to deliver complete quotas of mitayos), ordaining that the kurakas were to be held responsible only for those Indians with whom they had departed their home provinces. The mitayos who did appear in Potosí, moreover, were to be distributed on a pro rata basis to the azogueros, and the corregidores of the provinces were to be held responsible for any failure to remit sufficient numbers of Indians.[19] The Conde de Alba, convinced by the portrayal of conditions he received from his emissary, backed up those orders with viceregal provisiones in January 1660.[20] Encouraged by the support he received from the viceroy, Cruz issued a second wave of edicts in February that reinforced his earlier decrees; the kurakas, he insisted, were not to be held accountable for the failure of Indians to appear in Potosí to serve in the mita.[21]

The viceroy may have chosen to back up Cruz's edicts, but he also understood that they would have to be complemented with an updated repartimiento if a wholesale upheaval at Potosí were to be avoided. The Conde de Alba ordered his superintendent to return to

Lima, and began to draft the new repartimiento himself.[22] Cruz never did leave Potosí, however, for his actions prompted a response from the azogueros that was in keeping with the seriousness of the threat that his orders represented. The azogueros' protests to Cruz and the viceroy having proved unavailing, they decided to murder the superintendent by poisoning his hot chocolate; Cruz went to bed the night of April 23, 1660, in perfect health and died in his sleep. President Nestares Marín, by no coincidence, died that same evening, quite possibly murdered by the same means.[23] *

As with the earlier visita of Juan de Carvajal y Sande and the effort by President Pérez Manrique to remove mitayos from those guilty of engaging in indios de faltriquera, the azogueros had responded to an immediate threat with extraordinary means. In each case, the threat had come when the traditional administrative buffer between official policy and reality—the local Hapsburg officials—was circumvented. Carvajal and Pérez Manrique were defeated with less desperate means and with the assistance of a local official. The superintendent's determination to eradicate the abuses in the mita and his apparent administrative omnipotence had required a more extreme reply.

Francisco de la Cruz's murder halted the government's attack on the mita only temporarily, however, for another official was soon sent to replace him (and to occupy concurrently the presidency of the Audiencia of La Plata). By murdering the superintendent, moreover, the azogueros had convinced the Conde de Alba that everything that Cruz had reported about the situation at Potosí was true. Alba's determination to punish the azogueros was more than evident in his orders to the second superintendent of the mita, Bartolomé de Salazar: first, he was to base the new mita charter on the current population of the sixteen mita provinces, to be determined by a prerepartimiento census (i.e., no reducción general was to be conducted); second, he was to collect all mita deliveries in silver personally and to hire mingas with that money directly. Much as Guadalcázar and Chinchón had sought to do, Alba had resolved to tailor the mita to the extant

---

* Arzáns, *Historia*, vol. 2, pp. 128–33, discusses an earlier attempt, in 1651, to kill Nestares Marín with poison; and on pp. 187–94, he notes the deaths of the two officials. The author of the Dominican paper supporting the Viceroy Conde de Lemos's 1670 proposal that the mita be abolished said that he had been in Potosí at the time of the murder. He reported that the azogueros first tried to burn Cruz's house down, and that they later killed him. The Tuesday morning following the murder, moreover, indios de faltriquera were again collected from the kurakas (AGI, Charcas, leg. 268, no. 15E, undated and unsigned).

population in the sixteen obligated provinces, whatever that might be and whatever the impact on the azogueros. The guild, he told Salazar, deserved no more.[24]

Alba's firmness of purpose was undone, however, by his appointment of Bartolomé de Salazar as superintendent, for Salazar was determined to increase Potosí silver production—to demonstrate his skills as an administrator—and his prior government service at Huancavelica had hardened him to the grim realities of a mining community. Salazar argued that the azogueros' abuses should be dealt with only after the new repartimiento was completed, and he refused to implement the viceroy's anti-azoguero program. With an exuberance common to officials arriving in Potosí for the first time, moreover, Salazar proclaimed that he was prepared to execute every facet of the Council of the Indies' plan.[25] With that, the cumbersome machinery of the Hapsburg bureaucracy began again to serve the interests of the azogueros, by protecting the mita from viceregal interference.

If the new superintendent refused to do as the viceroy requested, the Conde de Alba was also determined to keep Salazar from proceeding as he pleased. The immediate objects of their struggle were the number of corregimientos to include in the prerepartimiento census and who should conduct it. The viceroy wanted two judges from the Audiencia of La Plata to do an enumeration in only the sixteen obligated provinces; Salazar was convinced that more areas would have to be added if silver production at Potosí were to be revitalized—an issue that no longer concerned the viceroy—and thought that the corregidores should undertake the count.[26] The Conde de Alba realized that his program was unattainable as long as Salazar was in charge of matters at Potosí, but with the end of his viceroyalty in sight, he decided simply to leave the resolution of the census matter to his successor. In the meantime, he prevented Salazar from implementing his own plan by using the delays in Lima-Potosí correspondence to full advantage. After a year of procrastination, Alba finally acceded to Salazar's demand that he be allowed to proceed, but only once it was clear that the superintendent's program would be carried out under the Viceroy Conde de Santisteban (1661–66).[27] Whatever satisfaction Salazar might have taken from winning his battle with Alba was soon lost, for immediately after the new viceroy took office in July 1661, he ordered the superintendent to suspend all activities leading toward a new repartimiento.[28]

Santisteban told Salazar that he wanted the census to be conducted by two oidores of the Audiencia of La Plata. The superintendent responded with a host of reasons why the new viceroy's plan was unrealistic, but the latter was not concerned with its viability; he had only issued the order to prevent Salazar from following through with his own program. Indeed, when the superintendent grew impatient late in 1661, the viceroy scolded him for his impertinence and told him to do nothing until his own successor—President/Superintendent-elect Pedro Vázquez de Velasco—arrived to take his place.[29] Santisteban's decision to wait for Vázquez effectively postponed any action on the issue of the census for two more years, for the appointee was detained in Quito, where he had been president of the Audiencia, by charges lodged against him (during his residencia) by the bishop. Vázquez de Velasco would not arrive in Potosí until August 1663.[30]

The viceroy's reluctance to act where the mita was concerned—a reluctance that Santisteban had inherited from his predecessors—was reinforced by Fiscal Nicolás de Polanco's counsel that the cost and effort required to complete a new census and repartimiento would never be recovered in the form of higher silver production at Potosí. Polanco was certain, moreover, that a census would document a halving of the originario population in the sixteen provinces and thus raise the uncomfortable issue of the inclusion of new corregimientos, which he promised would simply extend further the demographic disruption wrought by the mita.[31]

The viceroy could not simply tread water, however, because of constant pressure from the Council of the Indies to implement its revitalization program; and should he suggest that efforts to execute the 1650 cédula be halted, he might be labeled a defeatist. The pressure was especially strong now because the ultimate effects of Philip IV's European adventures were being felt in Madrid: a public debt of 3 million pesos, following the conclusion of the Peace of the Pyrenees in 1659, that threatened to bankrupt the royal treasury.[32] The desperation for revenue in Spain only reinforced viceregal reluctance, however, and Santisteban passed the years of his viceroyalty juggling alternatives to a census-based repartimiento. One of the proposals he sent to the Crown called for the legitimation of mita deliveries in silver and, in fact, for their becoming the standard means of compliance.[33] This may well have been the most perceptive proposal of the century, but its submission to Madrid for comment was meant only to keep up appearances. The viceroy was further relieved of responsibility for action when Vázquez de Velasco "convinced" him that he would be able to complete a census and include forasteros and yanaconas in a new repartimiento. He had, he told the viceroy, already accomplished both feats in Quito; Santisteban decided to give him a chance.[34]

Vázquez de Velasco's enthusiasm dissolved upon his arrival in Potosí and his initial confrontation with the realities of silver mining in the Villa Imperial. He was especially dismayed to find a mere 500 mitayos at work in the cerro and to discover that Salazar had misrepresented official silver production figures to protect his reputation as an administrator.[35] Nevertheless, Vázquez was determined to complete what he had promised to accomplish. He requested permission from the viceroy to conduct a 30-corregimiento census and then to include in the subsequent mita charter those Indians who had migrated out of the sixteen obligated provinces; he suggested that local priests should conduct the count, but when that idea was given short shrift in Lima because of its novelty, he urged instead that the corregidores undertake the enumeration. Santisteban had no intention of undertaking a census of any kind, however, and refused to proceed with Vázquez's program despite enthusiastic support for it from Bartolomé de Salazar, now an oidor of the Audiencia of Lima. The viceroy argued, rather transparently, that he had only been ordered to implement a repartimiento, not to conduct a census; he wrote to Madrid to request such an order and, of course, postponed all action until a reply could be received.[36]

Confronted with the harsh realities at Potosí and viceregal intransigence, Vázquez quickly grew frustrated. He was especially annoyed by the new corregidor, Gabriel Guerrero de Luna, whose principal concern seemed to be the running of a casino in his home. The superintendent objected not to the gambling per se, but rather to the fact that the azogueros paid their debts with indios de faltriquera; the corregidor was therefore contributing to their delinquency.[37] Frustration evolved into exasperation and in January 1665, Vázquez wrote to Santisteban to suggest that perhaps the best course of action would be to abolish the mita altogether. The abuses pervading the system could not be purged in any other way, he argued, and the Crown would lose little as a result, for the royal fifth was no longer a significant sum.[38] The viceroy's response to this proposal was to send Vázquez yet another alternative to a standard repartimiento. It called for 1,000 mitayos per week to be drafted from the sixteen obligated provinces and another 1,500 from the fourteen exempted corregimientos of Alto Perú, with the latter afforded the option of serving in person or in silver; yanaconas, forasteros, and originarios would all be obligated. The plan was clearly a delaying tactic, for all other efforts toward a census or repartimiento were suspended while the proposal was studied by Vázquez and other government officials.[39]

By January 1666, Vázquez was too ill and too tired to concern himself with Potosí any longer. He was attracted to the latest viceregal plan, but he responded to Santisteban's request—of September 28, 1665—for a report on the status quo at Potosí (ostensibly to be used in the implementation of the proposed system) with unrestrained fatalism. He argued that only through their abuses of the mita did the azogueros currently profit from silver production, and he said he doubted that their abuses would be curtailed by the proposed charter. He suggested that the government leave him out of any revitalization effort and rely solely on the knowledge and abilities of Corregidor Juan Jiménez Lobatón.[40]

Whether or not Santisteban intended to implement the program is unclear, for the viceroy died in March 1666, before he could receive the various replies to the plan. The Audiencia of Lima, following established practice, assumed the direction of the viceroyalty until the arrival of a successor. The Audiencia also received a cédula from Queen Mariana—Philip IV had died in 1665—that permitted the viceroy to act in any way he deemed best. As interim head of government in Peru, the Audiencia could therefore have pursued the matter of a new mita charter, but it was no more inclined to assume responsibility for that albatross than were Salvatierra, Alba, and Santisteban. It left the matter for the Conde de Lemos.[41]

THE ARRIVAL of the Viceroy Conde de Lemos in Lima in 1667 opened a new era in the Hapsburg administration of the mita, for Lemos was determined to succeed with the mita where his predecessors had not—much as Salazar and Vázquez de Velasco had thought they would be able to overcome the problems that had stymied their predecessors.[42] Within three years, however, he would echo Vázquez de Velasco's call for the abolition of the Potosí mita. The point from which Lemos began his path to abolitionism was this simple three-step plan, which he proposed to the Crown in 1668:

> The Potosí mita requires three things, the first being an inspection of the mills, mines, and other workings, and this can be completed by the president of Chuquisaca [La Plata] in two months. The second is the

distribution of the Indians to the miners [azogueros and soldados] according to the mines, mills, and workings that they own, and this I can do without leaving Lima. The third is the determination of the Indians in the provinces subject to the Potosí mita, and this can only be accomplished by the archbishop of Charcas, without cost to the miners, the Indians, or the royal treasury. If Your Majesty, accepting this assessment of the situation, should name to that archbishopric an individual of sufficient age and understanding of these matters, the mita could be adjusted to everyone's satisfaction within six months; and this is the most important matter before this government.[43]

Because of the possible ill effects that a government census might provoke—including Indian migration into unconquered areas beyond the frontier—and the clear impossibility of conducting a reducción general should the enumeration document a vastly diminished population in the mita provinces, and because the use of the ecclesiastical hierarchy to conduct a census had not been provided for by any royal order (despite having been discussed by Mancera and Vázquez earlier) and involved an administrative hierarchy over which he had limited authority, Lemos delayed the execution of the census until the queen could give her blessing to the plan.

This request for royal permission was not a ploy to delay action, for while Lemos waited for a reply from Madrid, he became embroiled in a struggle with Corregidor of Potosí Luis Antonio de Oviedo over three reforms of the mita. In November and December 1669, the viceroy ordered, first, that the capitanes enteradores were not to be held responsible for more mitayos than those with whom they had left their home provinces; second, that the mitayos were not to work both day and night in the cerro; and third, that the corregidor was not to dispatch judges to collect rezagos de mita from the kurakas. These three orders were meant to serve as a temporary alternative to a new repartimiento should the Crown decide that an ecclesiastical enumeration was impolitic. Their primary purpose was to relieve the pressure on the mitayos and kurakas, but they are also testimony to the viceroy's determination to do something about the mita.[44]

The Conde de Lemos was aware that his orders would probably result in a decline in silver production at Potosí, and that his reputation as an official might suffer accordingly. In fact, he had been ordered by the president of the Council of the Indies to reverse the pattern of deficit spending established by his immediate predecessors, in part by reviving silver production at Potosí; of course he was simultaneously expected to end the azogueros' abuses. However, the viceroy had also been ordered by the queen to guard her royal conscience and it was that trust that he chose to be his principal concern.[45]

Lemos's three orders were a revival of Francisco de la Cruz's directives, but the viceroy was not in Potosí to implement them or to answer for their execution. Corregidor Oviedo, who was there, and who feared the worst, refused to implement the reforms, citing their probable negative impact on silver production and the importance of Potosí to the well-being of the empire; he called instead for the promised census and new mita charter.[46] Oviedo's own health was undoubtedly his greatest concern, however, for he was well aware that Francisco de la Cruz was murdered for trying to execute similar reforms. The Conde de Lemos was incensed by Oviedo's obstructionism and ordered Vázquez de Velasco to travel to Potosí from La Plata and implement the three orders. Should the corregidor try to block their execution, he added, then Vázquez was to arrest Oviedo, suspend him, and remand him to Lima to be dealt with by the viceroy.[47]

The Conde de Lemos's direct orders to Oviedo and Vázquez suggest an unwavering determination on his part, but the viceroy continued to worry about the financial repercussions of his actions. He asked the queen to decide whether his three reforms complied with his instructions to guard her conscience: "In my secret instructions and in other dispatches that I have received from Your Majesty, I am told to unburden the royal conscience by following my own and to aid this unfortunate people. In that regard, I am attempting to remedy the many offenses that they suffer. Should these reforms that I propose not be appropriate, please tell me what I must do, so that the tyranny with which these Indians are treated does not weigh upon my own conscience."[48] Lemos was still searching for a means of satisfying his diverse instructions in April 1670. He had returned to the possibility of conducting a census through ecclesiastical channels, for the archbishop-elect of Charcas had died and Lemos thought that he could place an experienced and trusted adviser, Visitador Alvaro de Ibarra, in that vacancy and thus at the head of the church-administered enumeration. Lemos and Ibarra alone would know the true purpose of the census. In addition, the viceroy proposed that the Crown appoint Ibarra to the presidency of La Plata and empower him to appoint and dismiss corregidores of Potosí for however long he required to reintegrate the Potosí mita. The only danger in the plan, Lemos confided, was that the azogueros might try to kill Ibarra as they had Francisco de la Cruz.[49]

In the interim, the viceroy's dependence on Oviedo as a broker proved utterly frustrating, for the corregidor thwarted the implementation of the 1669 reforms even in the presence of Vázquez de Velasco. Oviedo did in fact publish the orders in March 1670, but he reworded them in such a way as to guarantee that they would have the predicted negative impact on silver production: he ordered that all work in the mines was to halt at sundown; and he refused to hold anyone in the provinces responsible for incomplete deliveries of mitayos—because, he argued, the corregidores had no means to enforce compliance with the regimen. Oviedo then complained to the Council of the Indies that Lemos's orders would surely destroy the Potosí silver industry.[50]

The viceroy responded that he had ordered that no individual Indian should work both day and night, not that all work should stop at sundown, and he insisted that the provincial corregidores be held responsible for their failure to dispatch adequate numbers of mitayos. But the problems surrounding a census and the frustrations that Lemos suffered in his dealings with Oviedo had already convinced the viceroy that he would not be able to reform the mita as long as the corregidor was at his post.[51] In fact, the viceroy had concluded that the existing governmental apparatus was incapable of preventing the abuses that pervaded the mita and therefore that the only means of eradicating those abuses was to abolish the system.

Lemos proposed the abolition of the mita to the Crown in a letter of July 4, 1670.[52] His arguments in support of the measure were, in essence, these: first, that whereas the mita had been legal as designed, it had degenerated into a loathsome institution characterized by a host of abuses; second, that the few azogueros who owned viable mining operations at Potosí would survive the abolition of the mita; third, that the royal fifth no longer amounted to 400,000 pesos per year, and that the gains won by the system's preservation were thus minimal; fourth, that the Indians would be better employed in other, more productive mining zones; and fifth, that reform of the system was impossible.[53]

The viceroy asked the queen and the Council of the Indies to order the mita's termination because he did not want to assume the responsibility for that decision. As viceroy, he had the authority to abolish the mita, but his decision would have been subject to review by the Crown. Once abolished, however, the mita probably would not have been recoverable, so should the Crown reverse his decision,

Lemos would have to suffer the consequences forever. Rather than face that possibility, the Conde decided to request a definitive royal cédula (indeed, he had felt compelled to request cédulas confirming even his 1669 reforms of the mita).[54] To bolster his case, Lemos included with his proposal reams of supporting documents, including a historical summary of the evolution of the mita and corroborating statements by government officials and religious figures.[55]*

While the viceroy awaited a decision from Madrid, he vented his anger by suspending Corregidor Oviedo and replacing him on an interim basis with Diego de Ulloa. Lemos explained to the Crown that the change was necessary to clear up the misconceptions that Oviedo had fomented in the Villa Imperial.[56] The proposal for the abolition of the Potosí mita fell victim, meanwhile, to the time lag involved in transatlantic correspondence and bureaucratic delays—factors that had contributed to the failure to execute a new repartimiento de la mita since 1633. Four months after Lemos dispatched his July 4, 1670, proposal, for example, the Council of the Indies was only just responding to his 1669 correspondence on the problems confronting the completion of a prerepartimiento census. His three reforms of late 1669 were confirmed with royal edicts on the last day of 1671— eighteen months after the viceroy had given up on them—and the Council did not consider the question of the mita's abolition until May 1673. By then the Conde de Lemos was dead, having succumbed in December 1672.[57]

The time consumed in correspondence between Lima and Madrid hurt the chances of the abolition proposal, but the Council of the Indies' refusal to assume responsibility for a decision in the matter proved even more important. After considering Lemos's arguments, the Council voted that only Queen Mariana herself could make such an important decision. It agreed, however, to form a junta—in league with prominent theologians—to discuss the issue in all its aspects, and it suggested that the mita seemed to have outlived its usefulness

---

*An example is the contribution of the bishop-elect of Concepción. He claimed that the Indians forced to serve in the mita were stripped of their liberty, that their assignment to the Potosí mines was tantamount to their enslavement, and that their treatment was abominable. Mita deliveries in silver, moreover, were equivalent to the payments that slaves made to their masters in lieu of personal service. In his summation, the bishop-elect argued that the mitayos were subjected to a bondage worse than that the Hebrews had endured in Egypt—the clear implication being that they would soon be delivered from the unjust captivity by God, if not by the queen (AGI, Charcas, leg. 268, no. 15D, undated and unsigned).

and justification.[58] Yet on October 9, 1673, the Council abruptly terminated the junta's inquiry and ordered the Conde de Castellar to investigate the matter in his capacity as the next viceroy of Peru.[59]

Why did the Council of the Indies call off the inquiry? Its decision stemmed in part from the news of Lemos's death, but primarily from its fear of the economic ramifications of the mita's abolition (given the financial difficulties bequeathed to the empire by Philip IV) and its refusal to give up hope that reform was possible.[60] Vázquez and Lemos had both grounded their proposals for the abolition of the mita on the impossibility of reform and the relatively low levels of royal revenue currently remitted by the once-rich Potosí silver industry, but the validity of their arguments had been put in doubt by counterproposals and by the viceroy's own reports; and for the Council any doubt whatsoever was paralyzing.

The principal counterproposal was the *Memorial* by Nicolás Matías del Campo y de la Rynaga, discussed in Chapter 3. The two most important messages carried by that treatise were that the mita could be reformed and that Potosí would collapse without mitayos. Those arguments were supported, quite naturally, by the azogueros in their own correspondence with the Crown.[61] But the most damaging evidence that the Conde de Lemos's portrayal of the situation in the Villa Imperial was mistaken came—ironically enough—from the viceroy himself and his interim corregidor, Diego de Ulloa, through their efforts to demonstrate that they were competent administrators. In 1669, for example, Corregidor Oviedo reported to Lemos that his diligence had resulted in the raising of the weekly Indian work force at Potosí to 3,424—both mingas and mitayos. Lemos relayed the corregidor's figure to the Council of the Indies with one modification: he claimed that the 3,424 were all mitayos, for an apparently substantial improvement in the effective weekly draft.[62]

Later, after Lemos had suspended Oviedo, Ulloa reported that he had raised the production of the royal fifth significantly and that he had abolished indios de faltriquera (by hiring mingas himself with mita deliveries in silver). He attributed his success to the implementation of the viceroy's three 1669 reforms. Pleased with Ulloa's achievements, Lemos relayed the good news to the Crown.[63] The viceroy probably felt vindicated, but his reports had the effect of countering the arguments in his July 4, 1670, proposal—that production at Potosí was no longer significant, that reform of the mita was impossible, and that abolition of the system was needed to halt abuses. The

Crown clearly appreciated the reports of augmented royal revenue, for the queen sent Oviedo (whom she had returned to office) orders on June 10, 1673, to maintain the high level of silver production that Ulloa had reported.[64] The queen's directive was sent to the corregidor just two days after the Council had presented her with the case for the abolition of the mita; the two issues were therefore considered by her concurrently.

In combination, the Campo *Memorial*, the government reports of reform and higher production, and the claims made by the azogueros thwarted the abolition movement headed by the Conde de Lemos. They did not end the discussion of that alternative entirely, but the element of doubt that they interjected into the debate in Madrid caused sufficient hesitation on the part of the Crown that it postponed a decision on the issue until the Conde de Castellar could report from Peru. In the final analysis, therefore, the division of authority within the Hapsburg government saved the mita, for neither center of authority was willing to accept responsibility for the financial consequences of its eradication.*

The Conde de Castellar reported to the Council from Lima, in February 1675, that despite his predisposition to abolish the mita, he had been forced to halt his efforts in that direction when he failed to find anyone who advocated the mita's demise. The members of a July 3, 1670, junta consultiva who had supported the Conde de Lemos's proposal now claimed that they had been coerced by that viceroy. Given the circumstances, Castellar confided, he had decided that he had better not risk anything novel, and would thus keep Potosí going with the traditional, if imperfect, means: the mita.[65] Upon its receipt of the viceroy's report, the Crown—now in the person of the young Charles II—issued two cédulas, of July 8 and November 16, 1676, ordering a thorough reintegration of the Potosí mita. The first order empowered the viceroy to increase the weekly

* It is ironic that Oviedo would later refute Lemos's claims. Upon his return to office in April 1673, he charged that Ulloa had manipulated production data and that silver output had not been as high as the interim corregidor had reported. Oviedo said that the apparent rise in the royal fifth reflected Ulloa's use of 1670 as the base year for the comparison. Production had been hindered that year by a severe drought, and ore that had been stockpiled during 1670 was later processed in 1671 and 1672—the two years for which Ulloa claimed credit. The *carta cuenta* (official tally) for 1671 had included, furthermore, some thirteen months' worth of production, and that for 1672 had contained fifteen months' worth. The total work force had actually fallen, Oviedo reported, to 2,664 Indians—1,427 mitayos and 1,217 mingas (Cole, "An Abolitionism," pp. 330–31).

draft by extending the mita obligation to new corregimientos—over-turning the decision of the Conde de Alba to confine the mita to the sixteen provinces already affected—and the second demanded that indios de faltriquera be eliminated from the regimen once and for all.[66] The Council of the Indies had, quite simply, dusted off its unexecuted program from the 1650's.

Forty-three years had elapsed since the last repartimiento de la mita was implemented. What was needed, clearly, was another viceroy of the caliber of Francisco de Toledo. The Council of the Indies and Charles II chose the Duque de la Palata for that role, placing in his care the restoration of the Potosí mita and the revitalization of silver production in the Villa Imperial.[67] Palata was a trusted royal adviser who had served on the regency council during the king's minority, and he enjoyed a reputation as a faithful administrator from his quarter century of government service.[68] He was as determined and decisive as Toledo had been, and he did his utmost to carry out his instructions, but Palata would in time learn that good intentions and hard work were not enough to guarantee his mission's success.

SIX

Administering the Mita,
1680-1700

Upon his arrival in Peru in 1681, the Duque de la Palata set about the business of determining what course of action would be best. Like the Conde de Lemos, he did so with the clear intention of implementing a program. The opinions of the archbishops of Lima and Charcas (the former, Melchor Liñán y Cisneros, having served as interim viceroy), the president of the Audiencia of La Plata, the corregidor of Potosí, and others were solicited. These men held varying views on the propriety of the mita and the reforms that were needed to reinvigorate it. Only Liñán, however, argued that the mita should be abolished*; everyone else agreed that it should be preserved, though their opinions differed on the number of provinces to be included and on who should conduct the prerequisite census.[1]

While the viceroy was considering the logistics of a census and new repartimiento, he received another directive (of May 28, 1681) from the king reinforcing his earlier call for the revitalization of the mita. Charles II had been strongly influenced by a printed memorial from the azogueros warning that Potosí would soon collapse without the prompt resolution of the long-standing issues of the census and repartimiento. The king's sensitivity to that overused threat was a function of his empire's desperation for income and perhaps his inexperience. He instructed Palata to follow a program suggested by President Bartolomé González de Poveda in 1676, which called for a

---

*Liñán y Cisneros thereby reversed himself. Four years earlier, as archbishop of Charcas, he had argued that the mita was beneficial for the Indians because it kept them occupied and thus out of mischief (Liñán to the Crown, La Plata, Feb. 28, 1677, AGI, Charcas, leg. 268, no. 53). In fact, he had called upon the Crown to reverse the Conde de Lemos's reforms, because they had generated mass confusion and were not helping the mitayos at all.

census in all 30 of the altoperuano corregimientos, conducted by their corregidores, and the incorporation in the mita of however many new areas were needed to regain an effective weekly draft of 4,220 Indians.[2]

By the end of 1682, the viceroy's plans for the census and new mita charter were complete. Palata reported to the Council of the Indies that all 30 corregimientos would indeed be included in the enumeration, as the 1681 cédula had ordered.[3] He was somewhat worried about the use of the corregidores to conduct the census, however, given their propensity to underrepresent the Indian population of their districts. González de Poveda and the 1681 edict had both taken the line that the enumeration would be completed quickly and at a minimal cost by employing those officials, but the viceroy understood that the corregidores used Indian labor in their own enterprises and hence were less than trustworthy. The question was of prime importance, he noted, for if the census were not done well, the subsequent repartimiento would suffer as a result.[4]

Accepting that there was no alternative to the use of the corregidores, Palata sought to monitor their activities by ordering a parallel secret enumeration by priests, under the direction of their bishops and prelates. The viceroy explained to the church officials that he needed to have a clear understanding of Peruvian demographics if he were to adjust the Indians' tribute and mita obligations so that they might be exacted more fairly. To ensure that the priests' reports would be factual, Palata cautioned the bishops not to tell them why they were reporting on their Indian charges.[5] The Duque had resurrected the ecclesiastical census plan to serve as a check on the reports that he would soon receive from the corregidores. Like Toledo, therefore, he did not devise a new program, but adapted extant ideas and tried to make them work efficiently.

The orders to begin the ecclesiastical census were dispatched first, in April 1683, and were followed by the instructions to the corregidores in July. The government's enumeration was scheduled to begin in all of the corregimientos on the same day—October 1, 1683—to prevent the Indians' movements from distorting the results. Two years later, the entire process was supposed to be completed, with the individual tallies having been compiled into master lists by two specially appointed controllers (contadores) in Lima. In addition to the 30 corregimientos of Alto Perú, the remaining 53 corregimientos of the viceroyalty were included in the viceroy's numeración general de *indios*, to improve the collection of tribute and other Crown revenue in those areas as well.[6]

The instructions for the corregidores were extremely detailed and demanding. Each magistrate was to produce eight books, as follows: for the originarios who were present (book 1), temporarily absent (book 2), or missing (book 3); for the forasteros who remembered their pueblos of origin (book 4) and those who did not (book 5); for *mitimaes*, i.e. descendants of Indians resettled during the pre-Hispanic period (book 6); and for yanaconas who worked in Spanish-owned enterprises (book 7) or in municipal and church activities (book 8). Within each tome, every Indian's age, sex, and ayllu affiliation were to be noted.[7] Once in the hands of the two controllers, the results were to be compared to determine the true patterns of Indian migration and other demographic trends. And since all of the Peruvian corregimientos were now included, any future Indian migration could be documented simply by repeating the process.[8]

The delineation of yanaconas, forasteros, and originarios was meant to serve another purpose as well. The viceroy and his advisers had agreed, during their discussions on the form that the census would take, that the traditional exemption from mita service and full tribute payments enjoyed by the yanaconas and forasteros should be eliminated (an idea considered by Mancera 40 years earlier)—that no Indian should be able to evade those responsibilities simply by living away from his pueblo of origin. Thus the forasteros were given a choice either to return to their pueblos of origin within six months or to be considered originarios in their current place of residence;[9] the yanaconas, who had no pueblos of origin, apparently were to be considered residents of the provinces in which they were domiciled. Clearly, Palata was attempting to complete the first modern census in Peruvian history, something very different from the lists on which the mita and tribute had been based in the past.[10] And still more fundamental changes were in store for the mita.

Since the 1630's—for nine consecutive viceroyalties—various members of the Hapsburg administration in Peru had kept a census and new repartimiento from being completed, but the conditions in 1683 were different: the corregidor of Potosí, the president of the Audiencia of La Plata, the archbishop of Charcas, the viceroy, and the Crown were all agreed that the program must be enacted. A goal whose feasibility had been preserved essentially because of the inability of the government to achieve it now seemed within reach, and for the first time in the seventeenth century the credibility of a thorough regeneration of the mita was to be put to the test.

In the sixteen mita provinces, the Indians responded to the enumeration from the moment it was announced, for the prologue to the corregidores' instructions made it clear that the census was the first stage in a process that would force the forasteros and yanaconas to bear their fair shares of the native community's responsibilities. Well-versed in the evasion of government programs, the forasteros, joined by many of the originarios and yanaconas, took to the roads and headed for the pueblos, cities, and provinces that historically had been exempted from mita service. Once tallied in those areas, they anticipated, they would be forever spared the rigors—physical and financial—of compliance with the Potosí mita. This effort to evade future personal service increased the number of Indians on the move, as the would-be exemptees joined the few forasteros who agreed to return to their pueblos of origin and the already large force of Indians who traveled during the course of any year as migrant laborers and traders. The payment of tribute seems to have been less of a concern for the Indians, for they would have to pay it even in the free pueblos and provinces.[11] Indeed, those already living in the exempted areas took little notice of Palata's enumeration or of its ultimate purposes.[12]

The effects of Indian movement on the census were compounded by the response to the viceroy's instructions by the corregidores in Alto Perú. Palata's orders did not reach them until just a few days or weeks before the enumeration was scheduled to begin, and when the corregidores did receive their orders, they were generally unable to decipher them. Many wrote to Lima asking for clarification and postponed the execution of the census until they received a reply (some sought to avoid compliance by this means as well). In other cases, the corregidores chose to follow local (and thus varied) custom in the formulation of their census rosters, and their districts had to be recounted later to bring them into line with Palata's instructions. Rather than the two years provided for by the viceroy's design, the enumeration in Alto Perú lagged on for five years and hence was not finished until 1688.[13]

Because the local officials were not to be paid for their efforts, the only incentives for them to comply with their orders were stiff penalties for failing to report Indians and prizes for discovering otherwise undocumented natives that Palata had included in the instructions.

When the census was finally under way in Alto Perú, therefore, the corregidores and kurakas (who had been ordered to assist the magistrates) included every Indian for whom they had a shred of evidence: migrants passing through, absentees for whom they had only a baptismal record, etc.[14] To make things worse, many Indians gave false names and places of origin to the corregidores and kurakas in another attempt to avoid the ultimate consequences of the census.[15]

We should note that most of the irregularities in the process were recognized while the census was being conducted. One of the controllers, Joseph de Villegas, expressed his grave doubts about the viability of the results from Alto Perú to the Duque de la Palata in 1685,[16] but the viceroy was unmoved. By that point Palata's honor and reputation were at stake, for the Crown had pestered him constantly with requests for reports and exhortations to act quickly. The viceroy simply called upon everyone concerned to do his best to minimize the problems that Villegas had identified and to complete the task as soon as possible. When the census was finally done, furthermore, Palata reported to the Crown that though it was not perfect, it had gone much more smoothly than anyone had anticipated and the results were surely the best attainable under the circumstances.[17] Earlier viceroys had postponed the execution of a census to avoid responsibility for its negative consequences; Palata's defense of a flawed enumeration was destined to make those ill effects even more devastating.

The findings of the 1683 numeración, however inaccurate, were significant. Even with overcounting, the figures for Alto Perú showed nearly a halving of the Indian population since 1573, with the demographic decline in the sixteen mita provinces being even more acute than elsewhere. While some of the fourteen other altiplano corregimientos had received a large influx of migrants—as many as three-quarters of their inhabitants were now forasteros—most had not experienced a net increase in population. Thus the large pockets of runaways that the azogueros of Potosí had claimed existed failed to materialize. The greatest loss was in the number of originarios, as even within the sixteen mita provinces the yanaconas and forasteros had come to represent some 50 percent of the native population.[18]

Beyond the portrayal of the rough contours of the Indian community of Alto Perú, the 1683 census failed to achieve its expressed goals. The viceroy had hoped, for instance, to compare the professed origins of the forasteros in any given corregimiento with the lists of absent originarios from the corresponding areas, but the uneven application of his instructions by the corregidores had made that impossible.[19] The issue of overcounting also put the accuracy of any given set of results in doubt.[20] Palata's insistence that his enumeration was accurate was relatively harmless as long as he did not use it as the basis of any wide-ranging reforms, but the reformation of the mita and tribute were the raison d'être for the census, and the results had shown that profound changes would have to be made if royal revenues from Peru were to be augmented.

In terms of the implementation of those changes, furthermore, the question of the overall accuracy of the census was less consequential than the inclusion of absent, migratory, or even nonexistent Indians on the enumeration rosters. For when Palata issued a new repartimiento de la mita and redefined tribute requirements in 1688–89, he tried to do more than meet Potosí's need for mitayos and make the yanaconas and forasteros bear their fair share of the Indians' obligations. He also attempted to hold each individual Indian accountable for his particular share of those responsibilities, by using the census rosters to compile tribute and mita lists.[21] If it succeeded, the Duque's effort to make the mita and tribute individual, rather than communal, responsibilities would alter the very nature of the relationship between the Andean Indians and their Hapsburg sovereign.

There were to be other innovations. The Duque de la Palata had no choice, given the results of the numeración general de indios, but to include some previously exempted corregimientos in the Potosí mita. He chose those that were closest to the Villa Imperial (see Map 2, p. 11): the provinces of Larecaja, Tomina, Pilaya y Paspaya, Misque, and Yamparaes; the parish of San Pedro in the city of La Paz; eight previously exempted curacies in Cochabamba and eight in Porco; and eighteen pueblos that had been spared even though they lay within the sixteen mita provinces. The cities of La Plata, Potosí, Oruro, and La Paz (with the exception of San Pedro) remained free from mita recruitment because their Indian residents continued to be needed for municipal labor projects. All of the Indians living within the designated areas were now obliged to serve in the mita, regardless of whether they had been forasteros, yanaconas, or originarios. It was unfair, the viceroy explained, that the first two groups of Indians should leave compliance with the native communities' responsibilities to the third.[22]

A concern for fairness underlay the other changes that Palata ordered for the mita as well. He lowered the weekly draft to 2,829

Indians, by limiting the recipients to the owners of the 57 most productive mills (at 50 mitayos per mill), and he replaced the Toledan
three-shift system with a two-shift cycle, because he felt that there
were now enough mingas to allow the mitayos to rest during a single
off-week. Palata also believed that the Indians who would have made
up the other third of a conventional annual draft would appreciate
staying home and that their communities would benefit from their
presence.[23]

The new tribute regimen was also supposed to be more equitable.
The forasteros and yanaconas were now to pay the same amount in
tribute per capita as the originarios; and they would be assessed that
sum wherever they moved. The amount of tribute owed by each Indian was lower, however, than that ostensibly paid by the originarios
under the Toledan system, and no Indian was to be made to pay the
tribute owed by another, for any reason whatsoever. Though tribute
was to be an unavoidable personal responsibility, therefore, it was
not to be burdensome.[24]

The reforms that the Duque de la Palata ordered for the mita and
tribute seem quite innocent in comparison to Toledo's ordinances,
but they failed to take into consideration that the two institutions
had long since stopped performing as Toledo had intended—indeed,
if they ever really had. More importantly, Francisco de Toledo had
based the original mita on the labor practices that were extant upon
his arrival in Peru; he had borrowed from the system he observed at
Huamanga and the experiences of Potosí during its first 30 years of
silver production. Rather than begin with the current form of the
mita, Palata based his new repartimiento on the Toledan ordinances
and thereby ignored a century and more of metamorphosis.

Palata's reforms also failed to consider the demographic changes
that had taken place in Alto Perú since the numeración general was
begun in 1683. The region had been visited, for example, by a number of deadly diseases at mid-decade, and many of the Indians who
appeared on Palata's mita and tribute rosters were no longer alive by
1689. Important economic centers that attracted voluntary Indian laborers by the hundreds had either been abandoned (e.g., the mines at
Porco) or founded during the interval.[25] Thus, the figures produced
during the census often bore little resemblance to the 1689 reality, no
matter how closely they may have reflected the situation a few years
earlier.

But the most important factor that Palata failed to consider was that both the mita and tribute systems depended, in practice, upon the ability of the kurakas to control and to extract money from the Indians. Indeed, both institutions had come to view the kurakas as well as their communities as the units taxed. The kurakas, in turn, depended upon a combination of financial, psychological, and corporal pressures to keep the originarios in line and to raise the money to meet their obligations. When the viceroy attempted to replace a communal taxation system with individual mita and tribute responsibilities—and included forasteros and yanaconas on an equal footing with the originarios—he asked more of the kurakas than they could possibly deliver.

These basic errors—the direct application of the Council of the Indies' misguided belief, inherited from the official viceregal position, that the Toledan age could be recaptured; the failure to adapt to the changes that had taken place during the 1680's; and the lack of appreciation for the role played in the mita by the kurakas—gave birth to a series of new problems and ruined any remaining chance that Palata might replicate Toledo's accomplishments of the 1570's. The speed with which the new repartimiento de la mita and tribute ordinances were introduced compounded the ill effects of Palata's program. The census in Alto Perú had taken so long, however, that the Duque's reforms had to be implemented quickly if they were to be in place when his successor arrived. Palata was afraid that the next viceroy would let any unfinished aspect of his program wither and die rather than follow through with a difficult endeavor.[26] Thus, the first payments of tribute under the new regime were due on June 24 (the Feast of St. John), 1689, and the first contingents of mitayos according to the new repartimiento were to arrive in Potosí by the end of the month—less than five months after the new orders were sent to the provincial corregidores from Lima.[27]

When the Indians who had been forasteros or yanaconas, or who had lived in or moved to the exempted areas, learned that they were subject to the mita, they fled at once.[28] A few went into the cities or to other parts of the viceroyalty, but many more moved southeast into the yungas (lowlands), to regions outside the control of the viceregal administration.[29] The kurakas were unable to prevent that flight and therefore incapable of delivering the Indians who had been designated to serve in the mita.[30] They were prohibited by the viceroy's new ordinances, meanwhile, from using their traditional means of complying with their mita obligations.[31] As their own resources gave out and they were unable to make up the difference between the means at their disposal and the demands that Palata had made of them, some of the kurakas fled with the rest of their ayllus.[32] Others tried instead to resign their posts, but more often than not these found themselves jailed by their corregidores instead.[33] Some of the corregidores then tried to take up the gauntlet and deliver the mitayos themselves, but they proved even less able than had the kurakas.[34]

The ill effects of the Palata reforms were great within the sixteen provinces that were traditionally obligated to support the mita, but they were still more devastating in the newly incorporated provinces and pueblos. In the frontier regions of Larecaja, Tomina, Pilaya y Paspaya, Misque, Sicasica, Tarija, and Cochabamba, the Spanish conquest was still incomplete in 1689. Settlements of colonists and recently attracted Indians were located within a few leagues of the unconquered "infidels," and were inhabited entirely by forasteros from other colonized areas and Indians who had been coaxed from the other side of the frontier—often only with the promise that they would never have to serve in the Potosí mita.[35] When Palata's reform orders arrived in those settlements, the Indians immediately moved across the frontier and out of reach. There they would have to pay tribute to their "infidel" hosts, but they would be spared compliance with the mita. The colonists and officials in the frontier settlements wrote to Palata to protest his decision to include their corregimientos in the mita, citing the Toledan reasons for their exemption and complaining bitterly about the impact of the 1689 decrees.[36] Their complaints were joined by similar protests from within the sixteen mita provinces of old.[37]

The Duque de la Palata tried to quell the uproar over his reforms on April 29, 1689, with a set of printed "Advertencias" that were supposed to clear up the confusion regarding the goals of those measures and the means to be used to comply with them. The viceroy insisted that his program had been designed to benefit everyone, and that any and all opposition would quickly evaporate if only his orders were followed. He noted, for example, that the per capita amount of tribute required of the Indians was less than the sum demanded by Toledo; if a community's quota had been raised, it was because the forasteros were now included. The latter's equation with the originarios was necessary and just, he explained, because of the ease with which they moved about. No Indian was obligated to pay the tribute of another, moreover, and in the case of absences or deaths, the kurakas had only to produce written proof to that effect to win a reduction of their overall remittances.[38]

Palata also noted that the kurakas claimed to be helpless in controlling the forasteros and that the corregidores had supported their assertions in that regard. This he would not countenance, for he had allowed an initial 40 percent discount in the number of mitayos to be drawn from forastero populations in anticipation of their probable opposition to mita service. He did give some ground where tribute was concerned, however, by moving the deadline for the first payments under the new system from the Feast of St. John to Christmas 1689—providing the kurakas with six more months to bring the reluctant forasteros to heel.[39]

For the most part, however, the "Advertencias" simply repeated the premises that lay at the core of the 1689 reforms. The Duque de la Palata's invocation of the Toledan ordinances and his assurances that his own orders were just failed to address the real causes for the opposition to his program in Alto Perú—primarily the inability of the kurakas to control the forasteros and yanaconas—and therefore had virtually no effect. Indeed, soon thereafter the viceroy was forced to halve the amount of tribute that the kurakas were asked to collect from the forasteros, but even that concession could not halt the social destruction wrought by his reform program.[40]

By 1690, Alto Perú was in the throes of a major crisis. Within the sixteen mita provinces of old, the disruptive migration of the previous century had been accelerated by Palata's flawed census and defective, hastily implemented reforms. Fifty years of efforts to replace the 1633 repartimiento de la mita, stifled by various members of the Hapsburg bureaucracy at different times, had finally ended, but the cure was proving worse than the disease. The fleeing Indians no longer stopped in the previously exempted corregimientos, but moved further away into unconquered territories; and they were joined by the Indians who had recently taken up residence just inside the viceroyalty's perimeter. Local government, based on the control of the Indians by the kurakas, had broken down completely, as the kurakas were unable to restrain the panicked originarios, let alone the yanaconas and forasteros for whom Palata had recently made them responsible.

What to do? The program that the Council of the Indies had pressed for since the 1650's had proved to be a terrible mistake; the decision of earlier viceroys to postpone its execution indefinitely had been vindicated. The 1633 repartimiento de la mita was hardly a suitable alternative to the 1689 charter, for it was nearly 60 years old and clearly obsolete. A solution was needed quickly, however, if the damage to altoperuano society was to be minimized. Fortunately, Palata's successor would prove to be just what Alto Perú needed.

THE CONDE DE LA MONCLOVA was confronted by a mass of complaints about Palata's reforms when he arrived in Peru in 1690. In fact, the news that a new viceroy had taken over in the capital caused a second wave of protests about the reform program to roll down off the altiplano and into Lima.[41] Added to the themes that had characterized the earlier complaints was a particular emphasis on the Indians' flight into the yungas. Priests were quick to point out that the loss of the natives to the other side of the frontier not only hurt the Peruvian economy but also damaged the Crown's claim that it was Christianizing the Indians. The corregidores and their lieutenants reported that they had been forced to resort to nighttime raids to round up mitayos.* Interspersed among the various protests were some especially poignant portrayals of the horrors of the Palatan mita. One curate recounted how an Indian who had been captured by the local officials came before him and other priests in chains and screamed "Look, Fathers, at the beneficent God that you have brought to our land!"[42]

Monclova was receptive to these complaints, for he had arrived in Peru predisposed against the Potosí mita. The viceroy questioned the need for the regimen, as he had just come from serving as viceroy of New Spain, where no such system existed.[43] But the people in the al-

---

*An example of the extremes to which officials were forced to go to round up mitayos—from a few years hence—is described by the kurakas of Aymaya in their complaint against the Conde de Canillas (Pedro Luis Enríquez), before the Audiencia of La Plata, Mar. 24, 1693–? (the latter date is obscured by a wax seal), ANB, M 126, no. 4. The corregidor had answered the kurakas' earlier protests concerning their responsibilities under the 1692 repartimiento (of the Viceroy Conde de la Monclova) by sending two officials to their village to round up Indians for the mita. The officials waited until Easter Sunday to strike; once everyone was at mass, they blockaded all the entrances to the church and began arresting Indians, using the gated baptismal area as a holding pen. The kurakas expressed their shock and outrage, and observed that it would be a very long time before any Indians returned to Aymaya, let alone to mass.

The dispatch of captured Indians did not guarantee that they would actually arrive in Potosí, however, for on at least two occasions in 1689–90, Indians revolted while en route to the Villa Imperial and fled, leaving their guards dead or wounded. Violent conscription was met, in the end, with violent opposition (AGNA, Sala 9, leg. 10.3.7, ff. 169 [Misque]; 433 [Cochabamba]).

toperuano provinces were not the only ones who were unhappy with Palata's handiwork. The Azogueros Guild—the association that had ostensibly stood to benefit from the completion of a new repartimiento—was very upset as well. The azogueros objected to the denial of mitayos for sixteen of their mills, to the assignment of the Indians in complete ayllus, and to the mere 2,829 Indians in the weekly draft.[44] Like the other complainants, the azogueros looked to Monclova to deliver them from a disastrous reformation of the mita.

With the complaints about Palata's census and reforms coming from all quarters, Monclova convened a junta in Lima late in 1690 to consider those matters. The azogueros were represented by the corregidor of Potosí, Pedro Luis Enríquez, and he was joined by the oidores of the Audiencia of Lima, the controllers of the royal treasury (of Lima), and other officials. The junta met 33 times between December 1690 and May 1691, and a resolution drafted by it was then submitted to a larger assembly for debate. Based on that assembly's recommendations, Fiscal-Oidor Matías Lagúnez and Protector General de Naturales Pedro de Figueroa Dávila wrote separate proposals for countering the difficulties caused by Palata's reform program.[45]

It was Lagúnez's proposal that Monclova used to develop an antidote for the deteriorating situation in Alto Perú. The fiscal accused the azogueros of unmitigated deceit in their dealings with the government and of subjecting the unfortunate mitayos to an oppression worse than slavery. Indeed, he argued that the Indians would be better off as slaves, for then the azogueros would have a stake in their survival. His first recommendation was that the mita be abolished, and for a brief while Monclova was disposed to agree, until Corregidor Enríquez persuaded the viceroy that such a move would have an unacceptably large impact on the royal coffers.[46] The same concern for the level of silver production during one's viceroyalty that had saved the mita from extinction earlier was destined to save it again.

Once the Conde de la Monclova had decided that it would be impolitic to destroy the mita, he chose to follow Lagúnez's second recommendation and tailor the regimen to the existing reality in Alto Perú. He opted, therefore, to follow the path that the Marqués de Guadalcázar and other viceroys had championed earlier in the century. Monclova herded the assembly toward the adoption of these twelve resolutions:

1. that the reforms of the Duque de la Palata, based on the general enumeration, be revoked;

2. that the mita be based, until another decision on the matter was reached, on the 33,423 [male] originarios in the sixteen provinces historically obligated to the mita;

3. that the same not be true for the 31,031 [male] forasteros residing in the sixteen provinces;

4. that the five additional provinces, the parish of San Pedro in La Paz, the sixteen pueblos, and the eighteen curacies be freed from mita obligation;

5. that a new census be conducted of the forasteros to determine the amount of tribute they should pay, and that until it was done, that they should pay the same amount as had the yanaconas [before 1689], or not more than seven pesos per year;

6. that the annual draft continue to be determined on the basis of one-seventh of the subject population;

7. that two weeks of rest be reinstated in place of the one week introduced by the Duque de la Palata;

8. that in place of 50 Indians for each mill, that the sum of 40 be provided, and therefore that 34 or 35 mills be assigned mitayos—the mills to be determined on the basis of information provided by experienced but disinterested persons;

9. that the figures included for the originarios in the Palatan census remain the basis of government policy until local officials requested revisitas, and that recounts be done individually and at any time;

10. that the daily wage for the mitayos be raised from four to five reales and payment be made for Mondays, bringing the total to 30 reales per week, and furthermore that the sum required of those who "serve" in silver be three pesos per week and that the money be presented to the capitán enterador for his use in hiring mingas—not to the azogueros (i.e., that there may be deliveries in silver but no indios de faltriquera).

11. that the Indians be paid their travel allowances at the prescribed rate; and

12. that the 40 Indians assigned to each mill come from the same ayllu and pueblo whenever possible.[47]

These twelve resolutions were sent to the provinces of Alto Perú in the form of a printed provisión of April 27, 1692.[48] A new repartimiento de la mita was drafted, meanwhile, by the *contador de retasas* (controller for adjusted taxation) and dispatched as a general order on May 8. In accordance with the viceroy's instructions and the guidelines set down in the twelve resolutions, mita obligation again fell only on the originarios residing in the sixteen provinces. The resulting 1,367-Indian weekly draft was shared by the owners of 34 mills (the remaining seven mitayos were assigned to the maintenance of the reservoirs), chosen by the corregidor of Potosí, the president of the Audiencia of La Plata, and ex-Corregidor Oviedo; another 23 mills were left without any mitayos at all. Monclova also ordered that travel allowances be paid at the rate of two reales for every four leagues traveled, and that the mingas' wage be lowered to the same 30 reales per week that the mitayos were to receive.[49] One must question the thinking behind the last decree; because this section of the provisión was never fully implemented, however, its impact was negligible.

The azogueros had protested when Palata assigned them a mere 2,829 mitayos per week. They now found themselves with less than half that number and with 23 more mills denied mitayos. This was hardly what they had had in mind when they contributed 35,000 pesos to send Corregidor Enríquez to Lima to be their representative. He took the precaution of informing them of the assembly's decisions in a letter from the capital on April 28, 1692; one can only imagine what might have happened to him had he been in Potosí at the time.[50] The azogueros apparently learned of the viceroy's intentions before receiving the corregidor's letter, however, for on April 1 they proposed to the Crown that the archbishop of Charcas (ex-President González de Poveda) be named to replace Monclova as viceroy. In August, they complained to Monclova that the 30-real wage for the mitayos would ruin them financially and warned him that they would not be the only ones to suffer, for the Crown's share of production would soon be nil. Their warnings to the viceroy having gone unheeded, the azogueros repeated their protests in an appeal to the Crown in December 1693. The guild had by then changed its opinion of Palata's repartimiento, for it now argued that six years of diligence on that viceroy's part was being undermined by the current administration in Lima.[51]

While the azogueros sought the reversal of Monclova's reforms through legal channels, they did their best to protect the day-to-day mita from the innovations in the new repartimiento. When Corregidor Enríquez returned to the Villa Imperial in October 1692, he found the capitanes enteradores and azogueros locked in a battle over mita deliveries. The azogueros insisted that Palata's quotas of mitayos be met, and when they were not, demanded rezagos de mita. The kurakas refused, arguing that the Monclova repartimiento was in force, and they accused the azogueros of not paying the mitayos the increased wages to which they were entitled.[52] Most of the local government officials supported the kurakas; the veedores and capitán mayor de la mita reported that the 23 mills that had been stripped of their mitayos had long histories of misuse. The 27 azogueros who owned the remaining 34 mills, the officials noted, had viable refining operations and mines and thus deserved continued government assistance.[53]

The Conde de la Monclova responded to the azogueros' objections to his reforms by demanding that the twelve resolutions be enforced without exception. When Enríquez gathered the azogueros together to read them the viceroy's reply, they responded that it was absolutely impossible for them to pay the increased mitayo wage. They had petitioned the viceroy on that issue through the archbishop, they said, and would await further word from Lima before saying more. González de Poveda died two days after Enríquez's meeting with the azogueros, however, and the guild understood that its chances for absolute redemption had perished with the archbishop. They accordingly went to the corregidor and proposed a compromise: three pesos (24 reales) per week for the mitayos. Enríquez accepted the offer, under powers he had been assigned by Monclova to adjust the 1692 repartimiento as the need arose.[54] He explained to the viceroy that the government's continued demand that the 30-real wage be paid would only force the meritorious azogueros to commit abuses, for they could not otherwise remain solvent.[55]

The Conde de la Monclova was not through with the mita, however. In an interim report to the Crown of August 1692, he not only defended the twelve resolutions but proposed that the mita be abolished. The viceroy argued that Lagúnez had demonstrated beyond any doubt that the Potosí silver industry was no longer important enough to warrant the continuation of such an oppressive institution. Monclova, like the Conde de Lemos before him, left the final decision to the Crown, but he strongly suggested that all the problems caused by the mita could best be solved through its eradication.[56] The viceroy repeated his call for the abolition of the mita in a report of late 1693 on Corregidor Enríquez's activities in Potosí. Included with that report was a statement of support from the archbishop of Lima, Liñán y Cisneros.[57]

On April 2, 1694, the Council of the Indies began to prepare for a comprehensive debate on the Potosí mita. The decision it faced was not whether Palata's or Monclova's repartimiento should be confirmed, but rather—once the Council had received the Conde's Au-

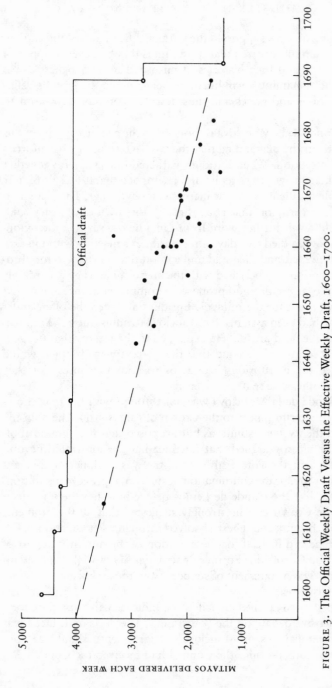

FIGURE 3. The Official Weekly Draft Versus the Effective Weekly Draft, 1600–1700.

Sources: For the effective weekly draft, same as for Figure 2; for the official weekly draft, same as for Table 3 except for 1689 (AGI, Charcas, leg. 270, no. 30) and 1692 (BNB, MSS 31, ff. 37–53).

gust 1692 report—whether the mita should be preserved or abolished. Given Charles II's preoccupation with the well-being of his treasury, the Council decided to confirm Monclova's twelve points as a compromise. The mita would therefore continue—and thus the dispatch of royal revenue from Potosí would be uninterrupted—but at a lower level than Palata had sought to achieve and hopefully free of the problems that his reforms had created.[58] The Conde de la Monclova's call for the abolition of the mita was meant, I suspect, to have just this effect. If so, then the administrative gambit of sending exaggerated orders or recommendations with the purpose of attaining some lesser goal was used in both directions.

The Council of the Indies passed final judgment on the mita—for the period of Hapsburg dominion in Peru—in January 1697. Monclova's twelve resolutions were transformed by the councillors into nine of their own:

1. that the mitayos and mingas were to receive the same wage, without exception;
2. that there were to be no deliveries in silver;
3. that the substitutes were to be paid the same wage as the mitayos;
4. that the travel allowances were to be paid at the rate of one-half wages for four leagues traveled per day;
5. that half of the travel allowance was to be paid to the mitayos upon their departure for Potosí;
6. that the mitayos were to be paid directly, in the presence of the corregidor of Potosí and a notary;
7. that the royal treasury officials of Potosí were to maintain lists of the mitayos and careful records of their assignments;
8. that the Indians were not to work beyond the hours or period of their obligation, under any pretense; and
9. that once their year of obligation had been completed, the Indians were to return to their homes.[59]

Charles II decreed the adoption of the Council's nine resolutions in a series of cédulas of February 18, 1697. The response to the nine edicts by royal officials in Peru was generally favorable, with the exception of the first and third. The Audiencia of La Plata, the royal treasury officials of Potosí, and others noted that the mingas would not work for the lower wages that the mitayos received, and they argued that skilled laborers should be paid more than unskilled workers.[60] This issue presented few difficulties, however, for no one in Peru was going to object to paying the mingas more in practice.

On the whole, the reforms that the Conde de la Monclova introduced in 1692 (later transformed into the 1697 cédulas) created an official policy on the mita that allowed the system to operate as it had before 1689. With only 34 of the mills receiving the 1,367 mitayos per week, the remaining recipients were assigned an adequate number to meet their needs. More importantly, Monclova's official weekly draft was roughly equivalent to the effective weekly total of the pre-1689 period (see Figure 3), and by again exempting the forasteros and yanaconas and dispensing with specific lists of mitayos, he made it possible for the kurakas to perform their traditional role as capitanes enteradores.

Like Francisco de Toledo, Monclova had benefited from a fortuitous set of circumstances. The Conde did not share with Toledo the advantages of a new technology or tailings, but he was the first seventeenth-century viceroy to enjoy a uniformity of purpose among the Hapsburg officials of Peru (like Palata) and to base his program on current realities rather than legal considerations (unlike Palata). Indeed, the machinery of the Hapsburg empire performed admirably, where the mita was concerned, during the 1690's—at the height of Charles II's reign. The viceroy and a junta devised a plan, it was tailored to reality in Potosí by local officials, and it received the endorsement of the Crown. In a period when corruption and administrative inefficiency were rife in other sectors, the government's handling of the crisis in Alto Perú stands—ironically—as an example of that administrative system at its best.

SEVEN

Conclusions

N o INSTITUTION can survive for 125 years without undergoing significant changes, and so it was with the Potosí mita. The regimen was developed by Francisco de Toledo to provide the inexpensive unskilled labor required by the revitalized Potosí silver industry, founded as well on the introduction of mercury amalgamation technology, the exploitation of tailings, and an infusion of capital by the azogueros. At its inception, the mita was both a capital subsidy—providing unskilled labor at vastly reduced wages—and a means of compelling Indians to do work they otherwise refused to do. Their refusal, we should note, was not the product of ingrained laziness or anticapitalistic sentiment, for the truth is quite the opposite: the Indians refused to work in the mines because their labor in other sectors of the mining community or in other enterprises brought them greater rewards. Once established in the 1570's, the mita evolved in concert with changes in the production formula and demographic developments in the obligated provinces.

With the exhaustion of the tailings by the early 1580's, the Toledan production formula was disrupted, and the azogueros tried to compensate by sending more of their mitayos into the mines to work as apiris and by demanding that they produce more silver ore each day. Quotas were imposed, corporal punishment became commonplace, and the various monetary incentives for the Indians that Toledo had included in the original design—such as the right to kapcha—were suppressed.

The Indians' response to worsening conditions in the Villa Imperial was to flee from the mining center and from the Toledan pueblos subject to mita recruitment. This presented the Hapsburg government and the Azogueros Guild with a pair of related problems, the first being a shortage of mitayos in Potosí and the second being vastly depleted tributary populations in the subjected provinces. As a result, the remaining originarios were compelled to serve more often than one week in three and one year in seven. The individuals responsible for ensuring that they did so were the kurakas, for despite their having no official responsibility for delivering mitayos, the kurakas were in fact the crucial linkage—the means of compulsion—that made the system function. As more and more Indians fled from their responsibilities and found legal exemption as forasteros and "yanaconas," the kurakas were forced to devise ever harsher means of forcing the remaining tributary population to serve in the mita—lest they suffer the consequences at the hands of the azogueros.

As early as 1600, compulsion was no longer sufficient. Not only had the pueblos been greatly affected by flight, they had suffered the ravages of epidemic disease and other disruptions. Around the turn of the century, also, the azogueros found themselves dependent upon silver merchants and moneylenders for operating capital. From these twin phenomena came the principal transformation of the mita of the Hapsburg period—mita deliveries in silver, collected from exempted as well as obligated Indians, and raised through economic activities supervised by the kurakas. The money was used by the azogueros to cover minga labor costs and production ingredient costs—whereby it became known as indios de faltriquera—as well as to hire minga substitutes for mitayos who were not delivered in person. Mita deliveries in silver very quickly became a vital part of the silver production formula, providing the azogueros with a greater degree of economic support as well as Indians to work as apiris in the mines.

The evolution of the mita permitted more azogueros to remain in business than otherwise would have been possible, but it also meant the contraction of each azoguero's enterprise. The development of deliveries in silver also served to keep the guild from winning new government concessions, because the Crown and viceregal authorities considered the practice to be an abuse of the mita—especially in the form of indios de faltriquera—and one that disqualified the azogueros for further assistance. The abuses were made all the more necessary, however, by the azogueros' inability to secure better terms from the Crown. By the middle of the seventeenth century, indios de faltriquera were indispensable to the well-being of the Potosí silver industry; the azogueros would literally kill to protect them.

By the middle of the 1600's, also, the azogueros faced stiff competition for the services of the Indians. The owners of ranches, farms, other mines, and textile mills, municipal organizations, corregidores, priests, and others vied with the Azogueros Guild for the ever falling number of Indians. These other economic interests seized upon the azogueros' abuses of the mita and the demographic impact of the system to argue for its abolition. The azogueros, in turn, accused their enemies of strangling the mita and thus undercutting the production of royal revenue. Their battle had very little to do with loyalty to the Crown or the depopulation of the provinces, however, and in fact was over the more immediate issue of which enterprises would have access to Indian labor. Because the rules of the game precluded one's arguing that he would benefit personally from royal favors, the competitors wrapped their true goals inside the betterment of the public good and the royal welfare. The fundamental importance of the struggle, born of the colonists' thorough dependence on Indian labor for their prosperity, caused the level of rhetoric to reach hyperbolic proportions. We must therefore take the arguments of the combatants with a grain of salt and be extremely careful when using the quantitative data produced by the two sides.

As the objects of a fierce competition for their services, the Indians were afforded an opportunity to choose their masters. Some decided to leave the colonized zone entirely and live among the "infidels," but most took up residence as forasteros or "yanaconas" on farms, ranches, and elsewhere within the sixteen obligated and fourteen exempted corregimientos of Alto Perú. The Indians' migration was an integral factor in the depopulation of the sixteen obligated provinces, but it also peopled other enterprises in a developing, diversifying Peruvian economy. The Indians' abandonment of their "original" (i.e., Toledan) pueblos was their most effective means of opposing the mita, the demands of their kurakas and corregidores, and other obligations. Because they did not rise up against their oppressors, their opposition to the mita and other obligations was quiet, unspectacular, and effective. We should not consider the Indians of Alto Perú conquered or describe them as passive victims of Spanish colonization. Remember, it was the Indians who chose their patrons, not the patrons who chose their clients. The Indians were therefore active participants in determining their own futures and the shape of colonial society.

Ironically, the mita survived into the Bourbon epoch precisely be-

cause Indian migration and the competition for Indian labor in Alto
Perú caused the mitayos to become all the more critical to silver production at Potosí. First, those few mitayos who served in person
produced the ore on which the industry depended (very few mingas
were willing to perform the tasks assigned to the apiris). Second,
mita deliveries in silver—both indios de faltriquera and those used to
hire substitutes—were necessary to subsidize production, to keep the
azogueros' profits sufficiently high that they could remain in business. Were it not for the mita, then surely fewer than 34 mills would
have been in production at the dawn of the eighteenth century. While
the mita had contributed to the revitalization of Potosí in the 1570's,
therefore, it also had a major role in maintaining that industry, even
at greatly inferior levels of production, throughout the remainder of
the Hapsburg period.

Was it worth it, in the final analysis, to keep the mita going? We
have seen that the system drew considerable sums of money from the
native communities and the Indians' other employers in the obligated
provinces, and that the deliveries in silver by the 1660's surpassed by
one-third the royal share of production at Potosí. Indeed, Francisco
de la Cruz suggested that the money collected from the kurakas
should be sent directly to the Crown. In hindsight, it seems clear that
the mita was not worth preserving. The question is moot, however,
because the current levels of production at Potosí were less important, as the seventeenth century matured, than the potential levels of
production promised by those who called for a revitalized mita and
other reforms. This phenomenon was the product of the metropolis's
ever growing need for revenue, which deepened from great to desperate by the end of the Hapsburg epoch. The mita was preserved, therefore, not because it was worthwhile, but because of the hope that
Potosí might someday undergo a renaissance of the sort experienced
in the 1570's. No one wanted to kill the goose that might someday
lay the silver egg.

As we saw in Chapter 1, John Leddy Phelan argued that the Crown's
contradictory and mutually incompatible orders for the conservation
of the Indians and the production of revenue were issued in part to
control its overseas bureaucracy. His thesis clearly requires modification in the light of the administration of the Potosí mita, for the
Crown's coeval orders for augmented silver production and the abolition of the azogueros' abuses of the mita were primarily meant to re-

strain the mining elite. Moreover, it should be clear that the Crown wished to see silver production increased and the Indians protected to the fullest extents possible. Though it placed the former goal above the latter, we would be mistaken to argue that it did not seek to achieve the best results possible in both. Indeed, the Crown believed that its orders to end the azogueros' abuses of the mita, if implemented, would advance its goals in both areas.

Such was the intent of Philip III, and the thinking behind his 1601 and 1609 cédulas, which sought to limit the independence not only of the azogueros, but of encomenderos and similar elites throughout the Americas. The orders were adamant and couched in absolute terms to permit local officials, including Viceroy Luis de Velasco, to employ them against the colonial elites. Though the cédulas may have been issued in part to push local officials toward action, they were designed primarily for the officials' use against the elites; the inclusion of chapters empowering the viceroys to alter the orders as they deemed fit demonstrates that they were not meant to control the officials alone.

The Crown held the ultimate trump card with regard to the mita: its possible abolition. But because it was interested in silver production at Potosí—with a 20 percent stake in the silver produced with mita labor—the Crown was reluctant to use that weapon. Viceroys of Peru, meanwhile, were reluctant to take any significant action because of the importance of silver production during their viceroyalties to their reputations as royal officials, and because of the possibility of provoking an armed insurrection in Alto Perú (like that of Gonzálo Pizarro). The abolition of the mita would therefore have to be a last resort, reserved until all other means of controlling the system had been exhausted and its ill effects clearly outweighed its benefits. Indeed, both Vázquez de Velasco and the Conde de Lemos arrived at their decisions that the mita should be eradicated only after failing in their efforts to reform the regimen. They were frustrated by the stranglehold that the azogueros had on the situation at Potosí, a stranglehold the guild was able to sustain for most of the seventeenth century. Only in the 1680's, with the Duque de la Palata's efforts— ostensibly on the azogueros' behalf—did the azogueros lower their guard, and they paid the price for that mistake with a grave deterioration of their condition.

The Crown's weakness vis-à-vis the altoperuano elites was caused by its geographical isolation from the Villa Imperial and its resulting dependence on the viceregal administration to fight its battles for it. The viceroys were scarcely more effective than the kings, however, in controlling events at Potosí, hampered as they were both by the division of authority between Lima and Madrid and by their own reliance on "government by proxy" mechanisms—especially the division of responsibility for the mita among several government officials in Alto Perú. That division was designed to prevent the officials' subversion by the azogueros, to maintain a steady flow of information to Lima and Madrid, and to ensure that the officials did their best. But the battles waged between the Audiencia of La Plata and officials in Lima, between the Audiencia and the corregidores of Potosí, between the presidents of the Audiencia and any visitador who appeared, and between officials in Alto Perú and the viceroys, nearly prevented the Hapsburg administration from functioning at all.

Perhaps the most important reason why the government could not respond to the metamorphosis of the mita was the refusal of both centers of authority to assume responsibility for major decisions. The viceroys, for example, employed myriad bureaucratic delaying tactics when they feared that their execution of the Council of the Indies' 1650–51 program would cause the collapse of the Potosí silver industry during their viceroyalties. When the Conde de Lemos proposed that the mita be abolished, moreover, the Council of the Indies tried to pass the responsibility for that decision on to the queen, and later sent it back into the viceregal arena with the Conde de Castellar. The conservatism inherent in the system was thus not just a product of bureaucratic foot-dragging on the American side of the Atlantic.

If the failure of the Hapsburg administration to prevent the evolution of the mita—or even to keep pace with it—was frustrating, the impact of the few moments of viceregal effectiveness was often disastrous. After the establishment of the mita by Toledo—one of very few viceroys willing to assume responsibility for innovation—there followed a half-century of mere adjustments to his creation, while the situation at Potosí and in the sixteen obligated provinces deteriorated.

The first moment of subsequent viceregal effectiveness came with the circumvention of local government officials by the Conde de Chinchón, resulting in the 1633 repartimiento de la mita drafted by Juan de Carvajal y Sande. That mita charter was destined to survive for another 56 years, despite the uproar that it created, because of the government's inability to decide between two courses of action: (1) the revitalization of the mita, beginning with a reducción general or an extension of mita obligation to more corregimientos; and (2) the tailoring of the mita to the extant originario population in the sixteen provinces (with a concomitant drop in silver production). The administrative paralysis provoked by that choice could not even be broken by direct orders from the Crown. Indeed, the next moment of effectiveness came in 1659 only because of the decision of Superintendent of the Mita Francisco de la Cruz to ignore his secret instructions from the Conde de Alba; it ended abruptly with his assassination by the azogueros in 1660.

In both of these cases, government effectiveness resulted from the efforts of viceroys to overcome the difficulties presented by the use of local government officials as brokers. But because the viceroys tried to enforce an unrealistic "official" position on the mita—that the Toledan production formula was still viable—the results were necessarily catastrophic. Thus, Phelan's thesis must also be modified to take into account those bureaucrats who did not understand the rules of the game they were playing.

The consummate example of this phenomenon was the third episode of administrative effectiveness: the viceroyalty of the Duque de la Palata. Palata was only the second viceroy of Peru who was willing to assume the responsibility for a far-ranging program, but unfortunately his conceptual basis for that program was entirely obsolete. This is not to say that it was unusual for a viceroy to be out of touch with reality, for every viceroy from the Conde de Chinchón forward shared this problem to one degree or another. Palata was different from the others in that he succeeded in foisting his unworkable reforms upon Alto Perú. The results were utter chaos in, and the probable destruction of, altoperuano society. Were it not for the fourth and final moment of Hapsburg efficiency under the Conde de la Monclova—and the only one in the seventeenth century to be firmly grounded in reality—the region might have suffered still more damage.

In sum, the Phelan thesis needs to be expanded to include American elites among those whom the royal cédulas were meant to control. It also needs to take into account the relative powerlessness of the Crown vis-à-vis those colonial elites. The conservatism of the bureaucracy, moreover, was as much a creation of the Crown's dual concerns for silver production and conservation of the Indians (conservation from subjugation by the elites) as it was a natural product of bureaucracy in general. The priority given to silver production was clear, nevertheless, to all concerned, and in fact intensified with each expensive Spanish campaign against Protestant heresy. But it also seems clear that the Crown in fact hoped to attain the best result possible in all areas.

The miniature versions of the Crown's administrative apparatus by which viceroys tried to administer remote areas of their own jurisdictions deserve further attention as well. The desire of the central authorities to enhance their effectiveness must also be understood as part of the reason for the exaggerated tenor—and the sometimes apparently contradictory nature—of their own orders. Monclova's use of a proposal that the mita be abolished to ensure that at the least his reforms would be confirmed by the Council of the Indies suggests that this sort of gambit was also used in viceroyalty-to-metropolis correspondence. And we must realize that though weaknesses in the administrative system kept it from performing very well most of the time, the results could be catastrophic when momentary effectiveness was not accompanied by a thorough understanding of current reality.

Finally, a word about individuals. As important as the design of administrative hierarchy was to the history of the mita, the people who occupied the key government posts were just as important. The presence of Dionisio Pérez Manrique in the presidency of La Plata in the 1640's was fundamental to the azogueros' inability to win a new repartimiento de la mita from the Marqués de Mancera; what might have happened had Juan de Lizarazu still been at that post? The assassination of Francisco de la Cruz was extremely important to the history of the mita, and we must not forget how Bartolomé de Salazar protected the azogueros from the wrath of the Conde de Alba. To forget the individuals who occupied the administrative posts associated with the mita would be no less a sin than to forget that the Indians were fundamental to the evolution of the mita.

THE YEAR 1700 brought the reign of Charles II to a close, and with it the tenure of the Hapsburg dynasty upon the Spanish throne. The history of the mita does not end with the dawn of the eighteenth century, however, for the system was destined to exist for another century and a quarter. A brief look at the mita during the 1700's, based primarily on the work of Enrique Tandeter and Ramón Ezquerra Abadía, will offer further insights into the conclusions drawn here from the history of the mita during the Hapsburg epoch.[1]

The accession of Philippe d'Anjou of France as Philip V of Spain, and thus the beginning of the Bourbon dynasty's dominion, did not have an immediate impact on day-to-day reality in the Villa Imperial de Potosí. At first the new king was preoccupied with the consolidation of his position on the Iberian peninsula, and only after 1713 was he able to turn his attention to the rest of the empire that Charles II had bequeathed to him. By the end of the eighteenth century, however, the Bourbons had contributed to a significant restructuring of the silver production industry. They had also committed their share of mistakes.

Philip V's attention was first drawn to Potosí in 1718, when he received a proposal from Viceroy Carmine Nicolás Caraccioli that the mita be abolished. After the matter was discussed at some length in the Council of the Indies, the king instructed Caraccioli to put the question to the Audiencia of Lima for a majority vote; he would abide, he said, by its decision. The Audiencia of Lima was clearly not enthusiastic about its role in this matter, for it delayed the required vote for nearly ten years, until very explicit orders from the king in 1727 and 1728, reinforced by those of the Viceroy Marqués de Castel-Fuerte, finally forced the tribunal to take the fateful vote. The result was nine ballots in favor of preserving the mita. That resolution was complemented by the written opinions of individual members of the Audiencia of La Plata.[2]

Ezquerra Abadía has published lengthy summaries of two of the La Plata judges' treatises on the subject in an article concerning the problems that plagued the mita in the eighteenth century. The first was written by Oidor Ignacio Antonio del Castillo in 1728, and the second was sent to the Crown by the Audiencia's fiscal, Joseph Casimiro Gómez García, in 1730. Both officials defended the mita as a necessary evil—evil because of the great weight that it placed on the native community, and necessary because of the great works supported by the silver produced in the Villa Imperial—and both argued that the abuses currently pervading the institution could be countered with a more effective administration of the regimen. Specifically, they called for greater care to be given to the nomination of corregidores of Potosí, for these were the officials most able to affect the status quo in the mining zone. Finally, both called for the assignment of more Indians to the silver industry by extending the territory from which the mitayos were drawn and by obligating anew the forasteros.[3] The dynasty may have changed, but the realities in Alto Perú and the options available to the government had not.

Despite the resolution by the Audiencia of Lima and the arguments of the officials in La Plata, the Council of the Indies suggested to Philip V that the mita be eradicated in May 1732—a move that certainly set it apart from its Hapsburg forbears. The king dismissed that counsel, however, and ordered Castel-Fuerte (in a cédula of October 22, 1732) to preserve the Potosí mita. The viceroy was instructed to ensure that all viceregal ordinances concerning the regimen, including those requiring the payment of travel allowances to the Indians and proscribing mita deliveries in silver, were obeyed. At the same time, the king ordered a wage reduction for the mitayos from 24 to 20 reales per week (the pre-1692 level); and four years later he cut the royal share of production to a tenth. These last two measures were designed to assist the azogueros in their efforts to reverse the downward trend of silver output at Potosí. Philip V also decreed that those Indians, blacks, and mulattos who worked as volunteers at Potosí would be relieved of their tribute obligations. Should this last measure attract sufficient numbers of free laborers, the king told Castel-Fuerte, then perhaps the mita might become unnecessary at some point in the future.[4] Like his Hapsburg predecessors, therefore, Philip V held the mita to be justifiable only for lack of alternatives.

Clearly, the first Bourbon king of Spain had the same priorities as had the Hapsburgs before him: income first, Indian welfare second. He was, however, more willing to sacrifice short-term income for long-term gain, as the halving of the royal share of production attests. The interests of the Azogueros Guild and the Crown remained inexorably linked, moreover, as they had been since the days of Toledo and the first azogueros.[5]

In response to the Crown's directive of October 1732, the Marqués de Castel-Fuerte implemented a new mita charter in 1736, including 3,199 Indians in his annual draft (down from the 4,145 required under Monclova). As the king had demanded, the viceroy also ordered an end to mita deliveries in silver, but he was unable to enforce that decree, despite threats to visit the Villa Imperial personally and the subsequent dispatch of an emissary. Thus, beyond the drop in the official annual draft, the mita was scarcely affected by the 1736 repartimiento.[6]

The mita continued to evolve during the eighteenth century, as it had in the Hapsburg period. The effective annual draft was able to remain in close relation to the official figure, however, for reports from 1740, 1754, and 1801 all fall within the 2,800–3,000 range.[7]

The delivery of money in lieu of Indians became far less prevalent, moreover, until a mere 499 "mitayos" arrived in the Villa Imperial in that form by the early nineteenth century.[8] This development was made possible by the improvement of the azogueros' financial situation. The reduction of the royal share of production to a tenth, noted above, certainly lessened the pressure on them, but we must also remember that only the 34 most viable mining operations had survived the Monclova repartimiento of 1692 and that the wages the azogueros paid the mingas were lower as well. Tandeter reports that the mingas received only 50 percent more in wages than the mitayos by the mid-eighteenth century, whereas a century earlier they had received three times as much. Indeed, the lower minga wage permitted kurakas to deliver a "mitayo" in silver for a mere 60 pesos per annum, compared with the 150-peso sum that had been common in the 1600's.[9]

Another important factor in the improved well-being of the azogueros was the establishment by the guild in 1751 of the Banco de San Carlos—an institution created to take the purchase of silver and the distribution of credit out of the hands of the silver merchants and return them to the control of the azogueros themselves. The first two decades of the bank's existence were filled with problems, but Charles III saw fit in the 1770's to assume control of it (whereby it became the Real Banco de San Carlos) and subsidize the production of silver with loans from the royal treasury. At the same time, mercury supplies were augmented by increasing exports to Peru from Almadén, Spain.[10]

In combination, the royal concessions to the azogueros and the other improvements in their economic situation helped them to raise the output of silver substantially. From 1740 to 1790, the amount of silver sent from the Villa Imperial doubled, and Potosí enjoyed a welcome renaissance.[11] Though the number of enterprises receiving allocations of mita labor fell to a mere 25 by the end of the century, the number of cabezas de ingenio—sets of stamping mechanisms—within those enterprises more than doubled between 1692 and 1799.[12] Many azogueros were able to rent their enterprises to tenants and retire to more comfortable surroundings (La Plata, Lima, Buenos Aires, or Spain). Furthermore, the nine mills that were deprived of mitayos were able to maintain production despite that handicap. Enrique Tandeter has been able—owing to the systematic record keeping of the Real Banco de San Carlos and the generally more reliable quantitative sources from the eighteenth century—to derive close approximations of the profits and costs involved in the administration of a mill with mita labor in the years 1790–93. Of the silver produced in that four-year period, 71.2 percent went to general production costs, 11.4 percent went for mitayos' wages, 11.8 percent went in rent to the owner, and 5.6 percent went to the tenant/operator (the royal share had already been exacted—43 percent of the profits, compared with 37 percent for the owner and 20 percent for the tenant).[13]

Tandeter identifies as the principal cause of the revitalization of Potosí none of the factors described above, however, but rather an innovation in the mita. Specifically, the quotas of ore that the mitayos were required to produce were doubled during the same 1740–90 period from roughly fifteen loads per day to 30. This forced the mitayos to work longer for the same wages (which Tandeter factors at just under 65.5 pesos per year) and led to the greater participation of the mitayos' families (wives and children) in the satisfaction of their obligations. Thus, twice as much ore was ground by twice as many stamping mechanisms, resulting in the production of twice as much silver. The royal concessions served as catalysts, Tandeter argues, but they could not have caused the resurgence of output without this change in the mita.[14]

The mita therefore became more of the draft labor system that it was originally meant to be, and its seventeenth-century role as a source of operating capital was lessened by the creation of the Real Banco de San Carlos, the halving of the royal fifth, and the lower minga wage. Only under a forced labor system could quotas be doubled with such effectiveness. The mita continued to be crucial to the Potosí silver industry even in a period of rapid growth, therefore, because it still drafted workers for those tasks at Potosí that mingas refused to do for the wages they would receive. Tandeter makes this point very clearly and backs it up with figures showing that the mitayos were assigned the heavier, physical work of carrying ore and grinding it in the mills (free laborers were hired for these jobs only by those enterprises that did not receive mitayos).[15]

The mita's role as an economic subsidy may have been lessened by the end of the eighteenth century, but the system still transferred capital from the Indian communities to the mining sector at Potosí, for the benefit of the mining industry and the Crown. The differential between the wages paid to mitayos and mingas (even when lessened) and the nearly 500 "mitayos" that now arrived in the form of silver remained a significant sum. Even at a yearly remittance of 60 pesos per Indian, the total was 30,000 pesos, and it was divided only 25 ways.

So the mita was important to the production of silver at Potosí throughout its existence. Indeed, it proved crucial to the renaissance of production in the mid-eighteenth century—the revitalization so yearned for but never achieved by the Hapsburgs, who nevertheless made it possible by preserving the system despite its inefficiency. The resurgence of silver production did not put an end to the controversy that constantly swirled about the mita, however, for the working conditions of the mitayos were condemned by Antonio de Ulloa and Jorge Juan at mid-century and the system came under renewed attack in the late 1700's by the Jesuit Victorián de Villava. The responses of Charles III and Charles IV to these attacks were thoroughly traditional: they ordered improvements in the administration of the mita. Indeed, the eighteenth century closed with a total restructuring of the system under the direction of the corregidor-intendant of Potosí, Francisco de Paula Sanz (and the famous Código Carolino of 1794).[16]

But this is not the end of the story. The regeneration of Potosí after 1740 was unable to satisfy the appetite of the Bourbons for revenue from South America, and the Crown pressed for larger payments of tribute and imposed other taxes. That effort, including the doubling of the mitayos' quotas and intense pressure on the kurakas to deliver the numbers of mitayos required under the 1736 repartimiento de la mita, touched off a series of native upheavals in Alto Perú, culminating in the Tupac Amaru and Tupac Catari rebellions of the 1780's.[17] The period of greatest Bourbon zeal under Charles III led to disaster in Alto Perú, therefore, just as the efforts of the Duque de la Palata on behalf of Charles II had ravaged altoperuano society a century earlier. And just as the Palatan reform program of 1689–90 had provoked serious—albeit peaceful—opposition from the Indian population, so too did the Bourbon reforms compel the native community to respond, this time with violence, in keeping with the severity of the threat. Though the rebellions were not successful, they did serve to remind the white elites of the vast reservoir of power within the Indian community, and of their ultimate dependence on that community. It may well be that the Indians also learned a lesson: that passive resistance is more successful than violent opposition.

This glimpse of the Potosí mita in the eighteenth century lends support to many of the arguments made earlier about the mita under Hapsburg administration. First, the mita served as an economic subsidy without which most of the azogueros would not have been able to remain in production. Second, the mitayos were needed to perform those tasks that the mingas refused to do, for the wages the azogueros were prepared to pay them. Third, the royal administration of the mita could not alter, except under the most unusual circumstances, the status quo at Potosí without the consent of the local elites. Fourth, it is clear, at the same time, that the mita underwent a continuing metamorphosis in concert with changing conditions at Potosí and in the provinces from which the mitayos were drawn. And finally, the Indians did not resort to armed insurrection to oppose the mita because passive resistance—migration primarily—was more effective. Their decision to respond to the demands of the azogueros and the Hapsburg administration with migration, adoption of "yanacona" status, and other peaceful means was vindicated by the experience of the 1780's.

Reference Matter

Notes

Most of the abbreviations used in the notes are explained in the first section of the Bibliography, pp. 183–86. The only exceptions are the "CR" designation used in AHP citations (it refers to the "Cajas Reales" collection) and the "C" used in AGNP citations (it stands for "Cuaderno"). I have employed the abbreviations used by the archives themselves, except that I have added a letter to "Archivo General de la Nación" abbreviations to distinguish between the Argentine and Peruvian institutions.

Quoted passages in the notes are presented with the same spelling and accentuation as in the original sources.

CHAPTER 1

1. Zavala, *Servicio personal*, vol. 1, p. 87; Castillo, f. 3v.
2. Hanke, "Viceroy Toledo," p. 3; Zavala, *Servicio personal*, vol. 1, p. 63; Padden, pp. xvii–xviii.
3. Parry, pp. 188–89.
4. The Viceroy Conde de Lemos to the Crown (Lima, July 4, 1670), AGI, Charcas, leg. 268, no. 16, and the accompanying discourse (AGI, Charcas, leg. 268, no. 15) of the same date. The discourse has been published in Vargas Ugarte, ed., *Pareceres*, pp. 155–65; and in Hanke and Rodríguez, eds., *Virreyes* (Perú), vol. 4, pp. 276–89. Baquíjano y Carrillo, p. 37 (providing a total of 1,067,697 Indians); Málaga Medina, p. 611 (1,067,697); Padden, p. xix (1,677,697); all draw upon the discourse.
5. Zavala, *Servicio personal*, vol. 1, pp. 14–15, 50.
6. Parry, pp. 189–90, offers an unflattering view of corregidores de indios. Rowe provides a more extensive description in "The Incas." See Keith also.
7. Castañeda Delgado, p. 334; Arzáns, *Historia*, vol. 1, pp. 43–46.
8. For the initial profitability of Potosí, see Bargalló, p. 74; Capoche,

p. 77. For figures on the mining center's population, see Holmes, pp. 9–12; Arzáns, *Historia*, vol. 1, p. 42.

9. Holmes, pp. 8, 14; Brading and Cross, pp. 553–54; Padden, pp. xiv–xv.

10. Campo y de la Rynaga, p. 11.

11. Cobb, "Potosí . . . Frontier," p. 47; Capoche, pp. 108–9, 134–35; Benino, pp. 365–66; "Descripción (1603)," p. 373; Holmes, pp. 20, 25–27, 32–37; Castillo, ff. 2–2v; Bakewell, *Miners*, Chap. 2.

12. Holmes, p. 14; Cobb, "Potosí and Huancavelica," pp. 8–9.

13. Capoche, pp. 108–9; Holmes, pp. 35–37.

14. Brading and Cross, pp. 552–54; Lohmann Villena, "La minería," p. 645.

15. Oidor Juan de Matienzo to the Crown (La Plata, Oct. 20, 1561) in Levillier, ed., *Audiencia de Charcas*, vol. 1, p. 57; Padden, pp. xvii–xviii; Holmes, pp. 45–47; Arzáns, *Historia*, vol. 1, pp. 108–11; Cobb, "Potosí and Huancavelica," p. 65.

16. Zavala, *Servicio personal*, vol. 1, pp. 20–21, 23–25, 34, 39; Holmes, pp. 17–20. The idea of replacing mitayos with black slaves was resurrected a number of times. Three examples of sources dealing with the issue are: President Juan López de Cepeda to the Crown, La Plata, Mar. 12, 1593, in Levillier, ed., *Audiencia de Charcas*, vol. 3, pp. 162–81; the Audiencia of La Plata to the Crown, La Plata, Feb. 1, 1610, ANB, C, no. 1143; and a copy of a royal cédula to the Audiencia of La Plata, Zaragoza, Oct. 12, 1645, ANB, RC, no. 392.

17. Bakewell, *Miners*, Chap. 2.

18. Campo y de la Rynaga, p. 13.

19. *Ibid.*, pp. 13–14; Zavala, *Servicio personal*, vol. 2, p. 117.

20. Zavala, *Servicio personal*, vol. 1, p. 64.

21. For general descriptions of Potosí, see Riva-Agüero, pp. 30–31; Ramírez del Aguila, pp. 81–82. Capoche, p. 77, says that silver was placed at Potosí by God to lure the Spanish into Alto Perú.

22. Cobb, "Supply and Transportation," and "Potosí . . . Frontier," p. 43 (for charcoal supplies); Padden, p. xvi.

23. The quote is from Campo y de la Rynaga, p. 15. Zavala, *Servicio personal*, vol. 1, p. 68, relates the Audiencia of Lima's report to the Crown on the matter.

24. Zavala, *Servicio personal*, vol. 1, pp. 64–65; Holmes, pp. 21–23. The 1552 cédula is described by Zavala, *Servicio personal*, vol. 1, p. 18.

25. Bakewell, "Technological Change," p. 60; Zavala, *Servicio personal*, vol. 1, p. 68.

26. Zavala, *Servicio personal*, vol. 1, pp. 30, 68–69. For more on Huamanga during the sixteenth century, see Stern.

27. "Carta del virrey D. Francisco de Toledo a S.M. sobre materias de hacienda real y fisco, especialmente acerca de las minas de Potosí," Potosí, Mar. 20, 1573, in Levillier, ed., *Gobernantes*, vol. 5, pp. 76–110; Bargalló, pp. 136–37; Brading and Cross, pp. 553–54; Lohmann Villena, "La min-

ería," p. 645; Campo y de la Rynaga, p. 16; Capoche, p. 116; Zavala, *Servicio personal*, vol. 1, p. 74; Arzáns, *Historia*, vol. 1, pp. 145–55.

28. Toledo to the Crown, Mar. 20, 1573 (see n. 27 above); Zavala, *Servicio personal*, vol. 1, p. 87; Bakewell, *Miners*, Chap. 3.

29. Toledo to the Crown, Mar. 20, 1573 (see n. 27 above). Bakewell, "Technological Change," pp. 60–61, notes the comparative economics and the mine owners' reluctance (see his *Miners*, Chap. 3, also). Valera notes that the investment in new mills required assurances that production would be profitable even after the tailings were exhausted. "Información" submitted by the Azogueros Guild, Potosí, 1642–43, AGNA, Sala 9, leg. 6.2.5. Other provisions were made to entice the mine owners, including the guarantee that they would not be jailed for debts; see Crespo, *Guerra*, p. 42. For the azogueros' efforts to protect both privileges, see Chap. 3 below.

30. The azogueros' 1642–43 "información" (see n. 29 above); Crespo, *Guerra*, p. 42; Bakewell, *Miners*, Chap. 3.

31. Bakewell, "Technological Change," p. 66; "Memoriales del Virrey Francisco de Toledo . . . ," n.d., in Hanke and Rodríguez, eds., *Virreyes* (Perú), vol. 1, p. 144.

32. Bakewell, "Technological Change," p. 66; Zavala, *Servicio personal*, vol. 1, pp. 90, 94.

33. Holmes, p. 48, says that Toledo's mita ordinances were based primarily on the mining code drawn up by Polo de Ondegardo in 1562 for the mines of Huamanga. For this code, see Joaquín F. Pacheco et al., eds., *Colección de documentos inéditos relativos al descubrimiento, conquista y colonización de las posesiones españolas en América y Oceanía, sacados, en su mayor parte, del Real Archivo de Indias* (42 vols.; Madrid, 1864–84), vol. 8, pp. 449–62.

34. Nothing about the mita has caused more confusion than the question of the number and nature of the repartimientos de la mita drafted by Toledo himself. The following discussion is based on the "caveza del rrepartimientto xeneral que hizo El señor Virrey Don francisco de ttoledo . . . ," copied by Notary Luis Maldonado in the 1660's for Superintendent of the Mita Francisco de la Cruz, AGI, Charcas, leg. 266, no. 45J; Toledo to the Crown, Mar. 20, 1573 (see n. 27 above); and a history of the mita written by Controller Pedro Antonio del Castillo to serve as the introduction to the tome on the general enumeration of Indians and new mita charter of the Viceroy Duque de la Palata (ca. 1689), AGI, Charcas, leg. 270, no. 33C.

35. AGI, Charcas, leg. 266, no. 45J; Capoche, p. 135. Also of import are two legajos from the AGNA: Sala 9, leg. 10.3.7, and Sala 13, leg. 18.7.4, both of which are compilations of complaints resulting from the inclusion of new classes of Indians and new regions in the mita during the viceroyalty of the Duque de la Palata.

36. AGI, Charcas, leg. 266, no. 45J; Castillo, f. 3v; Bakewell, *Miners*, Chap. 3.

37. Castillo, f. 3v.

38. *Ibid.*, ff. 4–4v.

39. Percentages are from AGI, Charcas, leg. 266, no. 45J; totals are from Castillo, ff. 5–6. See also Arzáns, *Historia*, vol. 1, pp. 157–58. Bakewell, *Miners*, Chap. 3, says that the weekly draft was 3,861 and the annual draft was 11,494.

40. For priorities, see Rowe, "The Incas," p. 171; for the need to make it worthwhile for the mitayos, see Bakewell, "Technological Change," p. 65. Zavala, *Servicio personal*, vol. 1, pp. 118–22, gives a lengthy accounting of Toledo's ordinances.

41. Zavala, *Servicio personal*, vol. 1, pp. 118–22, includes a sketch of the mitayos' weekly routine.

42. On pay, see Zavala, *Servicio personal*, vol. 1, p. 103; Capoche, p. 145.

43. Cobb, "Potosí and Huancavelica," p. 71; Zavala, *Servicio personal*, vol. 1, pp. 118–22.

44. Crespo, "La 'Mita,'" pp. 172–73, says that five pesos were to be paid for each month on the road. See Cañete y Domínquez, pp. 105–6, for an eighteenth-century view.

45. Capoche, pp. 140–41. AGI, Charcas, leg. 266, no. 45J, says that the segregation also facilitated the distribution of priests to provide religious instruction for the Indians.

46. AGI, Charcas, leg. 266, no. 45J; Zavala, *Servicio personal*, vol. 1, p. 89. Matienzo describes how these officials were paid with money deducted from the mitayos' wages in a letter to the Crown, Potosí, Dec. 23, 1577, in Levillier, ed., *Audiencia de Charcas*, vol. 1, pp. 455–65 (summarized in Zavala, *Servicio personal*, vol. 1, p. 103).

47. Zavala, *Servicio personal*, vol. 1, pp. 159–60; Bakewell, "Technological Change," p. 65.

48. Cobb, "Potosí . . . Frontier," p. 47; Basadre, "El Régimen," pp. 345–46; Holmes, pp. 84–88; Zavala, *Servicio personal*, vol. 1, p. 85; Tandeter, "Mineros de 'week-end.'"

49. Brading and Cross, pp. 558–60; Kubler, p. 372; Ayanz, p. 39.

50. On the reliance on kurakas, see Crespo, "Reclutamiento," pp. 473–74, and "La 'Mita,'" pp. 179–80; Holmes, pp. 95–99. On the communal basis of taxation, see Parry, pp. 188–89; Málaga Medina, pp. 611–12. For an excellent general description of the functions of kurakas, see Rasnake.

51. Matienzo to the Crown, Dec. 23, 1577 (see n. 46 above).

52. Zavala, *Servicio personal*, vol. 1, p. 103.

53. Castillo, ff. 6v–7v; AGI, Charcas, leg. 266, no. 45J; Bakewell, *Miners*, Chap. 3 (his figures are slightly different).

54. This listing is based on Valera, pp. 35–36, and Sánchez-Albornoz, "Mita, migraciones" (itself based on Cook, ed., *Tasa de la visita*); see Table 4. No detailed listing of the provinces included in 1573 or 1575 has yet been discovered.

55. Cañete y Domínguez, p. 101.

56. The question of the difference between mitayo and minga wages is discussed in detail in Chap. 2 below.

57. On the mita as a recruiting mechanism, see Pereyra, pp. 17–19; on debt-peonage, see Holmes, p. 106.

58. Cobb, "Supply and Transportation," pp. 31–32; Oidor Arias de Ugarte to the Crown, Potosí, Feb. 28, 1599, in Levillier, ed., *Audiencia de Charcas*, vol. 3, pp. 355–67.

59. Bakewell, "Technological Change," p. 65; Zavala, *Servicio personal*, vol. 1, p. 75; Brading and Cross, p. 546; Cobb, "Potosí and Huancavelica," pp. 22–23.

60. Cobb, "Supply and Transportation," pp. 37–41; Zavala, *Servicio personal*, vol. 1, pp. 75, 87; Brading and Cross, pp. 563–64, 572. See also Toledo's "Memoriales," in Hanke and Rodríguez, eds., *Virreyes* (Perú), vol. 1, pp. 145–47.

61. Bakewell, "Technological Change," pp. 60–61, 65; Baquíjano y Carrillo, p. 36.

62. On the climate, see Capoche, pp. 79, 110; Ballesteros Gaibrois, pp. 39–41. On the cost of the reservoirs, see Baquíjano y Carrillo, p. 36; Brading and Cross, pp. 553–54 (say that some 2 million pesos were spent on twenty reservoirs). On later problems with the water supply, see Chap. 3 below.

63. Bakewell, "Technological Change," p. 77.

64. Campo y de la Rynaga, p. 18; Zavala, *Servicio personal*, vol. 1, pp. 168, 172.

65. Capoche, p. 135. On the Audiencia of Lima's unhappiness over the expropriation of Huancavelica, see Cobb, "Potosí and Huancavelica," pp. 43, 46–49; for the Audiencia of La Plata's reasons for opposition, see *ibid.*, pp. 66–67.

66. Zavala, *Servicio personal*, vol. 1, pp. 82, 93–94 (1574), 97–99 (1575), 99–100 (1576 correspondence), 103–4 (1578 statement).

67. Elliott, pp. 262–85.

68. Cañete y Domínguez, p. 100; Zavala, *Servicio personal*, vol. 1, p. 174; Campo y de la Rynaga, pp. 18–19. Parry, p. 191, says that forced labor was authorized as a temporary means to get the Indians into the cities and other zones controlled by the Spanish.

69. Phelan, "Authority and Flexibility."

70. Phelan, *The Kingdom of Quito*.

CHAPTER 2

1. Oidor Juan de Matienzo to the Crown, Potosí, Dec. 23, 1577, in Levillier, ed., *Audiencia de Charcas*, vol. 1, pp. 455–65; "Descripción (1603)," p. 377.

2. ANB, M 125, no. 13 (this is a jurisdictional dispute between Corregidor of Potosí Francisco Sarmiento de Mendoza and Alcalde Mayor de Minas

Pedro de Montalvo from the mid-1650's, but it includes a series of accounts of injury to mitayos from the 1590's forward, used as precedents); Hanke, *Imperial City*, p. 25 (for a discussion of pneumoconiocis); President Juan López de Cepeda to the Crown, La Plata, Dec. 27, 1582, in Levillier, ed., *Audiencia de Charcas*, vol. 2, pp. 30–41; Oidor Arias de Ugarte to the Crown, Potosí, Feb. 28, 1599, *ibid.*, vol. 3, pp. 355–67.

3. Holmes p. 72 (I have made some alterations in his translation and converted distances to their metric equivalents).

4. *Ibid.*, pp. 73–74; ANB, M 125, no. 13; Cañete y Domínguez, pp. 111–12; Arias de Ugarte to the Crown, Feb. 28, 1599, in Levillier, ed., *Audiencia de Charcas*, vol. 3, pp. 355–67; Bakewell, *Miners*, Chap. 5.

5. Holmes, p. 73. Problems with water in the mines continued to the end of the seventeenth century (accord of the Cabildo of Potosí to receive a demonstration of a new method of extracting water from mines, Potosí, May 2, 1635, BNB, CPLA 20, ff. 215–15v; a complaint by an azoguero, Antonio de Guzmán Maldonado, about the corregidor's removal of 40 mitayos from his operation, including a lengthy description of the means Guzmán used to extract water from his mines, Potosí, Apr. 1–May 19, 1699, ANB, M 126, no. 6).

6. Holmes, p. 75; ANB, M 125, no. 13; Oidor Arias de Ugarte to the Crown, Potosí, Feb. 28, 1599, in Levillier, ed., *Audiencia de Charcas*, vol. 3, pp. 355–67; "Memoria gubernativa del Conde del Villardompardo," n.d. (ca. 1592), in Hanke and Rodríguez, eds., *Virreyes* (Perú), vol. 1, pp. 210–12.

7. Bakewell, *Miners*, Chap. 3; Capoche, pp. 141–43 (for Viceroy Martín Enríquez's repartimiento de la mita).

8. Petition (información) by Juan de Ayala y Figueroa, procurador of Potosí, Potosí, 1609–10, ANB, M 3, no. 17. The ineffectiveness of that petition is noted in the azogueros' petition of 1642–43, AGNA, Sala 9, leg. 6.2.5. The Audiencia to the Crown, La Plata, Feb. 25, 1589, in Levillier, ed., *Audiencia de Charcas*, vol. 2, pp. 422–34, and Mar. 5, 1590, vol. 3, pp. 40–74; Zavala, *Servicio personal*, vol. 1, p. 183 (Cañete to the Crown in 1593); "Instrucción al virrey del Perú don Luis de Velasco sobre hacienda," Madrid[?], Aug. 11, 1596, in Hanke and Rodríguez, eds., *Virreyes* (Perú), vol. 2, pp. 33–36 (mercury statistics); Cobb, "Supply and Transportation," pp. 37–39 (for 85 pesos/quintal) and Sandoval y Guzmán, f. 63 (for 66 pesos/quintal in 1630).

9. Zavala, *Servicio personal*, vol. 1, pp. 165–66.

10. Chapters of accords by the Cabildo of Potosí, Potosí, Sept. 9, 1635, BNB, CPLA 20, ff. 285v–86, 327v; Mar. 7, 1636, BNB, CPLA 20, ff. 422v–23; Jan. 14, 1649, BNB, CPLA 24, f. 274 (all deal with candles, the cost of wax, etc.).

11. Barnadas, "Una polémica"; Zavala, *Servicio personal*, vol. 1, pp. 163–64; Capoche, pp. 150–58, 160–67.

12. Zavala, *Servicio personal*, vol. 1, pp. 149–52, 157–58; Capoche, pp.

167–68; Oidor Juan Díaz de Lopidana to the Crown, Potosí, Feb. 19, 1586, in Levillier, ed., *Audiencia de Charcas*, vol. 2, pp. 241–44; Cobb, "Potosí and Huancavelica," p. 83; Holmes, pp. 83–84; Bakewell, *Miners*, Chap. 5.

13. Capoche, p. 158; Rowe, "The Incas," p. 175; Cobb, "Potosí and Huancavelica," pp. 78–79, 81–82; Fiscal Jerónimo Tovar y Montalvo to the Crown, La Plata, Feb. 20, 1595, in Levillier, ed., *Audiencia de Charcas*, vol. 3, pp. 247–58; Lohmann Villena, "La minería," pp. 654–55; Parry, pp. 174–75.

14. The Audiencia of La Plata to the Crown, La Plata, Feb. 17, 1611, ANB, C, no. 1160; Ayanz, pp. 36–50; Cobb, "Potosí and Huancavelica," p. 83; Sánchez-Albornoz, *Indios y tributos*, pp. 92–95. Zavala, *Servicio personal*, vol. 1, p. 40, notes that those who went to Potosí in the pre-1572 period rarely returned home after their period of service in the mining zone.

15. Crespo, "Reclutamiento," pp. 476–77, and "La 'Mita,'" p. 169.

16. Basadre, "El Régimen," p. 344.

17. Rowe, "The Incas," p. 175; Lohmann Villena, "La minería," pp. 654–55.

18. The Audiencia to the Crown, La Plata, Feb. 17, 1584, in Levillier, ed., *Audiencia de Charcas*, vol. 2, pp. 93–112; Sánchez-Albornoz, *Indios y tributos*, pp. 72, 92–95.

19. Zavala, *Servicio personal*, vol. 1, p. 148; Bakewell, *Miners*, Chap. 4.

20. President Juan López de Cepeda to the Crown, La Plata, Feb. 28, 1590, in Levillier, ed., *Audiencia de Charcas*, vol. 3, pp. 19–30, and July 2, 1590, vol. 3, pp. 82–92; Dobyns, pp. 501–5; Zavala, *Servicio personal*, vol. 1, pp. 151, 177–78; Cobb, "Potosí and Huancavelica," pp. 81–82; Bakewell, *Miners*, Chap. 4.

21. "Descripción (1603)," p. 377.

22. *Ibid.*; Padden, p. xx, interprets these figures differently, by not including the 19,000 among the 30,000 total, and thereby deriving an Indian population of 79,000. The figures for the 1611 census come from Baquíjano y Carrillo, pp. 37–38 (which also list 3,000 Spaniards, 35,000 criollos, 40,000 Europeans, and 6,000 mulattos, zambos, and negros). "Descripción (1603)," p. 378, documents 6,000 Spaniards, 4,000 male and 2,000 female. Zavala, *Servicio personal*, vol. 2, p. 6, includes an undated profile by Felipe Fernández de Santillán (140 mill owners, 80 mine owners, 280 mill employees, two mayordomos per mill, 100 miners who oversaw Indians, 200 Spaniards involved in rescates, 80 Spaniards carting ore, 200 merchants, 200 officials [or artisans], 500 foreign merchants, and 13,000 mitayos); unfortunately, this listing must be considered incomplete, as no mingas are included.

23. Bakewell, *Miners*, Chap. 4.

24. *Ibid.*, Chaps. 4–5; Holmes, pp. 73–74.

25. "Descripción (1603)," p. 384, gives mitayo wages (the listing on p. 377 provides some of the wages paid to mingas). Pérez Bustamante quotes extensively from the account of the Carmelite Vázquez de Espinosa, who visited

Peru between 1617 and 1619; on pp. 302−3 is a passage on Potosí, describing the wages paid to the mitayos and mingas. "Pareceres de los Padres de la Compañía de Jesús de Potosí. 1610," p. 120, says that the mingas earned nine pesos per week until Corregidor Ortiz de Sotomayor reduced the sum to seven and one-half. Another reason why the work in the mines was so unpopular was that the tunnel owners charged passage for the Indians to enter the mines through the adits, and the azogueros forced their Indians to climb down through the shafts rather than pay for their passage via the tunnels (appointment of Cristóbal Jiménez de Arandia as a veedor by the Viceroy Marqués de Montesclaros, Lima, Oct. 20, 1610, BNB, CPLA 12, ff. 353−54v). Bakewell, *Miners*, Chaps. 4−5.

26. Ramírez del Aguila, pp. 82−84.

27. Undated petition by Gabriel Fernández Guarachi, a kuraka from the province of Pacajes, AGI, Charcas, leg. 267, no. 53A (a summary of the petition's contents is AGI, Charcas, leg. 267, no. 53; it is dated Madrid, June 19, 1668); ANB, M 125, no. 13; BNB, CPLA 12, ff. 353−54v; Mesía Venegas, p. 113.

28. ANB, M 125, no. 13 (including cases); Ramírez del Aguila, pp. 82−84.

29. Decision of the Cabildo of Potosí to appeal the 1615 ruling by the Audiencia, Oct. 16, 1615, BNB, CPLA 14, f. 147v; provisión of the Viceroy Marqués de Guadalcázar confirming the Audiencia's ruling, Los Reyes [Lima], Feb. 9, 1626, BNB, MSS 7, ff. 56−66; provisión of the same viceroy ordering compliance with the preceding, Los Reyes, Nov. 13, 1626, BNB, MSS 7, ff. 74−78v. For Viceroy Luis de Velasco's comments that the priests took all of the Indians' possessions to pay for funerals and masses, see his order concerning compliance with the mita by the Indians of Chucuito, Los Reyes, Apr. 10, 1603, BNB, MSS 2, ff. 135−39.

30. Zavala, *Servicio personal*, vol. 2, p. 34 (for rescates), vol. 1, p. 183 (for the high cost of food); petition by Francisco Pérez de la Rinaga, protector general de los naturales of Potosí, Potosí, Nov. 7−11, 1603, ANB, M 122, no. 9. When food was plentiful, however, the Indians were generally the last to get it (accord of the Cabildo of Potosí to prohibit the sale of wheat bread to the Indians, Dec. 3, 1610, BNB, CPLA 13, ff. 342−42v). For Indians eating their llamas, see the accord of the Cabildo of Potosí, June 8, 1618, BNB, CPLA 16, f. 31v, and another of Apr. 4, 1634 (in this case the Indians were eating other people's livestock), BNB, CPLA 20, ff. 8−8v. Bakewell, *Miners*, Chap. 4, draws on the estimated wages and expenses of a mitayo established by Felipe de Godoy in 1608; in a six month period, a mitayo would earn a maximum of 65 pesos and his expenses for the same period would come to some 200 pesos; clearly, to meet all his expenses, a mitayo would have to rely on funds and goods brought from his home pueblo, wages earned during "rest" periods, and familial assistance.

31. Relación of the Viceroy Luis de Velasco, Nov. 28, 1604, in Hanke and Rodríguez, eds., *Virreyes* (Perú), vol. 2, p. 52; Dobyns, pp. 508−9.

Potosí was affected by measles in 1619 and smallpox in 1628 (accords of the Cabildo of Potosí, Aug. 20, 1619, BNB, CPLA 16, ff. 148–48v, 150, and Apr. 4, 1628, BNB, CPLA 18, ff. 279v–80, respectively). In 1635, the Villa Imperial was infested with "bubillas, sarampión, tabardillo y dolor de costado" (Cabildo accords of Oct. 20 and 24, 1635, BNB, CPLA 20, ff. 332 and 334v, respectively). Castillo, p. 11, comments on a 1617 order by the Viceroy Príncipe de Esquilache that was meant to counter the Indians' absences from their home pueblos. Zavala, *Servicio personal*, vol. 2, pp. 27–28 (for fugitives hidden on farms); accord of the Cabildo of Potosí to request a viceregal order to overcome the opposition to the delivery of mitayos by corregidores, kurakas, and others, Sept. 19, 1609, BNB, CPLA 12, ff. 241–43v.

32. Francisco Michaca vs. Pedro Andrada Sotomayor, case heard before the Audiencia of La Plata, Jan. 24–Nov. 14, 1608, ANB, M 131, no. 1.

33. Sánchez-Albornoz, *Indios y tributos*, pp. 92–95, comments on the protection afforded to runaway Indians by landowners, and on the agreements that the landowners often reached with kurakas to pay them some compensation.

34. Petition by Friar Fernando Doncel, of the Company of Jesus in La Plata, before the Audiencia of La Plata, 1589–1696, ANB, EC 1762, no. 16.

35. Francisco Quispi vs. Pascual Huanca, case heard before the Audiencia of La Plata, La Plata and Potosí, June 23, 1682–June 1, 1683, ANB, M 126, no. 1.

36. Case brought before the Audiencia of La Plata by Gabriel Fernández Guarachi, La Paz, La Plata, and Caquiaviri, Aug. 2–Dec. 24, 1633, ANB, M 123, no. 11.

37. Petition by Pedro Mamani before the Audiencia of La Plata, Porco, May 1–20, 1684, ANB, M 126, no. 2 (a request for the Audiencia to reinforce its earlier order).

38. Juan Bautista Catari vs. Pedro Anava, case before the Audiencia of La Plata, Porco, Apr. 24, 1684, ANB, M 126, no. 3. A similar case is that between Capitán Enterador Juan Choque Mamani and Martín Chui Fernández, gobernador of the pueblo of Laja, 1685–89, ANB, EC 1689, no. 31 (in this instance, the charges seem to have been brought by a disgruntled Indian who had been forcibly returned to his pueblo and then denied the status of kuraka to which he aspired).

39. Sánchez-Albornoz, *Indios y tributos*, pp. 99–107, discusses the complaints of the capitanes enteradores about other kurakas, and he provides a full transcription of the questions and answers in an appendix (pp. 113–49). Zavala, *Servicio personal*, vol. 2, pp. 190–93, also describes the testimony of the capitanes. The questioning took place in Potosí in March 1690, and a transcript was produced by Notary Juan de Torres Domínguez on March 24.

40. Cobb, "Potosí and Huancavelica," p. 98.

41. Fernando Surco vs. Pedro Alata Arusi, case before the Audiencia of La Plata, La Plata, Mar. 27–Apr. 21, 1643, ANB, M 125, no. 11.

42. Petition by Antonio Carrillo and his brothers, before the Audiencia of La Plata, Porco, 1603–Oct. 1638, ANB, M 125, no. 2.

43. Petition by Bartolomé González, before the Audiencia of La Plata, Porco, July 19, 1679, ANB, M 125, no. 20.

44. The case brought against the corregidor of Asangaro, Francisco de Castro, heard by the Audiencia of La Plata, La Plata and Asangaro, Apr. 18, 1673–Mar. 6, 1674, ANB, M 125, no. 19.

45. *Ibid.*

46. Zavala, *Servicio personal*, vol. 2, p. 69. His account of the origin of mita deliveries in silver is based on an anonymous and undated document entitled "De la mita de Potosí, y reducciones del Reino," printed in *Livro primeiro do Governo do Brasil, 1607–1633* (Rio de Janeiro: Departamento de Imprensa Nacional, 1958), pp. 7–28; a margin note that the document was obtained from "Dom Rafael Ortis" and the identification of the Príncipe de Esquilache as the most recent viceroy strongly suggest that the document was produced by Rafael Ortiz de Sotomayor, corregidor of Potosí from 1608 to 1617, in the 1610's.

47. President Alonso Maldonado de Torres to the Audiencia of La Plata, Potosí, Dec. 12, 1606, ANB, M 123, no. 2; Zavala, *Servicio personal*, vol. 2, p. 32.

48. Ramírez del Aguila, pp. 118–20; "Pareceres de los Padres de la Compañía de Jesús de Potosí. 1610," p. 120, was probably the source of Ramírez's explanation that the mingas' wage was lowered to seven and one-half pesos because the azogueros were turning away able mitayos simply to save themselves the two and one-half pesos per week salary.

49. Zavala, *Servicio personal*, vol. 2, pp. 68–69.

50. Royal edict to the Audiencia of Charcas to advise the viceroy on various proposals by Visitador Alonso Martínez de Pastrana to improve silver production at Potosí, Madrid, July 15, 1620, BNB, MSS 5, ff. 251v–53. A copy of an identical order to the Viceroy Príncipe de Esquilache is AGI, Charcas, leg. 266, no. 25B. See also Zavala, *Servicio personal*, vol. 2, p. 119. Crespo, *Guerra*, p. 19, cites a letter from Corregidor Francisco Sarmiento de Sotomayor to the Crown (Potosí, May 9, 1619, AGI, Charcas, leg. 52) claiming that one-third of the mitayos were missing.

51. Zavala, *Servicio personal*, vol. 2, pp. 79–80. Corregidor Blas Robles de Salzedo reported in 1639 that one-third of the mita arrived in person, implying that the remainder came in the form of money (Bakewell, *Miners*, Chap. 5).

52. Cañedo-Arguelles, pp. 57–64.

53. President Pedro Vázquez de Velasco to the Viceroy Conde de Santisteban, Potosí, Jan. 20, 1665, AGI, Charcas, leg. 267, no. 43.

54. Superintendent of the Mita Francisco de la Cruz to the Crown, Potosí, June 3, 1659, AGI, Charcas, leg. 266, no. 41; the royal fifth, he reported, amounted to a mere 300,000 pesos per year. Crespo, "La 'Mita,'" p. 177,

says that the relationship was 308,547 pesos for the royal fifth to more than 700,000 in indios de faltriquera; Lynch, p. 220, says the relationship was 400,000 for the royal fifth to 600,000 in indios de faltriquera; Zavala, *Servicio personal*, vol. 2, p. 139, says 600,000 in indios de faltriquera and 400,000 for the royal fifth, and notes that Porco sent 60,000 pesos per year. Francisco de la Cruz used the terms "indio en plata" (an "Indian" delivered in silver) and "indio de faltriquera" (an "Indian" delivered in silver that was not used to hire a minga) interchangeably, leading to considerable confusion at the time and for historians later. See Chap. 3 below for more detail.

55. Juan de Padilla, "Papel de apuntamientos . . . sobre los Travajos q^e padecen los In^{os} = asi en lo espiritual como en lo temporal," AGI, Charcas, leg. 266, no. 37A; this has been published in Vargas Ugarte, *Historia general*, vol. 3, pp. 391–420.

56. Cañedo-Arguelles, pp. 93–96; Gabriel Fernández Guarachi was also engaged in wine and coca transport to raise money for the delivery of the mita in silver (*ibid.*, pp. 67–69).

57. BNP, B575 (see the Bibliography, "Archival Sources").

58. Corregidor of Lampa Antonio Ordóñez del Aguila to the Audiencia of La Plata, Lampa, Apr. 8, 1673, ANB, C, no. 1899a.

59. BNP, B585 (see the Bibliography, "Archival Sources").

60. Commission granted to Diego Núñez de Ovando by Corregidor José Sáez de Elorduy, Potosí, Jan. 5, 1640, ANB, M 125, no. 1.

61. Viceregal provisión, Lima, Oct. 10, 1640, ANB, M 125, no. 3 (confirming Chinchón's order of Aug. 7, 1634); also a chapter of a letter from the Viceroy Conde de Chinchón to Corregidor José Sáez de Elorduy, Lima, Apr. 4, 1638, AHP, CR 264, f. 178v.

62. The Viceroy Marqués de Mancera to the Azogueros Guild, Lima, Sept. 1, 1646, and the guild's reply, Potosí, Oct. 3, 1646, AGNA, Sala 9, leg. 6.2.5 (a draft of the viceroy's letter is also included in this legajo).

63. Corregidor Juan de Velarde to the Marqués de Mancera, Potosí, July 31, 1646 (for Chucuito and Chayanta); Antonio de Toledo Pimentel to the corregidor of Potosí, Colquemarca, June 22, 1646; evidence presented by Notary Diego Pacheco de Chaves of actions taken to shore up the mita delivery from Paria, Potosí, Aug. 31, 1646; and Augustín de Sobranis to Corregidor Juan de Velarde, Desaguadero, July 20, 1646; all in AGNA, Sala 9, leg. 6.2.5.

64. Corregidor Juan de Velarde to the Marqués de Mancera, Potosí, Oct. 31, 1646, AGNA, Sala 9, leg. 6.2.5.

65. Superintendent of the Mita Francisco de la Cruz to the Crown, Potosí, Feb. 17, 1660, AGI, Charcas, leg. 266, no. 46; order (auto) by Superintendent Francisco de la Cruz banning rezagos de mita, Potosí, Nov. 3, 1659, AGI, Charcas, leg. 266, no. 51A; certification (testimonio) of the order banning rezagos, Potosí, Nov. 3–Dec. 7, 1659, AGI, Charcas, leg. 266, no. 45A; exhortation by Superintendent Francisco de la Cruz that Corregidor Gómez

Dávila halt the practice of sending judges to collect rezagos from the kura-kas, Potosí, Jan. 12, 1660, AGI, Charcas, leg. 266, no. 45E.

66. Superintendent Francisco de la Cruz to the Crown, Potosí, Feb. 17, 1660, AGI, Charcas, leg. 266, no. 46.

67. Cañedo-Arguelles, pp. 71−74 (including the 1657 petition); petition to the Crown by the kurakas of the provinces obligated to the mita, Potosí, Jan. 23, 1660, AGI, Charcas, leg. 266, no. 42. The relaciones of the Viceroys Conde de Salvatierra (Mar. 22, 1655) and Conde de Alba (Jan. 9, 1662) con-tain descriptions of the azogueros' mistreatment of the kurakas. Both rela-ciones are in Hanke and Rodríguez, eds., Virreyes (Perú); see vol. 4, pp. 36 and 120, respectively.

68. Superintendent Francisco de la Cruz to the Crown, Potosí, Apr. 15, 1660, AGI, Charcas, leg. 266, no. 52.

69. Zavala, Servicio personal, vol. 2, p. 146.

70. The capitanes enteradores vs. Capitán Mayor de la Mita Joseph Fer-nández de Valencia, Potosí, Feb. 19, 1677−July 29, 1679, ANB, M 125, no. 21.

71. Ibid.

CHAPTER 3

1. Baquíjano y Carrillo, pp. 36−37, gives the figure of 132 mills, and an incomplete copy of the 1624 mita charter drafted by President Diego de Por-tugal of the Audiencia of La Plata (AHP, CR 201, last item) lists 124. See also Pérez Bustamante, p. 302.

2. Petition by the Azogueros Guild to the Audiencia of La Plata, Potosí, Oct. 28, 1602, ANB, M 143; the silver merchants of Potosí vs. the azogueros, case before the Audiencia of La Plata, Potosí, Apr. 7−May 9, 1603, BNB, MSS 2, ff. 119−28; chapter of a letter from Viceroy Luis de Velasco to Corregidor Pedro de Lodeña, Lima, May 14, 1603, BNB, MSS 2, ff. 181−81v; provisión of Viceroy Luis de Velasco, Lima, June 16, 1603, BNB, MSS 2, ff. 143−44. For the viceroy's permission to rent mills, see his order of Los Reyes, May 9, 1603, BNB, MSS 2, ff. 140−42v.

3. Mesía Venegas, p. 96.

4. President Alonso Maldonado de Torres to the Audiencia of La Plata, Potosí, Jan. 8 and 9, 1609, ANB, M 3, nos. 15 and 16, respectively; accord of the Cabildo of Potosí (on the collection of contributions), Potosí, Nov. 20, 1609, BNB, CPLA 12, ff. 263v−64.

5. The numbers of mills are provided in the respective repartimientos de la mita: 1624—of the Viceroy Marqués de Guadalcázar (AHP, CR 201, last item); 1633—of the Viceroy Conde de Chinchón (from the Mar. 22, 1655, relación of the Viceroy Conde de Salvatierra, in Hanke and Rodríguez, eds., Virreyes (Perú), vol. 4, pp. 38−40); 1689—of the Viceroy Duque de la Palata (provisiones of Dec. 2, 1688, BNB, MSS 4, ff. 442−49, and Los Reyes, Jan. 29, 1689, AGI, Charcas, leg. 270, no. 30); and 1692—of the Viceroy Conde

de la Monclova (a copy of the 1692 charter, of Lima, Apr. 27, 1692, BNB, MSS 31, ff. 37–53, and a provisión of Monclova of Lima, May 8, 1692, AGNA, Sala 9, leg. 14.8.10, ff. 50–145v).

6. Brading and Cross, pp. 562–65, 572; Cobb, "Supply and Transportation," pp. 36–42. For shortages of mercury in 1608–9, see a letter from the Viceroy Marqués de Montesclaros to the Audiencia of La Plata, Lima, July 1, 1608, ANB, C, no. 1093; a call for an open Cabildo meeting, proposed by Corregidor Rafael Ortiz de Sotomayor, Potosí, Dec. 11, 1608, BNB, CPLA 12, f. 166v; and a letter from President Alonso Maldonado de Torres to the Audiencia of La Plata, Potosí, Jan. 8, 1609, ANB, M 3, no. 15. See also Oidor Arias de Ugarte to the Crown, La Plata, Nov. 10, 1600, in Levillier, ed., *Audiencia de Charcas*, vol. 3, pp. 457–59. The two fundamental sources for Huancavelica are Lohmann Villena, *Las minas de Huancavelica*, and Whitaker.

7. Bakewell, *Miners*, Chap. 5.

8. The Audiencia of La Plata to the viceroy, La Plata, Dec. 11, 1628, ANB, C, no. 1376 (a copy).

9. Chapters of accords reached by the Cabildo de Potosí with regard to water shortages: Feb. 21, Mar. 11 and 14, 1608, BNB, CPLA 12, ff. 94v, 98, 102; Mar. 6, 1609, BNB, CPLA 12, f. 208. Long-term drought continued to be a problem, however, as these later accords of the Cabildo attest: Jan. 30, 1635, BNB, CPLA 20, ff. 160–60v; Dec. 13, 1651, BNB, CPLA 24, ff. 480–82. See also the letter from Protector de Naturales Christóval Laredo Trevino to the Crown, Potosí, May 31, 1661, AGI, Charcas, leg. 266, no. 63 (reporting a current lack of water, among other matters).

10. Provisión of the Viceroy Marqués de Guadalcázar, Los Reyes, May 6, 1626, BNB, MSS 7, ff. 71–72; copy of a provisión of the Marqués, Los Reyes, May 30, 1626, AHP, CR 201, ff. 40–45. The azogueros also requested that the Audiencia of La Plata stop prosecuting them for mistreatment of mitayos, in consideration of what the guild faced in the rebuilding effort (Potosí, June 5, 1626, BNB, CPLA 18, ff. 19–19v), but that request was turned down.

11. Accord of the Cabildo of Potosí to ask the help of the Audiencia of La Plata and the viceroy in halting the loss of Indian laborers to Oruro, Sept. 19, 1609, BNB, CPLA 12, ff. 241–43v; chapter of an accord of the Cabildo to write to the president of the Audiencia of La Plata about the retention of mitayos in Oruro, Oct. 21, 1609, BNB, CPLA 12, f. 251v. For Oruro's ability to repulse the Cabildo's previous efforts to recoup Indians, see its accord of Oct. 3, 1608, BNB, CPLA 12, f. 142.

12. The Audiencia of La Plata to the Crown, La Plata, Mar. 17, 1608, ANB, M 86, no. 10 (relating the actions of the viceroy). Campo y de la Rynaga, pp. 26–27, says that the viceroy was ordered by the Crown in 1607 and 1611 not to permit the employment of mitayos at Oruro, and reports that the mines there played out by 1612. Zavala, *Servicio personal*, vol. 2,

p. 50, argues that Montesclaros banned mitas for all new mining zones in 1612, including Oruro. Bakewell, *Miners*, Chap. 4, says 4–6,000 Indians were working at Oruro in 1615 and some 10,000 in 1617–18.

13. Sánchez-Albornoz, "Migraciones internas"; accord of the Cabildo of Potosí, Sept. 19, 1609, BNB, CPLA 12, ff. 241–43v (resolution to seek help in preventing rural interests from interfering with the delivery of mitayos).

14. Información compiled by the Azogueros Guild, 1642–43; President Dionisio Pérez Manrique's letter to the viceroy confirming the contents of that piece, Mar. 31, 1643; and testimony gathered by the president from religious figures in Potosí in support of the azogueros' información, Aug. 25, 1643; all in AGNA, Sala 9, leg. 6.2.5. For another thorough description of the relationship between an azoguero and a silver merchant, see the account of the efforts by the corregidor of Potosí to collect the mercury debts of those azogueros who were denied mitayos in the 1692 repartimiento, Potosí, Apr. 5–May 8, 1693, ANB, M 116, no. 5.

15. Crespo, *Guerra*, is the best single source on the "civil war" (see pp. 33–39 for background on the Basques). I have relied primarily on Padden, pp. xxvii–xxviii, for this brief summary. Arzáns, *Historia*, includes accounts of battles among the various Iberian nationalities throughout Potosí's colonial existence. An example of the continuing violence is a case from 1628, when one miner and his men caved in the mine of another; a barretero whose tools had been buried in the mine sued the perpetrators for restitution (one of the precedents cited in ANB, M 125, no. 13).

16. Minutes of the open Cabildo meeting held on Dec. 5, 1608, to respond to the Viceroy Marqués de Montesclaro's letter of Lima, Nov. 1, 1608, which itself responded to the Cabildo's letter of Sept. 1, 1608, concerning poor ore quality, BNB, CPLA 12, ff. 158–64.

17. Petition sent to the Crown by way of the Audiencia of La Plata by Juan de Ayala y Figueroa, procurador of Potosí, asking for concessions, Potosí, 1609–10, ANB, M 3, no. 17.

18. Accord of the Cabildo of Potosí to send to the viceroy a warning by the azogueros that if help were not forthcoming, the silver industry would soon collapse, Potosí, July 29, 1617, BNB, CPLA 15, ff. 346–48v.

19. Sandoval y Guzmán (I used the copy in the Moreno Collection, BNB).

20. The second part carries three proposals that deal with nonmining matters: (a) "Que no deven ser compelidos los Señores de viñas, que estan en los valles de Pilaya y Paspaya, y otros circunvezinos a Potosi, à que paguen a Su Magestad cada año à dos por ciento de vino que cogen"; (b) "Que no puede Su Magestad acrecentar en la villa de Potosi el oficio de Provincial de la Hermandad que se ha m[an]dado vender"; and (c) "Que no se deven mandar quintar las perlas y joyas que ay en la villa de Potosi." (I have partially modernized the orthography of the original.)

21. The letter to President García de Haro y Avellaneda, Conde de Castrillo,

is dated Madrid, July 3, 1634, and included at the beginning of Sandoval y Guzmán's *Pretensiones* as a prologue.

22. These four proposals are listed in Sandoval y Guzmán, f. 1.

23. *Ibid.*, ff. 1–33v, 63–65.

24. *Ibid.*, ff. 34–62v.

25. *Ibid.*, ff. 37v–39 (viceroys' objections), 41v–42v (description of problems), 42v–62v (solutions to those problems).

26. *Ibid.*, ff. 65v–66.

27. This despite continual efforts to improve the method—with some progress—as these sources attest: chapter of a letter from the Audiencia of La Plata to the viceroy, La Plata, Dec. 26, 1602, ANB, C, no. 799; chapter of a letter from the Audiencia to the viceroy, La Plata, Dec. 26, 1603, ANB, C, no. 866; chapters of accords by the Cabildo of Potosí, May 8, 1621, BNB, CPLA 16, f. 314; Apr. 30, 1634, BNB, CPLA 20, ff. 14v–15; June 5, 1635, BNB, CPLA 20, ff. 225v–26; July 8, 1635, BNB, CPLA 20, ff. 239v–41v; and Nov. 27, 1635, BNB, CPLA 20, ff. 322–22v. A royal cédula to all officials at Potosí urged them to continue with experiments, Buen Retiro, May 3, 1651, BNB, MSS 4, ff. 7–7v. See also the Viceroy Conde de Santisteban to the Crown, Lima, Nov. 22, 1662, AGI, Charcas, leg. 267, no. 33. AGI, Charcas, leg. 416, Libro 6, contains many documents from the 1670's on a new process, introduced by Juan de Corro Cegarra, which failed to live up to early expectations.

28. The azogueros' indebtedness began early, and it was a problem throughout most of the Hapsburg period. The Audiencia of La Plata noted difficulties with payments for mercury in its letters to the Crown of La Plata, Feb. 25, 1589, and Mar. 5, 1590 (in Levillier, ed., *Audiencia de Charcas*, vol. 2, pp. 422–34, and vol. 3, pp. 40–74, respectively). President Diego de Portugal ordered the royal treasury officials of Potosí to allow the distribution of mercury on credit despite royal edicts banning that practice for chronic nonpayment (La Plata, Nov. 25, 1617, AHP, CR 153, ff. 83v–85); two agreements to provide mercury on credit are dated Sept. 11, 1618 (AHP, CR 153, ff. 128–36v) and Jan. 25, 1620 (AHP, CR 153, ff. 158–58v). In 1628, the Audiencia of La Plata wrote to the viceroy to tell him that his efforts to collect every peso owed for mercury would prove disastrous if he persisted (La Plata, Dec. 11, 1628, ANB, C, no. 1376). The deputies of the Azogueros Guild wrote to the Viceroy Marqués de Mancera in Sept. 1643 to inform him that they were too poor to pay the 400,000 pesos they owed the Crown for mercury (AGNA, Sala 9, leg. 6.2.5). A royal edict to the Viceroy Conde de Salvatierra (Aranjuez, Apr. 28, 1650, BNB, MSS 4, ff. 466–70) responded to the azogueros' contention that they had overpaid for mercury between 1609 and 1631, and to their wish that overpayments be deducted from what they owed the Crown. President/Visitador Francisco Nestares Marín bonded the azogueros to ensure that they paid their mercury debts

(Potosí, Apr. 9, 1654, AHP, CR 339, ff. 58−59). Superintendent of the Mita/ President Pedro Vázquez de Velasco wrote to the Viceroy Conde de Santisteban (Potosí[?], Mar. 3, 1664, AGI, Charcas, leg. 267, no. 37LL, a copy) to report that the azogueros' mercury debt was impossible to collect, and that to ask him to do so was to ask him to touch the sky with his finger. In the 1680's, during the attempted revitalization of the Potosí silver industry under the Viceroy Duque de la Palata, Corregidor Pedro Luis Enríquez and President Bartolomé González de Poveda were instructed by the Crown to settle the issue of mercury debts once and for all, even if that meant reducing the sums owed significantly; Corregidor Enríquez's success in that venture played a large part in his being entitled the Conde de Canillas in 1687; the documentation for this process is to be found in AGI, Charcas, leg. 416, Libro 6, and leg. 417, Libro 7. For an overview, see Baquíjano y Carrillo, pp. 38−39.

29. Mita deliveries in silver and "indios de faltriquera" (remittances that were not used to hire minga replacements) figure prominently in all the manuscript collections employed for this study. Some examples: a provisión of the Viceroy Marqués de Guadalcázar, Los Reyes, Sept. 28, 1624, BNB, MSS 7, ff. 35−37 (prohibiting indios de faltriquera and other forms of "mal uso"); a letter from the royal treasury officials of Potosí to the Crown, Potosí, Apr. 10, 1647, AGI, Charcas, leg. 267, no. 1; a copy of a letter from President Nestares Marín to the Crown, Potosí, Aug. 30, 1654, AGI, Charcas, leg. 266, no. 22; a copy of an order from the Council of the Indies to the viceroy of Peru to execute a royal cédula banning indios de faltriquera, Madrid, Apr. 18, 1657, AGI, Charcas, leg. 266, no. 39C; a letter from Superintendent Francisco de la Cruz to the Crown, Potosí, Apr. 15, 1660, AGI, Charcas, leg. 266, no. 50; a copy of a letter from Joseph de Escovar y Acerón to the Crown, La Plata, Sept. 29, 1666, AGI, Charcas, leg. 267, no. 51; a letter from the Viceroy Conde de Lemos to the Crown, Lima, Dec. 6, 1669, AGI, Charcas, leg. 268, no. 4; the decision of the Council of the Indies that the viceroy of Peru and corregidor of Potosí should make sure that no indios de faltriquera were permitted, Madrid, July 31, 1675, AGI, Charcas, leg. 268, no. 48.

30. Bakewell, *Miners*, Chap. 4.

31. Cole, "The Potosí Mita," p. 339 (these figures have been rounded off, as they included fractions).

32. On contraband, see Helmer, "Comércio e contrabando"; Baquíjano y Carrillo, p. 57; Cobb, "Potosí and Huancavelica," pp. ii−iii, 144; Padden, pp. xxv−xxvi. Examples of contemporary materials dealing with this topic are: an order of Oidor Alonso Pérez de Salazar (of the Audiencia of La Plata) that the Crown's prohibition of contraband shipments via Buenos Aires and Tucumán be enforced, Buenos Aires, Dec. 18, 1623, ANB, M 142, no. 8; an order from the Viceroy Conde de Alba to President Nestares Marín to counter contraband in any way possible, Lima, Jan. 4, 1660, ANB, C, no.

1762; and a statement by Superintendent Francisco de la Cruz on "Extravios de quintos y Plata Por Buenos ayres," Potosí, Apr. 14, 1660, AGI, Charcas, leg. 266, no. 56. For the dangers of quantification, see Diffie; Baquíjano y Carrillo, p. 40 (relating the contents of a "Memorial presentado al REY . . . ," on Oct. 12, 1636, in which the azogueros claimed that because they produced 617,517 pesos in royal income with 1,500 mitayos, it followed that with 4,674 Indians they could increase the royal fifth to nearly 2 million pesos per year); and Holmes, p. 105.

33. Bakewell, *Miners*, Chap. 5.

34. For the most famous reference to the Indians being chained and tied to the tails of horses, see the Viceroy Conde de Lemos's "Discurso y Informe . . . sobre que se escusen las Mitas forzadas de los In^{os}" (AGI, Charcas, leg. 268, no. 15), sent with his letter to the Crown of July 4, 1670, proposing that the mita be abolished, AGI, Charcas, leg. 266, no. 16. The discourse has been published in Vargas Ugarte, ed., *Pareceres jurídicos*, pp. 155–65, and in Hanke and Rodríguez, eds., *Virreyes* (Perú), vol. 4, pp. 276–89.

35. The kurakas of the provinces obligated to the mita to the Crown, Potosí, Jan. 23, 1660, AGI, Charcas, leg. 266, no. 42; certification of a kuraka who hanged himself, sent by Friar García de Vargas to Superintendent of the Mita Francisco de la Cruz, Toledo, Feb. 4, 1660, AGI, Charcas, leg. 266, no. 43B. Typical of these reports is the "Memorial" of the curate of Tomahave, Luis de Vega, sent to the Audiencia of La Plata, Tomahave, Nov. 13, 1616; ANB, C, no. 1215; he says of the mita: "Para la mita de Potosi los llevan 20. leguas. pierden su hazienda y libertad, q^e es inestimable, se ahorcan por no yr alla. se despeñan, toman Ueneno, y se echan en los rios, malpazen las preñadas por estos caminos y otros mil daños."

36. The work is addressed to Dr. Diego Hernández de Cardona y Córdova, Marqués de Santillán. Schäfer, vol. 1, p. 363, says that the Marqués was a member of the Council of the Indies from Nov. 17, 1671, to 1695.

37. Campo y de la Rynaga, pp. 1–5.

38. *Ibid.*, pp. 9–51.

39. *Ibid.*, pp. 53–92 (each article is paginated individually; the running pagination used here is that which is in pencil on the copy in the Library of the Sociedad Geográfica "Sucre," Sucre, Bolivia).

40. *Ibid.*, pp. 93–160.

41. *Ibid.*, pp. 161–221.

42. The role of the *Memorial* in undoing the effort to abolish the mita is discussed in Chap. 5 below and in Cole, "An Abolitionism."

CHAPTER 4

1. Horacio H. Urteaga, "Prólogo," in Levillier, ed., *Gobernantes del Perú*, vol. 9, p. xv (based on a letter from Viceroy Martín Enríquez to the Crown, Los Reyes, Sept. 22, 1582).

2. "Memoria gubernativa" of the Viceroy Conde del Villardompardo,

n.d. (ca. 1592–93), in Hanke and Rodríguez, eds., *Virreyes* (Perú), vol. 1, pp. 211–13; Zavala, *Servicio personal*, vol. 1, p. 182 (Cañete).

3. Capoche, pp. 141–43; Viceroy Martín Enríquez to the Crown, Feb. 17, 1583, in Hanke and Rodríguez, eds., *Virreyes* (Perú), vol. 1, pp. 181–82; copy of an información by the Audiencia of La Plata concerning services rendered the Crown by Hernando Ortiz de Vargas (including the drafting of a mita charter for the Conde del Villar, among others), La Plata, Jan. 12, 1620, ANB, ACh.LA 13, ff. 89–89v; Cañete y Domínguez, p. 102; "Memoria" of the Viceroy Conde del Villardompardo (cited in n. 2 above); Zavala, *Servicio personal*, vol. 1, p. 182.

4. Barnadas, "Una polémica"; Zavala, *Servicio personal*, vol. 1, pp. 167–68.

5. Zavala, *Servicio personal*, vol. 1, p. 182.

6. President Cepeda to the Crown, La Plata, Feb. 28, 1590, and July 2, 1590, in Levillier, ed., *Audiencia de Charcas*, vol. 3, pp. 19–30, 82–92; the Audiencia of La Plata to the Crown, La Plata, Mar. 5, 1590, *ibid.*, pp. 40–74.

7. Zavala, *Servicio personal*, vol. 1, pp. 187–92, 195–96.

8. *Ibid.*, p. 196.

9. Instructions for Viceroy Luis de Velasco, Madrid[?], July 22, 1595, and Aug. 11, 1596 ("sobre hacienda"), in Hanke and Rodríguez, eds., *Virreyes* (Perú), vol. 2, pp. 11–32 and 32–45, respectively; Campo y de la Rynaga, p. 20. For the 85-peso price for mercury, see Cobb, "Supply and Transportation," p. 39.

10. For figures on Velasco's repartimiento, see Valera, p. 8; Angulo, f. 2v. In a provisión of Lima, Feb. 10, 1601 (BNB, MSS 2, f. 65), Velasco said that he had assigned the drafting of the mita charter to "doctor Arias de vgarte." His ordinances for Potosí (dated Aug. 31, 1599) are AGI, Lima, leg. 34, lib. 5, ff. 319–26 (I used a transcription provided by Lewis Hanke); they also are described by Zavala, *Servicio personal*, vol. 1, pp. 203–6.

11. Instructions for Viceroy Luis de Velasco "sobre hacienda," Madrid[?], Aug. 11, 1596, in Hanke and Rodríguez, eds., *Virreyes* (Perú), vol. 2, pp. 32–45; Cobb, "Potosí and Huancavelica," pp. 96–97.

12. See Zavala, *Servicio personal*, vol. 2, pp. 3–6, for a chapter-by-chapter discussion of the 1601 cédula.

13. Domínguez Ortiz, pp. 84–87.

14. Arzáns, *Historia*, vol. 1, pp. 46–62; Parry, pp. 175–85; Padden, p. xvii; Baquíjano y Carrillo, p. 32; Málaga Medina, p. 602.

15. Zavala, *Servicio personal*, vol. 2, pp. 5–6; Fox, p. 64. Campo y de la Rynaga, p. 23, says that the viceroy received secret orders from the Council of the Indies to suspend the cédula; Pérez de Tudela y Bueso, p. 367, agrees (he bases his conclusion on Solórzano Pereira, vol. 1, p. 270).

16. Campo y de la Rynaga, pp. 24–26. Among those participating were Dean Pedro Muñiz, Friar Miguel de Agia, Father Alonso Mesía Venegas (Jesuit), Doctor Carlos Marcelo, Friar Gerónimo Valera, Doctor Francisco

de Sosa, and Doctor Feliciano Vega (all but Mesía Venegas are identified by Campo).

17. Zavala, *Servicio personal*, vol. 2, pp. 17–22 (a thorough discussion of Agia's position); Vargas Ugarte, on p. 21 of his introduction to *Pareceres jurídicos*, discusses Agia in his overview of Mesía Venegas's arguments, which are on pp. 94–115.

18. Fox, pp. 65–69 (commentary on Muñiz's paper), pp. 75–86 (a transcription), pp. 86–88 (an outline).

19. The following provisiones of Viceroy Luis de Velasco were based directly on the 1601 cédula: Los Reyes, Nov. 5, 1603, BNB, MSS 2, ff. 168–69 (restricting those types of Indians who were exempted from mita service); Lima, Nov. 14, 1603, BNB, MSS 2, ff. 147–48v (forbidding the sale, borrowing, or lending of mitayos); Lima, Nov. 14, 1603, BNB, MSS 2, ff. 153–54v (ordering the payment of travel allowances); Lima, Nov. 14, 1603, BNB, MSS 2, ff. 157–58 (forbidding the use of Indians as beasts of burden); Lima, Dec. 3, 1603, ANB, EC 1689, no. 31, ff. 423–24 (exempting from the mita the children of kurakas; a copy from the 1680's). Provisión of Velasco, that his earlier order concerning the delivery of mitayos from Chucuito be obeyed in the other mita provinces, Los Reyes, Apr. 10, 1603, BNB, MSS 2, ff. 135–39v. Bakewell, *Miners*, Chap. 4, describes the dispatch of mitayos from the province of Chucuito in 1600; the procedure took from July 21 to August 14 to complete, at which time 1,749 Indians took their leave and headed for Potosí, along with 11,703 llamas and other provisions.

20. Zavala, *Servicio personal*, vol. 2, ff. 36–40; Cobb, "Potosí and Huancavelica," pp. 96–97.

21. Relación of the Viceroy Príncipe de Esquilache, n.d. (ca. 1621), in Hanke and Rodríguez, eds., *Virreyes* (Perú), vol. 2, p. 160; Zavala, *Servicio personal*, vol. 2, p. 71.

22. Provisiones of the Viceroy Marqués de Guadalcázar, Los Reyes, Dec. 22, 1622, BNB, MSS 7, ff. 45–46 (reinforcing Esquilache's order of Los Reyes, July 6, 1617), and Feb. 10, 1624, BNB, MSS 7, ff. 47–49 (reiterating the 1622 edict). For an example of the process, see the replacement of Pedro Díaz de Alvarado as corregidor of Carangas with Juan Serrano de Amalgro, Potosí, Aug. 18–Sept. 9, 1626, BNB, CPLA 18, ff. 37–37v, 40v–52.

23. Provisiones of Viceroy Luis de Velasco, Lima, Feb. 10, 1601, BNB, MSS 2, ff. 65–69v (assigning another 30 Indians to Pedro Zores de Ulloa), and May 12, 1602, BNB, MSS 2, ff. 81–81v (ordering the corregidor to transfer the ten Indians the viceroy had assigned to Leandro de Valencia); the Viceroy Conde de Monterrey to the Audiencia of La Plata, Callao, June 30, 1605, ANB, M 122, no. 10 (instructing the tribunal to stop meddling in the mita). The Viceroy Príncipe de Esquilache provides the terms of his relationship with officials in Alto Perú in his relación, in Hanke and Rodríguez, eds., *Virreyes* (Perú), vol. 2, pp. 163–64.

24. An example: the Audiencia of La Plata to the viceroy, La Plata, Aug. 1,

1605, ANB, M 122, no. 11 (explaining that the seriousness of the abuses at Potosí required quick responses, which the viceroys clearly were not in a position to make).

25. Cobb, "Potosí and Huancavelica," pp. 101–2; "Razón del estado en que el Marqués de Guadalcázar deja el gobierno del Perú al Virrey Conde de Chinchón . . . ," Dec. 14, 1628, in Hanke and Rodríguez, eds., *Virreyes* (Perú), vol. 2, pp. 249–73.

26. Copy (testimonio) of chapters of letters from Viceroy Luis de Velasco to Corregidor Pedro de Lodeña, Lima, June 16, July 1, Aug. 1, and Sept. 1, 1603, and May 1, 1604 (copy made in Potosí, June 18, 1605), BNB, MSS 2, ff. 179–80v. The Audiencia's response to this delegation of responsibility is cited in n. 24 above.

27. Sluiter, ed., p. 243; the Audiencia of La Plata to the Council of the Indies, La Plata, Mar. 13, 1607, ANB, Minas complemento; the Audiencia to its president, Alonso Maldonado de Torres (in Potosí), La Plata, Apr. 19, 1607, ANB, M 86, no. 2; the Audiencia to the Council of the Indies, La Plata, Dec. 6, 1607, ANB, C, no. 1072; copy of chapters of letters from the Audiencia of La Plata to the Crown, La Plata, Feb. 15 and 20, 1608, ANB, C, no. 1083; the Audiencia to the Crown, La Plata, Mar. 13, 1608, ANB, M 123, no. 3; the Audiencia to the king and Council of the Indies, La Plata, Mar. 17, 1608, ANB, M 86, no. 10.

28. Accords of the Cabildo of Potosí concerning the loss of Indian laborers to Oruro, Potosí, Oct. 3, 1608, BNB, CPLA 12, f. 142; Sept. 19, 1609, BNB, CPLA 12, ff. 241–43v; and Oct. 21, 1609, BNB, CPLA 12, f. 251v. For the Audiencia's suspension of the commission of a judge sent to Oruro, see the Cabildo's accord of Apr. 23, 1610, BNB, CPLA 12, ff. 293–93v; for the Audiencia's suspension of judges sent out by the corregidor of Potosí to prosecute corregidores who failed to send sufficient numbers of mitayos, see the accord of Aug. 31, 1607, BNB, CPLA 12, ff. 54–54v.

29. Provisión of the Viceroy Príncipe de Esquilache to the governor of the province of Chucuito and all the corregidores of mita provinces, Lima, Mar. 20, 1616, BNB, MSS 9, ff. 294–311v (a copy made on Oct. 9, 1790).

30. Provisión of the Marqués de Guadalcázar, Los Reyes, Aug. 25, 1623, BNB, MSS 7, ff. 17–27 (two copies; this was in keeping with a royal cédula to President Diego de Portugal and the Audiencia of La Plata, Madrid, May 28, 1621, BNB, MSS 3, ff. 59–59v).

31. Relación of the Viceroy Príncipe de Esquilache, in Hanke and Rodríguez, eds., *Virreyes* (Perú), vol. 2, p. 166. Esquilache's ban was repeated by the Marqués de Guadalcázar on Sept. 30, 1626 (Los Reyes; BNB, MSS 7, ff. 79–80).

32. Adjustments of the mita by Luis de Velasco, BNB, MSS 2, ff. 65–69v, 81–81v (cited in n. 23 above); and his grounds for the removal of mitayos from an azoguero, included in BNB, MSS 2, ff. 147–48v (cited in n. 19). The Viceroy Marqués de Guadalcázar made at least two adjustments, one

favoring Francisco de Iturgoyen (Los Reyes, Jan. 31, 1625, BNB, MSS 7, ff. 43–44v) and another for Fernando Cabeza de Vaca (Lima, July 10, 1625, BNB, MSS 7, f. 70).

33. For the reassignment of indios meses, see AHP, CR 201, last item (the 1624 repartimiento). Ezquerra Abadía, pp. 489–90, n. 9bis, discusses the importance of silver production to a government official's record of service in Peru.

34. Campo y de la Rynaga, pp. 80–83 (Velasco); Zavala, Servicio personal, vol. 2, pp. 27–28 (Monterrey); response of the Marqués de Montesclaros to the Príncipe de Esquilache's request for more data on the status of Peru, May 11, 1616, in Hanke and Rodríguez, eds., Virreyes (Perú), vol. 2, p. 139.

35. Accord of the Cabildo of Potosí concerning compliance with the Príncipe's order, Potosí, Aug. 2, 1617, BNB, CPLA 15, ff. 349v–50v.

36. Castillo, f. 12.

37. Ibid., ff. 12v–13 (for the seven revisitas and the total diminution of the weekly draft by 147 Indians). For specific mention of Caquiaviri, Macha, and other pueblos affected, see the accord of the Cabildo of Potosí in response to the adjustments, Potosí, Sept. 9, 1627, BNB, CPLA 18, f. 203.

38. Andrien, p. 2.

39. Domínguez Ortiz, pp. 92–97.

40. Andrien, p. 4.

41. The original cédula was dated May 27, 1631; its contents were repeated in 1634; Zavala, Servicio personal, vol. 2, pp. 119–20; Campo y de la Rynaga, pp. 84–85.

42. Copy of the cover letter to the commission sent by the Viceroy Conde de Chinchón to Juan de Carvajal y Sande, empowering the visitador to adjust the 1633 repartimiento de la mita, Lima, Oct. 3 [or 30], 1635, BNB, CPLA 20, ff. 359v–60v (a copy).

43. Bartolomé Astete de Ulloa to the Crown, Callao, May 12, 1634, AGI, Charcas, leg. 266, no. 2. Angulo, f. 2v, says that 28 "dueños" (owners) were left without mitayos; Valera, p. 9, says that 28 "cabezas de ingenio" were deprived. The broad terms of the 1633 charter are included in the relación of the Viceroy Conde de Salvatierra, in Hanke and Rodríguez, eds., Virreyes (Perú), vol. 4, pp. 38–40. Angulo puts the weekly draft at 4,115 Indians, as does the archbishop of Lima in a letter to the Crown, Lima, Dec. 30, 1661, AGI, Charcas, leg. 267, no. 16. For Carvajal's motives and his order that travel allowances be paid, see the copy of a chapter of his letter [probably to the Crown] of Mar. 15, 1634 (AGI, Charcas, leg. 266, no. 2A), and the relación of the Conde de Chinchón, Jan. 1, 1640, in Hanke and Rodríguez, eds., Virreyes (Perú), vol. 3, p. 56.

44. President Juan de Lizarazu of the Audiencia of La Plata to the Crown, Potosí, Mar. 1, 1638, AGI, Charcas, leg. 266, no. 10 (suggesting an alternative distribution based solely on production capacity); the Azogueros Guild to the Viceroy Marqués de Mancera, Potosí, July 29, 1646, AGNA, Sala 9,

leg. 6.2.5 (responding positively to Mancera's plan to distribute mitayos on a prorated basis); Pedro de Vallesteros (an azoguero) to the Marqués de Mancera, Potosí, July 31, 1646, AGNA, Sala 9, leg. 6.2.5 (discusses differences in the quality of various ayllus; this same legajo contains an undated—but probably produced in 1646 as well—piece by the azogueros describing each pueblo's mitayos as good, bad, or mediocre).

45. Corregidor Francisco Sarmiento de Mendoza sent the Crown a series of lists with a letter of Potosí, May 31, 1657 (AGI, Charcas, leg. 266, no. 36), including one delineating the owners of two or three cabezas de ingenio who applied all their mitayos to the sustenance of just one (AGI, Charcas, leg. 266, no. 36D) and another detailing which mills had two cabezas but produced silver with only one (AGI, Charcas, leg. 266, no. 36H).

46. Petition from the Cabildo of Potosí to the Crown asking that Carvajal be recalled, Potosí, Mar. 17, 1638, AGI, Charcas, leg. 266, no. 11; Bartolomé Astete de Ulloa to the Crown, Callao, May 12, 1634, AGI, Charcas, leg. 266, no. 2 (promises that production will fall as a result of the 1633 charter); the Viceroy Conde de Chinchón to the Crown, Lima, Apr. 9, 1634, AGI, Charcas, leg. 266, no. 1.

47. Visitador Juan de Carvajal y Sande to the Crown, Feb. 25, 1635, AGI, Charcas, leg. 266, no. 3—for the visitador's comments on the charter as a whole—and another letter of the same date (AGI, Charcas, leg. 266, no. 4) for his actions with respect to an individual azoguero, Pedro de Andrade Sotomayor. See also Carvajal to the Crown, Mar. 18, 1636, AGI, Charcas, leg. 266, no. 8.

48. Two copies of a royal cédula to the Viceroy Conde de Chinchón, Madrid, Apr. 6, 1636, AGI, Charcas, leg. 266, nos. 1B and 39A.

49. Accord of the Cabildo to ask Lizarazu to remain in Potosí, Mar. 22, 1635, BNB, CPLA 20, ff. 180v-81. Lizarazu's Mar. 1, 1636, proposal to the Crown that he be empowered to administer the silver production industry unhindered is AGI, Charcas, leg. 266, no. 7. For the president's mercury distribution plan, see a copy of a provisión of the Conde de Chinchón upholding the royal treasury officials' efforts to keep Lizarazu from distributing mercury on credit, Lima, June 12, 1636, ANB, M 114, no. 4; and President Juan de Lizarazu to the Crown, Potosí, Mar. 1, 1637, AGI, Charcas, leg. 266, no. 9. On Sept. 1, 1643, Corregidor of Potosí Blas Robles de Salzedo wrote to the Marqués de Mancera on behalf of an azoguero who had been caught up in the mercury squabble (AGNA, Sala 9, leg. 6.2.5), so the effects of this conflict were long-lasting.

50. Céspedes del Castillo, pp. 31-32; relación of the Viceroy Conde de Chinchón, Jan. 1, 1640, in Hanke and Rodríguez, eds., Virreyes (Perú), vol. 3, pp. 48-49.

51. The terms are presented in a letter from President Lizarazu to the Crown, Mar. 1, 1638, AGI, Charcas, leg. 266, no. 10. See also a copy of a letter from Chinchón to Lizarazu, Lima, Mar. 30, 1639, AGI, Charcas, leg. 266, no. 12.

52. The Cabildo of Potosí to the Crown, Mar. 17, 1638, AGI, Charcas, leg. 266, no. 11.

53. Copies of a letter from the Viceroy Conde de Chinchón to President Juan de Lizarazu (Lima, Mar. 30, 1639) and the latter's response (Potosí, June 12, 1639), AGI, Charcas, leg. 266, no. 12; the order empowering Lizarazu to alter the repartimiento of 1633 (dated Mar. 6, 1639) is also reproduced.

54. President Juan de Lizarazu to the Crown, Potosí, June 12, 1639, AGI, Charcas, leg. 266, no. 13.

55. See the Conde de Chinchón's relación (cited in n. 50 above), pp. 48–49, 56–57, 61, for comments on the mita. The Marqués de Mancera was not content with that amount of information and asked for more, which he received in May 1640 (Lohmann Villena, ed., "Un informe veraz"). Royal cédula to the Viceroy Marqués de Mancera, Madrid, Dec. 7, 1639, AGI, Charcas, leg. 266, nos. 39B and 6B (a copy). Castillo, f. 15v; Valera, p. 10.

56. Provisión of the Marqués de Mancera, Los Reyes, Jan. 3, 1641, AHP, CR 286, ff. 94–94v (in response to Lizarazu's suggestion).

57. The Azogueros Guild to the viceroy, Potosí, Feb. 5, 1642 (complaining about Visitador Juan de Palacios); Mancera to the Azogueros Guild, Lima, Apr. 3, 1642 (in answer to their reports of a mercury shortage); both in AGNA, Sala 9, leg. 6.2.5.

58. The deputies of the Azogueros Guild to the Marqués de Mancera, Potosí, Oct. 8, 1642, AGNA, Sala 9, leg. 6.2.5.

59. The Viceroy Marqués de Mancera to the Azogueros Guild (a draft), Lima, Dec. 1, 1642, AGNA, Sala 9, leg. 6.2.5.

60. Mendoza relates the events surrounding the dejación (waiver) in a note on Arzáns, *Historia*, vol. 2, p. 90; the action is recorded in an "acta en testimonio" of Potosí, Oct. 26, 1642, ANB, M 125, no. 5. The azogueros informed the Audiencia of La Plata of their waiver in a letter of Potosí, Dec. 2, 1642, ANB, M 125, no. 6; the audiencia had already decided to review the matter (La Plata, Dec. 2, 1642, ANB, ACh.LA 7, ff. 430v–34).

61. President Pérez Manrique to the Audiencia of La Plata, Potosí, Dec. 7, 1642, ANB, M 125, no. 9.

62. President Pérez Manrique to the Audiencia of La Plata, El Terrado (on the road to Potosí), Dec. 3, 1642, ANB, M 125, no. 7 (announcing that he had passed the guild's deputies on the road that day); Potosí, Dec. 6, 1642, ANB, M 125, no. 8 (reporting on the status quo and asking the oidores not to let the deputies go on to Lima); and Potosí, Dec. 7, 1642, ANB, M 125, no. 9. The Azogueros Guild to the Audiencia of La Plata, Potosí, Dec. 10, 1642, ANB, M 125, no. 10 (announcing the azogueros' agreement to await a ruling on the dejación by the viceroy or the Crown).

63. Información by the Azogueros Guild, 1642–43, AGNA, Sala 9, leg. 6.2.5. (another, undated, petition along the same lines is in the same legajo); the president gathered testimony from members of Potosí's religious community that supported the azogueros' requests.

64. Castillo, f. 15 (for the corregidor's help); Corregidor Blas Robles de Salzedo to the Viceroy Marqués de Mancera, Potosí, Jan. 1, 1644, AGNA, Sala 9, leg. 6.2.5; President Pérez Manrique to the Marqués de Mancera, Potosí, Mar. 31 and Sept. 8, 1643, and Jan. 31, 1644, AGNA, Sala 9, leg. 6.2.5.

65. The Viceroy Marqués de Mancera to the Azogueros Guild (a draft; includes the charges), Lima, Nov. 1, 1643; the Azogueros Guild to the Marqués de Mancera, Potosí, Dec. 1, 1643; the Marqués de Mancera to the Azogueros Guild (a draft), Lima, Jan. 1, 1644; all AGNA, Sala 9, leg. 6.2.5. The undated denunciation sent to the Marqués de Mancera by Christóval de Castañeda and a letter on the matter from the Azogueros Guild (of Dec. 1, 1643) are also in AGNA, Sala 9, leg. 6.2.5.

66. The incomplete results of the census are to be found in AGNA, Sala 9, leg. 20.4.4; they have been used by Sánchez-Albornoz in his "Migraciones internas." Castillo, ff. 15v–16, mentions a letter of June 30, 1646, which noted that the census had been ordered; it most probably is the letter from the Marqués de Mancera to the Azogueros Guild, in AGNA, Sala 9, leg. 6.2.5. Valera, p. 11, says that Mancera ordered reports from the corregidores on the number and status of the Indians in their jurisdictions. Zavala, *Servicio personal*, vol. 2, p. 109, says that Phelipe de Bolíbar (an azoguero who represented the guild before the viceroy) presented the Marqués—on Nov. 29, 1646—with a document entitled "Padrones de los indios naturales, forasteros y anaconas con distinción de provincias tocantes al repartimiento general de mita de Potosí"; he says that it is from AGNA, Padrones, 1623–46, leg. 21.1.3, but the legajo of padrones for 1623–46 is Sala 9, leg. 20.4.4, as Sánchez-Albornoz notes in "Migraciones internas." Zavala provides the province-by-province breakdown, and Sánchez-Albornoz analyzes it further. The totals come to 45,302 [Sánchez-Albornoz says 45,292] originarios, 15,446 forasteros, and 10,086 yanaconas. Mancera, in his relación—of Oct. 8, 1648, in Hanke and Rodríguez, eds., *Virreyes* (Perú), vol. 3, p. 149—avowed that there were enough Indians to support the repartimiento, but Zavala, *Servicio personal*, vol. 2, p. 112, takes exception and says that the figures show an insufficient population base for the charter; perhaps the viceroy's decision that there were enough Indians was based on his belief that the official figures were a minimal representation of the true Indian population of the provinces.

67. The draft of the mita charter is dated Lima, June 30, 1646. It was sent with the viceroy's letter to the Azogueros Guild of that date, AGNA, Sala 9, leg. 6.2.5.

68. *Ibid.*; the addition of 380 mitayos from Porco and 700 yanaconas brought the weekly draft to 5,196 (figured in terms of a 1633 weekly draft of 4,116). The azogueros' response to the proposed charter is their letter to the Marqués, Potosí, July 29, 1646, AGNA, Sala 9, leg. 6.2.5.

69. Pedro de Vallesteros (an azoguero) to the Marqués de Mancera, Potosí, July 31, 1646, and the viceroy's response, Lima, Aug. 31, 1646 (a draft); the royal treasury officials of Potosí to the Viceroy Marqués de Mancera, Potosí,

July 31, 1646 (the officials argued that an inspection of the mines and mills was needed, noting one case in particular—the Barriales mill—where no silver had been produced for twenty years; the mitayos assigned to it were rented and the proceeds used to support the azoguera—a nun!); Corregidor Juan de Velarde to the Marqués de Mancera, Potosí, July 31, 1646; all in AGNA, Sala 9, leg. 6.2.5.

70. The Marqués de Mancera to the Azogueros Guild, Lima, Sept. 1, 1646, and the guild's reply, which begins at the end of the viceroy's letter, Potosí, Oct. 3, 1646, AGNA, Sala 9, leg. 6.2.5. A draft of the viceroy's letter is also included in this legajo.

71. Corregidor Juan de Velarde to the Marqués de Mancera, Potosí, Aug. 31, 1646, and an undated testimonio of his visita of Potosí, Tarapaya, and Porco; the Azogueros Guild to Mancera, Potosí, Sept. 1, 1646; Mancera's letter to the guild of Sept. 1, 1646, and the association's reply, Potosí, Oct. 3, 1646; the azogueros' undated memorial listing the pueblos and provinces obligated to send mitayos to Potosí, with notation of their record of service; all in AGNA, Sala 9, leg. 6.2.5.

72. The royal treasury officials to the Marqués de Mancera, Potosí, Oct. 31, 1646, AGNA, Sala 9, leg. 6.2.5.

73. *Ibid*. The 43,000-peso figure is also included in the letter from the viceroy to the Azogueros Guild, Surco, Oct. 31, 1646, AGNA, Sala 9, leg. 6.2.5.

74. The Marqués de Mancera to Corregidor Juan de Velarde, Lima, Nov. 30, 1646 (responding to Velarde's letter of Oct. 31), AGNA, Sala 9, leg. 6.2.5.

75. The Marqués de Mancera to the Azogueros Guild, Surco, Oct. 31, 1646, AGNA, Sala 9, leg. 6.2.5.

76. Relación of the Marqués de Mancera, Oct. 8, 1648, in Hanke and Rodríguez, eds., *Virreyes* (Perú), vol. 3, pp. 140 (index), 148–50 (for material on the mita). Valera, p. 11, says that the Marqués thought it better to have an incoming viceroy implement a new mita charter than an outgoing one. Bartolomé de Salazar, who would later serve as president of Audiencia of La Plata and superintendent of the mita, was an adviser to Mancera, and he told the Crown in 1662 that the repartimiento was ready to be put "en limpio" when the news of the Conde de Salvatierra's imminent arrival reached the Marqués (Salazar to the Crown, Potosí, Apr. 1, 1662, AGI, Charcas, leg. 267, no. 24).

77. Another request from the azogueros to finish with the charter is their letter to the Marqués de Mancera, Potosí, Nov. 1, 1646, AGNA, Sala 9, leg. 6.2.5. The viceroy's response of Lima, Nov. 30, 1646, is also in this legajo.

78. Domínguez Ortiz, p. 103.

CHAPTER 5

1. Two royal cédulas to the Viceroy Conde de Salvatierra, Aranjuez, Apr. 28, 1650, AGI, Charcas, leg. 266, no. 19C (concerning the repartimiento; a copy), and BNB, MSS 4, ff. 466–70 (concerning mercury debts).

2. President Francisco Nestares Marín to the Crown, Potosí, May 30, 1652, AGI, Charcas, leg. 266, no. 15 (this letter discusses the Council's order at length, and the motivation behind it).

3. Copy of the Conde de Salvatierra's response to a cédula of Apr. 28, 1650, Los Reyes, Sept. 2, 1651, AGI, Charcas, leg. 266, no. 30D, second item. For the viceroy's comments to his successor, see his relación, in Hanke and Rodríguez, eds., *Virreyes* (Perú), vol. 4, pp. 40–41. A good overview of the administrative processes at work during this period is the relación prepared by the Audiencia of Lima, after serving as interim head of government, for the Viceroy Conde de Lemos, Nov. 15, 1667, *ibid.*, pp. 205–9 (a copy of chap. 38 of that relación—dealing with the mita—is AGI, Charcas, leg. 267, no. 56A).

4. AGI, Charcas, leg. 266, no. 15.

5. The Crown to the corregidor of Potosí, Nov. 8, 1653, AGI, Charcas, leg. 266, no. 39D; discourse prepared by Corregidor Francisco Sarmiento de Mendoza concerning his compliance with that order and the fact that his activities had been suspended by the Conde de Salvatierra, n.d. (ca. 1654), AGI, Charcas, leg. 266, no. 20C. Copy of a royal cédula to the president of the Audiencia of La Plata, Nov. 8, 1653, AGI, Charcas, leg. 266, no. 26B.

6. Licenciado Gaspar González Pavón (a government official with long experience in various capacities) refers to the system of playing the corregidor against the president in a letter to the Viceroy Conde de Alba, Potosí, Apr. 25, 1655, AGI, Charcas, leg. 267, no. 3A (a copy; a list of his various posts is AGI, Charcas, leg. 267, no. 3B).

7. AGI, Charcas, leg. 266, no. 20C.

8. Corregidor Sarmiento de Mendoza to the Crown, Potosí, July 31, 1654, AGI, Charcas, leg. 266, no. 19.

9. President Nestares Marín to the Crown, Potosí, May 30, 1652, AGI, Charcas, leg. 266, no. 15 (for his previous activities and comments on the repartimiento), and Aug. 30, 1654, AGI, Charcas, leg. 266, no. 22 (responds to the Nov. 8, 1653 cédula; a copy sent with other correspondence on Feb. 8, 1658). Corregidor Sarmiento de Mendoza to the Crown, Potosí, Sept. 30, 1654, AGI, Charcas, leg. 266, no. 24 (his response to Nestares Marín's opposition).

10. Notary's report to Corregidor Sarmiento de Mendoza on the contents of two viceregal letters of May 31, 1654, AGI, Charcas, leg. 266, no. 20A. The corregidor's response is AGI, Charcas, leg. 266, no. 20C. In a letter to the Crown (Potosí, July 31, 1654, AGI, Charcas, leg. 266, no. 20), Sarmiento complained that everyone was using "wait for the new viceroy" as a pretext for doing nothing at all.

11. The Viceroy Conde de Alba discussed the order in a discourse on the mita dated Lima, Dec. 13, 1661, AGI, Charcas, leg. 267, no. 31A (a copy). See also a copy of a letter from Gaspar González Pavón to the Conde de Alba, Potosí, July 31, 1655, AGI, Charcas, leg. 266, no. 59, second item, and

AGI, Charcas, leg. 267, no. 3A. For a broadside attack on Nestares Marín by Sarmiento de Mendoza (Potosí, May 31, 1655), see AGI, Charcas, leg. 266, no. 26; and for charges that Nestares permitted a relative to engage in misuse of the mita, see Sarmiento's letter to the viceroy, Potosí, July 31, 1655, AGI, Charcas, leg. 266, no. 32F (a copy). The corregidor also charged that Nestares Marín was in league with the moneylenders of Potosí (in a letter to the Conde de Alba, Potosí, July 31, 1655, AGI, Charcas, leg. 266, no. 32H; a copy). An anonymous and undated indictment of President Nestares Marín is AGI, Charcas, leg. 266, no. 18.

12. Royal cédula to the viceroy of Peru, assigning him responsibility for both halves of the Council's program, Madrid[?], Apr. 18, 1657, AGI, Charcas, leg. 266, no. 39C; Nestares Marín's jurisdiction was not to be rescinded, but the viceroy was to monitor progress on the elimination of the practice of indios de faltriquera. The deliberations of the Council of the Indies, in preparation for that order, noted that the Conde de Alba was dragging his feet on the matter (Madrid[?], Feb. 26, 1657, AGI, Charcas, leg. 266, no. 35). For the viceroy's response, see his letter to the Crown, Lima, Aug. 22, 1658, AGI, Charcas, leg. 266, no. 39. Also see his relación, in Hanke and Rodríguez, eds., *Virreyes* (Perú), vol. 4, pp. 119–21; AGI, Charcas, leg. 267, no. 31A.

13. Minutes of the *acuerdo consultivo* called by the Conde de Alba on Aug. 26, 1658 (in response to the cédula of Apr. 18, 1657), AGI, Charcas, leg. 266, no. 64A; provisión of the Viceroy Conde de Alba naming Friar Francisco de la Cruz as his *juez comisario*, Lima, Oct. 8, 1658, BNB, CPLA 26, ff. 143–49 (a copy); AGI, Charcas, leg. 267, no. 31A; Valera, pp. 13–15; Castillo, ff. 18v–19.

14. All of Cruz's orders are detailed in a letter from the Conde de Alba to the Crown, Lima, July 3, 1660, AGI, Charcas, leg. 267, no. 9B, and compiled in AGI, Charcas, leg. 267, no. 15A (this includes, as well, the instructions given to Cruz's successor, Bartolomé de Salazar). For the viceroy's reasons for providing Cruz with both public and secret instructions, see AGI, Charcas, leg. 267, no. 31A.

15. Superintendent of the Mita Francisco de la Cruz to the Crown, Potosí, June 11, 1659, AGI, Charcas, leg. 267, no. 8A. For Alba's statement that this was against his orders, see AGI, Charcas, leg. 267, no. 31A.

16. Superintendent Francisco de la Cruz to the Crown, Potosí, June 3, 1659, AGI, Charcas, leg. 266, no. 41.

17. *Ibid.* (for deliveries in silver versus royal fifth figures). Francisco de la Cruz to the Crown, Potosí, Apr. 1, 1660, AGI, Charcas, leg. 266, no. 49 (for the 11,000-pesos-per-week figure); Apr. 14, 1660, AGI, Charcas, leg. 266, no. 55 (for the sale of Indians in Lipes); Apr. 14, 1660, AGI, Charcas, leg. 266, no. 56 (for contraband via Buenos Aires). The Conde de Alba ordered President Nestares Marín to counter the contraband trade in a letter of Lima, Jan. 4, 1660, ANB, C, no. 1762.

18. Transcript of an order by Francisco de la Cruz, Potosí, July 1, 1659 (the June 4 order is related in this clarification), AGI, Charcas, leg. 267, no. 8C.

19. Order by Francisco de la Cruz limiting the liability of the capitanes enteradores, Potosí, Nov. 3, 1659, AGI, Charcas, leg. 266, no. 53B (a copy); transcript of Cruz's order on the delivery of the mita and distribution of the mitayos, Potosí, Nov. 3, 1659, AGI, Charcas, leg. 266, no. 45F; Cruz to the Crown, Potosí, Apr. 14, 1660, AGI, Charcas, leg. 266, no. 53 (discusses the ban on rezagos and the viceroy's decision to back up that order); Cruz's order banning rezagos, Potosí, Nov. 3, 1659, AGI, Charcas, leg. 266, no. 51A (a copy); Cruz to the Crown, Potosí, Apr. 14, 1660, AGI, Charcas, leg. 266, no. 51.

20. Cited in Cruz's reinforcement of his ban on mita deliveries in silver, among other orders, Potosí, Feb. 18, 19, 23, and 24, 1660, AGI, Charcas, leg. 266, no. 50B (a copy). The viceroy notes his decision to support Cruz in AGI, Charcas, leg. 267, no. 31A.

21. Orders by Francisco de la Cruz banning the use of corporal punishment against kurakas, Tarapaya, Feb. 3, 1660, AGI, Charcas, leg. 266, nos. 45I and 52A (copies); AGI, Charcas, leg. 266, no. 50B. The penalties for accepting mita deliveries in silver are laid out in Cruz's order of Potosí, Mar. 1, 1660, AGI, Charcas, leg. 266, no. 50A (a copy).

22. The Conde de Alba to the Crown, Lima, Mar. 2, 1660, AGI, Charcas, leg. 267, no. 9A. The viceroy planned to conduct the census via ecclesiastical channels (AGI, Charcas, leg. 267, no. 31A); for Cruz's response to this idea (he called rural priests "idiots"), see his letter to the viceroy, Potosí, Feb. 14, 1660, AGI, Charcas, leg. 266, no. 43.

23. Transcript of a petition by the Azogueros Guild to Francisco de la Cruz, Potosí, July 1, 1659, AGI, Charcas, leg. 267, no. 8B; and another of Dec. 17, 1659, with the superintendent's response, AGI, Charcas, leg. 266, no. 45C. Gaspar González Pavón to the Crown, Potosí, Apr. 30 and May 10, 1660, AGI, Charcas, leg. 267, no. 3. The Conde de Alba to the Crown, Lima, July 3, 1660, AGI, Charcas, leg. 267, no. 9B. Friar Vicente Vitor, O.P., to the Crown, Cádiz, Apr. 2, 1676, AGI, Charcas, leg. 268, no. 49.

24. AGI, Charcas, leg. 267, nos. 9B and 15A. For Bartolomé de Salazar's thoughts on his appointment (on May 24, 1660), see his letter to the Crown, Potosí, Apr. 1, 1662, AGI, Charcas, leg. 267, no. 24; for his comments on his commission, see the copy of his letter to the Conde de Alba, Potosí, Dec. 1, 1660, AGI, Charcas, leg. 266, no. 60A.

25. Copy of a letter from Bartolomé de Salazar to the Conde de Alba, Potosí, Nov. 30, 1660, AGI, Charcas, leg. 266, no. 60B; Salazar to the Crown, Potosí, June 1, 1661, AGI, Charcas, leg. 267, no. 12. The azogueros were pleased with the new superintendent (the deputies of the Azogueros Guild to the Crown, Potosí, Dec. 17, 1660, AGI, Charcas, leg. 267, no. 41B).

26. Alba's plan was described in Salazar's commission and in AGI, Charcas,

leg. 267, no. 24. The new superintendent's plan is described in his letter to the Crown, Potosí, Dec. 13, 1660, AGI, Charcas, leg. 266, no. 60 (as well as in nos. 60A and 60B).

27. This entire course of events is related in AGI, Charcas, leg. 267, no. 24. Valera, p. 17, also provides an overview. In another letter to the Crown (Potosí, June 3, 1661, AGI, Charcas, leg. 267, no. 11), Salazar says that he received the go-ahead on Mar. 3, but that it came with another order to suspend all action, and that the May 26 letter from the viceroy stuck with the idea of using priests, although permitting him to name a few corregidores if he liked. For the Conde de Alba's side of this story, see AGI, Charcas, leg. 267, no. 31A.

28. Related in AGI, Charcas, leg. 267, no. 24. See also Castillo, ff. 20–20v.

29. AGI, Charcas, leg. 267, no. 24; President Bartolomé de Salazar to the Crown, Potosí, May 9, 1663, AGI, Charcas, leg. 267, no. 34.

30. President Pedro Vázquez de Velasco to the Crown, Lima, Nov. 21, 1662, AGI, Charcas, leg. 267, no. 32 (for problems in Quito); Vázquez to the Viceroy Conde de Santisteban, Potosí, Aug. 31, 1663, AGI, Charcas, leg. 267, no. 37D (a copy; relates his arrival in the Villa Imperial).

31. Fiscal Nicolás Polanco de Santillana to the Crown, Lima, Feb. 20, 1662, AGI, Charcas, leg. 267, no. 22.

32. Domínguez Ortiz, pp. 109–10; Andrien, p. 7.

33. The Conde de Santisteban to the Crown, Lima, July 20, 1663, AGI, Charcas, leg. 267, no. 35. Included were three unsigned discourses on the subject (AGI, Charcas, leg. 267, no. 35A).

34. Copies of written opinions provided by Vázquez de Velasco to the Conde de Santisteban on the enumeration, Lima, Jan. 31, 1663, AGI, Charcas, leg. 267, no. 37J and 37K (the latter is the last page), and n.d., AGI, Charcas, leg. 267, no. 37B (this essay is published in Zavala, *Servicio personal*, vol. 2, pp. 43–44—from another copy—in a discussion of the royal cédulas of 1601 and 1609).

35. AGI, Charcas, leg. 267, no. 37D.

36. President Vázquez de Velasco to the Conde de Santisteban, Potosí, Feb. 2 and Mar. 3, 1664, AGI, Charcas, leg. 267, nos. 37C and 37L (respectively; both are copies). The latter was soon followed by a list of provinces responsible to the mita, the numbers of Indians required from each, and those that actually arrived (Potosí, Mar. 31, 1664, AGI, Charcas, leg. 267, no. 37M). A thorough report on all of his activities in Potosí is Vázquez de Velasco's letter to the Crown, Potosí, Apr. 20, 1664, AGI, Charcas, leg. 267, no. 37. For the viceroy's argument that there had been no royal order to conduct a census, see a collection of arguments for and against the execution of a census (n.d., AGI, Charcas, leg. 267, no. 37A) and a copy of a letter from Vázquez de Velasco to Santisteban (Potosí[?], Feb. 2, 1664, AGI, Charcas, leg. 267, no. 37C), as well as a letter from the Conde de Santisteban to the

Crown, Lima, Nov. 11, 1664, AGI, Charcas, leg. 267, no. 39 (this includes a reference to Salazar's support for Vázquez's plan). In his discussion of the Viceroy Conde de Lemos's later proposal that the mita be abolished, Zavala says that Santisteban timidly proposed the same in the letter of Nov. 16, 1664 (*Servicio personal*, vol. 2, p. 149—the letter is in AGI, Lima, leg. 66); that would confirm that the viceroy's request for a direct order was a delaying tactic.

37. President Vázquez de Velasco to the Crown, Potosí, Dec. 11, 1664, AGI, Charcas, leg. 267, no. 40. See also Corregidor Gabriel Guerrero de Luna to the Crown, Potosí, Feb. 11 and May 6, 1665, AGI, Charcas, leg. 267, nos. 45 and 46, respectively.

38. Vázquez to Santisteban, Potosí, Jan. 20, 1665, AGI, Charcas, leg. 267, no. 43 (a copy sent to the Crown; see also Vázquez to the Crown, Potosí, Jan. 30, 1665, AGI, Charcas, leg. 267, no. 42).

39. The plan and the response to it of Fiscal Juan Baptista Moreto de Espinosa, Lima, Aug. 15, 1665, AGI, Charcas, leg. 267, no. 48A. A hodgepodge of materials from Vázquez to Santisteban, including the president's response to the plan (dated Sept. 3, 1665; a copy) is AGI, Charcas, leg. 267, no. 50A.

40. AGI, Charcas, leg. 267, no. 50A, includes a copy of the provisión of Sept. 28, 1665 and Vázquez de Velasco's response of Jan. 31, 1666.

41. Relación of the Audiencia of Lima, Nov. 15, 1667, in Hanke and Rodríguez, eds., *Virreyes* (Perú), vol. 4, pp. 205−9. Copy of a royal cédula to the Conde de Santisteban, Madrid[?], Dec. 12, 1665, AGI, Charcas, leg. 267, no. 56B. For the Council of the Indies' deliberations preceding that order, see AGI, Charcas, leg. 267, no. 49. Orders sent to President Vázquez de Velasco to dedicate himself to the reorganization of the Potosí mita, mentioned in the Dec. 12, 1665, cédula, are in AGI, Charcas, leg. 416, lib. 6, ff. 11−14. The Audiencia of Lima to the Crown, Lima, Oct. 21, 1666, AGI, Charcas, leg. 267, no. 52 (responding to the cédula), and the Crown to the viceroy, president, and oidores (in response to that letter), Madrid, Aug. 27, 1668, AGI, Charcas, leg. 416, lib. 6, ff. 43−44. See also Zavala, *Servicio personal*, vol. 2, p. 148.

42. This section is based on my article, "An Abolitionism Born of Frustration." Two errors in the article have been corrected here: (a) Visitador Alvaro de Ibarra was misidentified as Juan de Ibarra; and (b) the years of Lemos's death and the royal confirmation of his 1669 reforms were misprinted.

43. The Viceroy Conde de Lemos's initial report to the Crown from Peru, Mar. 4, 1668, in Hanke and Rodríguez, eds., *Virreyes* (Perú), vol. 4, pp. 271−73 (the quote is on p. 272); the viceroy's response to the Audiencia of Lima's relación is on *ibid.*, pp. 251−71 (an undated copy of Lemos's reply to chapter 38 of that account is AGI, Charcas, leg. 267, no. 54B). These sources note that the plan was the handiwork of Visitador Alvaro de Ibarra (for a discussion of his report to Lemos on the subject, see Zavala, *Servicio*

personal, vol. 2, pp. 148–49). For the problems surrounding the execution of a census, see the Conde de Lemos to the Crown, Lima, Jan. 13, 1670, AGI, Charcas, leg. 268, no. 8.

44. Orders from the Conde de Lemos to the corregidor of Potosí, Luis Antonio de Oviedo y Herrera, Los Reyes, Nov. 4, 1669, AGI, Charcas, leg. 268, no. 5A (a copy); and Dec. 3, 1669, AGI, Charcas, leg. 268, nos. 6A and 7A (the latter is a copy). Each order is described in a separate request that the Crown issue a cédula confirming it, Jan. 12, 1670, AGI, Charcas, leg. 268, nos. 5, 6, and 7 (the first is discussed by Escobedo Mansilla, pp. 88–89); the reasoning behind them is explained again in the viceroy's letter to the Crown, Lima, Feb. 3, 1670, AGI, Charcas, leg. 268, no. 10. The reduction of pressure on the kurakas had been called for in a cédula from Queen Mariana to the Conde de Lemos, Madrid, Nov. 12, 1668 (AGI, Charcas, leg. 420, lib. 8, ff. 20–22), which responded in part to the complaints of Gabriel Fernández Guarachi, a kuraka from Pacajes. See also Zavala, *Servicio personal*, vol. 2, p. 149; Valera, p. 22; Ezquerra Abadía, pp. 489–90, note 9*bis*. According to a letter from Lemos to the Crown (Lima, Dec. 6, 1669, AGI, Charcas, leg. 268, no. 4), Alvaro de Ibarra advised him on each of these decisions. The best single source on the Lemos-Oviedo confrontation is a relación of their correspondence prepared for the viceroy, Lima, Aug. 13, 1670, AGI, Charcas, leg. 268, no. 21A; Zavala, *Servicio personal*, vol. 2, p. 149, also describes their struggle.

45. Secret instructions from the Conde de Peñaranda to the Conde de Lemos, n.d. (ca. 1667), in Hanke and Rodríguez, eds., *Virreyes* (Perú), vol. 4, p. 246. The viceroy refers to the queen's instructions in his letter to the Crown, Lima, Feb. 7, 1670, AGI, Charcas, leg. 268, no. 11, and in his later discourse on the need to abolish the mita (cited in n. 53 below).

46. Corregidor Luis Antonio de Oviedo to the Crown, Potosí, Mar. 12, 1670, AGI, Charcas, leg. 267, no. 58. AGI, Charcas, leg. 268, no. 21A includes a letter from Oviedo to Lemos of Jan. 6, 1670, in which the corregidor warned that the viceroy's orders would destroy Potosí. Because Oviedo was aware that his opposition to Lemos might get him into trouble with the Council of the Indies, he asked a friend—a secretary to the Council—to make sure that his side of the story received its due (Oviedo to Secretary Gabriel de Quiros, Potosí, Mar. 12, 1670, AGI, Charcas, leg. 267, no. 59; a compendium of his correspondence with Lemos—no. 59A—was included).

47. Copies of letters from the Conde de Lemos to Corregidor Oviedo (to obey or resign) and President Vázquez de Velasco, Lima[?], Feb. 3, 1670, AGI, Charcas, leg. 268, nos. 10A and 10B, respectively.

48. AGI, Charcas, leg. 268, no. 11.

49. The Conde de Lemos to the Crown, Lima, Apr. 4, 1670, AGI, Charcas, leg. 268, no. 14. According to the plan, Vázquez de Velasco would return to Spain and serve on the Council of the Indies; Oviedo's fate was unimportant.

50. AGI, Charcas, leg. 268, no. 21A, includes Oviedo's report (of Mar. 10,

1670) that he had implemented the three orders; Zavala, *Servicio personal*, vol. 2, p. 149, says that the orders were promulgated on Mar. 9. AGI, Charcas, leg. 267, no. 58 (Oviedo's warning to the Crown); letters of support came from the Azogueros Guild (to the Crown, Potosí, Mar. 19, 1670, AGI, Charcas, leg. 268, no. 13) and the Cabildo of Potosí (to the Crown, Potosí, Mar. 15, 1670, AGI, Charcas, leg. 268, no. 12).

51. AGI, Charcas, leg. 268, no. 21A.

52. The Conde de Lemos to the Crown, Lima, July 4, 1670, AGI, Charcas, leg. 268, no. 16.

53. Lemos's discourse in support of the abolition of the mita, AGI, Charcas, leg. 268, no. 15; this is published in Vargas Ugarte, ed., *Pareceres jurídicos*, pp. 155–65, and in Hanke and Rodríguez, eds., *Virreyes* (Perú), vol. 4, pp. 276–89.

54. President Vázquez de Velasco argued that the viceroy did not have the authority to eradicate the mita on his own (in a letter to the Crown, Potosí, Aug. 9, 1670, AGI, Charcas, leg. 268, no. 20), but as the Crown's alter ego, he certainly had as much authority to terminate it as Toledo had had to establish it. For Lemos's requests for cédulas confirming his 1669 reforms, see AGI, Charcas, leg. 268, nos. 5–7 (cited in n. 44 above).

55. The first page of AGI, Charcas, leg. 268, no. 15 is an index of the accompanying documents; the items listed are included in AGI, Charcas, leg. 268, as nos. 15A–15J; Angulo wrote his "Relacion o ressumen" based on these and other materials. The alcalde del crimen for Lima, Juan de Padilla, wrote in favor of the abolition proposal, in a letter to the Crown, Lima, July 7, 1670, AGI, Charcas, leg. 268, no. 18; Vázquez de Velasco did the same from Potosí on July 7 and Aug. 9, AGI, Charcas, leg. 268, nos. 17 and 20, respectively (included with the latter was a copy—no. 20A—of the president's Jan. 1, 1665, letter to the Conde de Santisteban calling for the abolition of the mita; another copy, cited in n. 38 above, is AGI, Charcas, leg. 267, no. 43).

56. The Conde de Lemos to the Crown, Los Reyes, Aug. 14, 1670, AGI, Charcas, leg. 268, no. 21. Ibarra suggested that Oviedo be replaced (AGI, Charcas, leg. 268, no. 21B) and Lemos agreed (in the margin of the proposal is a note that reads "Hagase como parece al s.r Visitador D Alvaro de Ybarra para cuio efecto se despachen los ordenes necesarios. Lima 15 de Agosto de *1670*"; it carries the rubrica of the Conde de Lemos). For Ulloa's role in explaining the true goals of the 1669 reforms, see the viceroy's letter to the Crown, Lima, May 1, 1671, AGI, Charcas, leg. 268, no. 22.

57. The Council of the Indies to the Conde de Lemos, Madrid, Nov. 7, 1670, AGI, Charcas, leg. 268, no. 23 (responding to reported difficulties with a census by telling the viceroy to do as he deemed best). The Crown to the Conde de Lemos, Madrid, Dec. 31, 1671, AGI, Charcas, leg. 416, lib. 6, ff. 152v–55v; one of the specific orders, that banning night-and-day work in

the mines, is AGI, Charcas, leg. 416, lib. 6, ff. 151–52 (Madrid, Dec. 31, 1671). Confirmation of the 1669 reforms is also noted in a letter from Interim Corregidor Diego de Ulloa Pereyra to the Crown, Potosí, May 20, 1673, AGI, Charcas, leg. 268, nos. 31 and 32 (the former is the cover). For the Council's deliberations on abolition: its decision to hold a consulta, Apr. 12, 1673, AGI, Charcas, leg. 268, nos. 33A and 33B (the latter is the envelope); its order to provide Relator Andrés de Angulo with all the materials necessary to write his relación, Apr. 19, 1673, AGI, Charcas, leg. 268, no. 33; a draft of the Council's June 8, 1673, letter to Queen Mariana (the final draft is cited in n. 58 below), May 1673, AGI, Charcas, leg. 268, no. 35; Angulo's relación, May 3, 1673, AGI, Charcas, leg. 268, no. 36.

58. The Council of the Indies to the queen, Madrid, June 8, 1673, AGI, Charcas, leg. 268, no. 37.

59. Decision reached by the Council of the Indies, Oct. 9, 1673, AGI, Charcas, leg. 268, no. 41; the Council's orders for the Conde de Castellar, Madrid, Oct. 9, 1673, AGI, Charcas, leg. 268, nos. 42 (a draft) and 43.

60. News of Lemos's death was received at least a month earlier, for the queen informed the Audiencia of La Plata on Sept. 9, 1673, that the Conde de Castellar had been named viceroy and would be leaving for Peru in October (AGI, Charcas, leg. 416, lib. 6, ff. 140–41).

61. The deputies of the Azogueros Guild to the Crown, Potosí, Aug. 8, 1670, AGI, Charcas, leg. 268, no. 19.

62. Corregidor Luis Antonio de Oviedo to the Crown, Potosí, Oct. 8, 1668, AGI, Charcas, leg. 267, nos. 56C and 56D (the latter is the envelope), for his breakdown of the work force in late 1668 (2,125 mitayos and 899 mingas). The Conde de Lemos to the Crown, Lima[?], Mar. 18, 1669, AGI, Charcas, leg. 267, no. 57 (this states that the data came from Oviedo); a certification is included (no. 57A), but it merely notes that there were 347 more "yndios" in 1669 than in 1668. Ezquerra Abadía, pp. 489–90, note 9 bis, discusses the role of production in determining a government official's reputation.

63. Interim Corregidor Diego de Ulloa Pereyra to the Crown, Potosí, Feb. 4, 1672, AGI, Charcas, leg. 268, no. 28 (his certification of an increase in the royal fifth is no. 28A); he repeated his claims in AGI, Charcas, leg. 268, nos. 31 and 32. The Conde de Lemos to the Crown, Lima, Apr. 26, 1672, AGI, Charcas, leg. 268, no. 30 (for the relay; the accompanying certification is no. 30A, and it is identical to no. 28A).

64. The Crown to Corregidor Luis Antonio de Oviedo, Madrid[?], June 10, 1673, AGI, Charcas, leg. 268, no. 45A (a copy). Similar orders came later as well: to the Conde de Castellar and to Corregidor Oviedo, both Madrid, Sept. 12, 1675, AGI, Charcas, leg. 416, lib. 6, ff. 160v–61 and 161–62, respectively. Royal cédula to the Conde de Lemos to return Luis de Oviedo to his post as corregidor of Potosí, Madrid, Jan. 21, 1672, AGI,

Charcas, leg. 420, lib. 8, ff. 152–54; Oviedo's return to office is also noted in the Audiencia of Lima's relación for the Conde de Castellar, Aug. 1, 1674, in Hanke and Rodríguez, eds., *Virreyes* (Perú), vol. 5, pp. 19–20.

65. The Crown's response to Castellar's report describes his report at length, Madrid, Nov. 16, 1676, AGI, Charcas, leg. 268, no. 51 (a copy).

66. The Crown to the Conde de Castellar, Madrid, July 8, 1676, AGI, Charcas, leg. 416, lib. 6, ff. 187v–88v (Castillo, ff. 23–24v, provides a transcription) and the viceroy's response to both edicts, Lima, Feb. 22, 1678, AGI, Charcas, leg. 268, no. 57. The July 8 order is also described in a letter from the president of La Plata, Bartolomé González de Poveda to the Crown, La Plata[?], Jan. 30, 1678, AGI, Charcas, leg. 268, no. 55 (responding to the Crown's order that he assist the viceroy in this matter). Both cédulas were repeated for Interim Viceroy Melchor Liñán y Cisneros, Madrid, Sept. 13, 1678, AGI, Charcas, leg. 416, lib. 6, ff. 215–16v (his response came in a letter of Lima, Aug. 7, 1681, AGI, Charcas, leg. 270, no. 3). See also Valera, pp. 24–25; Holmes, pp. 53–55.

67. Relación of the Viceroy Duque de la Palata, Dec. 18, 1689, in Hanke and Rodríguez, eds., *Virreyes* (Perú), vol. 6, p. 207. The Crown's orders came in a royal cédula, San Lorenzo, Oct. 25, 1680, AGI, Charcas, leg. 416, lib. 6, ff. 269–71; the Duque discussed its import in a letter to the Crown, Lima, Aug. 21, 1683, AGI Charcas 270, no. 16 (that letter is reproduced in his relación, pp. 217–29). Orders to other officials to assist Palata in this endeavor are also included in AGI, Charcas, leg. 416, lib. 6.

68. For background on the Duque de la Palata, see Crahan.

CHAPTER 6

1. Noted by Palata in his letters to the Crown, Lima, Dec. 15, 1682, and Aug. 21, 1683, AGI, Charcas, leg. 270, nos. 14 and 16. Archbishop Melchor Liñán y Cisneros to the Crown, Lima, Nov. 27, 1682, AGI, Charcas, leg. 270, no. 13 (for a good overview of the former interim viceroy's opinions); copy of Palata's request that the archbishop provide him with a current opinion on the mita and the response, Lima, June 6, 1682, AGI, Charcas, leg. 270, no. 13A. Archbishop Christóval of La Plata to the Crown, La Plata, Feb. 28, 1682, AGI, Charcas, leg. 270, no. 6. Corregidor Pedro Luis Enríquez to the Crown, Potosí, Jan. 24, 1682, AGI, Charcas, leg. 270, no. 5 (supporting documentation for the corregidor's paper is AGI, Charcas, leg. 270, no. 9A, accompanied by a cover letter, Apr. 15, 1682, AGI, Charcas, leg. 270, no. 9). Controller Sebastián del Collado to the Crown, Lima, May 11, 1682, AGI, Charcas, leg. 270, no. 10. President González de Poveda to the Crown, La Plata, Aug. 21, 1682, AGI, Charcas, leg. 270, no. 12, and his report on the mita of Dec. 24, 1681, AGI, Charcas, leg. 270, no. 4 (to which he defers).

2. Memorial by the Azogueros Guild, n.d. (received in Madrid in 1681), AGI, Charcas, leg. 268, no. 70B. The cédula that it provoked is that of Madrid, May 28, 1681, AGI, Charcas, leg. 416, lib. 6, ff. 287v–93. The tie

between the memorial and the cédula is made in AGI, Charcas, leg. 270, no. 14 (Palata's letter of Dec. 15, 1682). A look back from the end of the process is the viceroy's letter to the Crown, Lima, Feb. 19, 1689, AGI, Charcas, leg. 270, no. 32. The deliberations of the Real Acuerdo of Lima on the general enumeration are described in AGI, Charcas, leg. 270, no. 16 (Palata's letter of Aug. 21, 1683). Palata was also ordered (cédula of Madrid, June 5, 1681, AGI, Charcas, leg. 416, lib. 6, ff. 293−94v) to settle the question of mercury debts within a year, and during that time not to bother the azogueros about the sums owed. Moreover, President González de Poveda's suggestion that new shipments of mercury be distributed on credit was accepted by the Crown and so ordered in a cédula of Madrid, May 13, 1682 (AGI, Charcas, leg. 416, lib. 6, ff. 303−6).

3. AGI, Charcas, leg. 270, no. 14.

4. *Ibid.* Palata noted that he had participated in just such a fiasco in Naples; on that occasion, the bungled census had cost the royal coffers some 80,000 ducats per year.

5. Copy of an Apr. 7, 1683, letter from the Duque de la Palata to all the bishops and prelates of Peru, signed by Joseph Bernal (his secretary), AGI, Charcas, leg. 270, no. 15, second item. Ezquerra Abadía, pp. 491−92, briefly describes this process.

6. AGI, Charcas, leg. 270, no. 15, second item. Printed instructions for the corregidores, Lima, July 24, 1683, AGI, Charcas, leg. 270, no. 15, first item. A general order against hiding Indians or otherwise hampering the census was dispatched the same day, AGNA, Sala 9, leg. 14.8.10, ff. 242−43. Four days earlier, the viceroy had sent a printed notice to all the curates in Peru, ordering them not to obstruct the government enumeration (AGNA, Sala 9, leg. 14.8.10, f. 244). See also Sánchez-Albornoz, "Mita, migraciones," and Evans. Brian Evans is currently preparing a book-length study of the numeración general of the 1680's.

7. AGI, Charcas, leg. 270, no. 15, first item.

8. AGI, Charcas, leg. 270, nos. 16 and 32.

9. In addition to AGI, Charcas, leg. 270, nos. 16 and 32, see a copy of Controller Joseph de Villegas's "Papel de dudas" that the general enumeration would be able to accomplish its principal goals, Lima, June 12, 1685 [*sic*, the copy is dated June 10, 1685, and it was dispatched to Madrid with the viceroy's letter of that date, which referred to it], AGI, Charcas, leg. 270, no. 20A.

10. So noted by Evans, p. 28, and Sánchez-Albornoz, "Mita, migraciones," p. 7.

11. The impact of the 1683 general enumeration is documented in two tomes of complaints in the AGNA: Sala 9, leg. 10.3.7 (from the city of La Paz and the provinces of Tomina, Pilaya y Paspaya, Larecaja, Misque, Sicasica, Pacajes, Omasuyos, and Cochabamba); and Sala 13, leg. 18.7.4 (from the provinces of Porco, Chayanta, Tarija, Paria, and Carangas; complaints from

Cuzco were apparently removed when Alto Perú came under the jurisdiction of the Viceroyalty of Río de la Plata in 1776; there are other materials in this legajo also). See also a letter from the bishop of Cuzco to the Crown, Cuzco, Oct. 3, 1692, AGI, Charcas, leg. 271, no. 8, and a copy of his report for the Viceroy Conde de la Monclova on the failings of the general enumeration, Cuzco, Mar. 19, 1691, AGI, Charcas, leg. 271, no. 8A. For the effects of flight on the enumeration, see AGNA, Sala 9, leg. 10.3.7, ff. 3v, 11v (La Paz); 350-50v, 392v (Pacajes), 395-99 [the ff. are out of order; the material begins on f. 399] (Omasuyos); and AGNA, Sala 13, leg. 18.7.4, f. 496 (Porco).

12. Noted by the corregidor of Pilaya y Paspaya, Lorenzo Fernández de Córdova y Figueroa, in a letter to the Conde de la Monclova, n.d. (but received in Dec. 1689), AGNA, Sala 9, leg. 10.3.7, f. 127.

13. Evans, pp. 31-33; Villegas. See also AGNA, Sala 9, leg. 10.3.7, ff. 11v (La Paz); 112 (Tomina); 127 (Pilaya y Paspaya); 141 (Larecaja); 401, 403 (Omasuyos); 468, 525, 528v (Cochabamba); 590 (Carangas). Two reports from the Duque de la Palata to the Crown expressed his continued faith in his program, Lima, Oct. 11, 1687, and Feb. 19, 1689 (AGI, Charcas, leg. 270, nos. 26 and 32, respectively).

14. AGNA, Sala 9, leg. 10.3.7, f. 3 (La Paz). For the various complaints about the overcounting that this caused, see AGNA, Sala 9, leg. 10.3.7, ff. 12, 24v, 67-67v, 70v, 98v (La Paz); 247 (Sicasica); 397 (Omasuyos); and AGNA, Sala 13, leg. 18.7.4, ff. 497v (Porco); 589 (Carangas). Even the demonstration of receipts by once-tallied Indians could not dissuade officials bent on providing the controllers in Lima with as complete a list as possible—AGNA, Sala 9, leg. 10.3.7, f. 67v (La Paz).

15. AGNA, Sala 9, leg. 10.3.7, f. 2 (La Paz); and AGNA, Sala 13, leg. 18.7.4, f. 586v (Carangas).

16. Villegas.

17. AGI, Charcas, leg. 270, nos. 26 and 32. For royal pressure on the viceroy, see the Crown's cédulas of Madrid, Oct. 7, 1682 (AGI, Charcas, leg. 416, lib. 6, ff. 315-15v; the king wanted to know, as soon as possible, what the viceroy was planning), and May 2, 1684 (AGI, Charcas, leg. 416, lib. 6, ff. 348v-49v; the king wanted to see the resolution reached in the Real Acuerdo). When the Crown was informed as to what was being done, however, it only gave general approval and said that it would await the outcome of the process to decide whether or not it approved of the specifics of Palata's program (cédula to the Duque de la Palata, Madrid, June 10, 1685, AGI, Charcas, leg. 416, lib. 6, ff. 350v-53v).

18. Sánchez-Albornoz, *Indios y tributos*, pp. 26-34, compares the 1573 and 1683 figures for ten altoperuano provinces, and finds a decline within them from 161,095 to 93,331; on pp. 76-77 he notes that the number of forasteros in the sixteen mita provinces had come to equal the number of originarios. Evans, pp. 36-37, notes the failure of the alleged pockets of runaways to materialize, and provides a table (2.1) entitled "Distribution

of Altiplano and Yungas Population, 1683," which considers the number of tributaries versus the percentage of originarios within each province. For the clarity of the migration patterns, see Sánchez-Albornoz, "Mita, migraciones," p. 15.

19. Villegas.

20. Palata later argued that whatever overcounting might have taken place had been offset by the failure to include other Indians at all—in printed "Advertencias para la ejecución de los despachos de la nueva retasa y repartimiento de mitas de Potosí que han de tener presentes los corregidores y dar a entender a los indios," Lima, Apr. 29, 1689, BNB, MSS 4, ff. 301a–304; repeated in his relación of Dec. 18, 1689, in Hanke and Rodríguez, eds., *Virreyes* (Perú), vol. 6, pp. 231–38. Evans (pp. 35–36) and Sánchez-Albornoz (*Indios y tributos*, pp. 86–91, and "Mita, migraciones," p. 11) tend to agree that the results were more accurate than contemporary critics of the census claimed.

21. The viceroy's intention is noted in his "Advertencias" (cited in n. 20 above). It is clear, moreover, from his subsequent actions.

22. Provisión of the Viceroy Conde de la Monclova, Lima, Apr. 27, 1692, BNB, MSS 4, ff. 279–87 (the newly incorporated regions are identified in this order exempting them anew). Provisión of the Duque de la Palata, Lima, Dec. 2, 1688, BNB, MSS 4, ff. 442–49 (this particular copy of a printed order, with handwritten insertions, applies to the province of Misque). For a negative appraisal of Palata's decision, based on its effects, see Archbishop Melchor Liñán y Cisneros to the Crown, Lima, Sept. 1, 1692, AGI, Charcas, leg. 271, no. 6. For the viceroy's own retrospectives, see AGI, Charcas, leg. 270, nos. 16 and 32. The repartimiento itself is Palata's provisión of Lima, Jan. 29, 1689, AGI, Charcas, leg. 270, no. 30.

23. For the reasoning behind Palata's changes of the mita, see his "Advertencias" (cited in n. 20 above) and his provisión of Dec. 2, 1688 (cited in n. 22 above). The initial draft of the repartimiento was prepared by Fiscal Juan González de Santiago of the Audiencia of Lima; it was then sent to La Plata and reviewed by a committee composed of the president, the corregidor of Potosí, and the archbishop of Charcas (copy of a letter from Palata to the archbishop, Lima[?], Mar. 18, 1688, AGI, Charcas, leg. 270, no. 27A; and a copy of the committee's report, La Plata, Oct. 19, 1688, AGI, Charcas, leg. 270, no. 32A).

24. See Palata's "Advertencias" (cited in n. 20 above) and AGI, Charcas, leg. 270, no. 16.

25. For epidemics and the fact that many Indians had otherwise died by 1689, see AGNA, Sala 9, leg. 10.3.7, ff. 77–78, 108v (La Paz); 141 (Larecaja); 200 (Sicasica); 396, 397, 399v, 401v, 420 (Omasuyos); and AGNA, Sala 13, leg. 18.7.4, ff. 480v, 498v (Porco); 533 (Tarija). The bishop of Cuzco reported (Mar. 19, 1691, AGI, Charcas, leg. 271, no. 8A) that an epidemic in 1687 had killed eight to ten Indians per day in his diocese. For the abandonment of Porco, see AGNA, Sala 13, leg. 18.7.4, ff 483–84.

26. The Duque de la Palata to the Crown, Lima, Mar. 18, 1688, AGI, Charcas, leg. 270, no. 27. The viceroy had more time at his post than most of his predecessors because the Crown had difficulties finding a replacement; see Antonio Domínguez Ortiz, "Un virreinato en venta," *Mercurio Peruano* (Lima), no. 453 (1965), pp. 43–51.

27. The deadline for tribute is noted in Palata's "Advertencias" (cited in n. 20 above) and it is referred to throughout AGNA, Sala 9, leg. 10.3.7, and AGNA, Sala 13, leg. 18.7.4. The new mita charter (AGI, Charcas, leg. 270, no. 30) was signed by Palata in Los Reyes on Jan. 29, 1689, and sent out to the provinces on Feb. 2. The daily administration of the revised mita was placed in the hands of the corregidor of Potosí, Pedro Luis Enríquez; his correspondence with the corregidor of La Paz, Bernabé Felipe de Aragón, concerning the impending deadline for mita deliveries includes Enríquez's original order for La Paz, Potosí, Mar. 12, 1689, AGNA, Sala 9, leg. 10.3.7, ff. 30–37).

28. For flight from the mita, see AGNA, Sala 9, leg. 10.3.7, ff. 5v, 17, 23, 23v, 26, 28v, 45v, 70, 94, 95–96, 98v, 109 (La Paz); 141, 153, 157, 159, 160–60v, 161v, 162 (Larecaja); 167–67v, 169 (Misque); 194, 198, 203v, 231, 232, 252 (Sicasica); 349, 371, 372 (Pacajes); 396, 396v, 397v, 399v, 402, 403v, 407, 408, 418, 424v (Omasuyos); 433v, 436, 468, 471v–72, 500, 501v, 524, 525, 534v, 558–59, 560v, 567 (Cochabamba); and AGNA, Sala 13, leg. 18.7.4, ff. 477, 480v, 484, 485, 491, 496, 497, 498 (Porco); 505 (Chayanta); 578 (Paria). For families being broken up as a result, see AGNA, Sala 9, leg. 10.3.7, ff. 43, 53v, 71, 99v, 109 (La Paz); 167v (Misque); 193, 199v (Sicasica); 396v, 399v, 405v (Omasuyos); 524v, 556 (Cochabamba). For flight from ranches in particular, see AGNA, Sala 9, leg. 10.3.7, ff. 3v, 10, 12, 27 (La Paz); 122, 129 (Pilaya y Paspaya); 167v (Misque); 203, 229, 231 (Sicasica); 391 (Pacajes); 395v (Omasuyos); 556v (Cochabamba). For the loss of Indian laborers employed in other activities, see AGNA, Sala 9, leg. 10.3.7, ff. 19v (La Paz: mail, hospital, carnesía, service in the homes of officials); 117 (Tomina: livestock tending); 155 (Larecaja: gold mining); 169v, 180 (Misque: winemaking and service in convents); 371 (Pacajes: service in convents and in La Paz, mail).

29. For Indian flight into the yungas, see AGNA, Sala 9, leg. 10.3.7, ff. 6, 24v, 26v, 40–50, 52v–53, 54, 55v, 56, 57v, 58, 59, 69, 71 (La Paz); 115 (Tomina); 121, 123 (Pilaya y Paspaya); 153, 157, 158, 163 (Larecaja); 180 (Misque); 193v, 199v, 247, 251 (Sicasica); 393 (Pacajes); 405v, 411, 412v (Omasuyos); 435v, 470, 472, 509, 523, 556, 566v (Cochabamba).

30. For the kurakas' inability to control the forasteros and yanaconas, see AGNA, Sala 9, leg. 10.3.7, ff. 16, 22, 24v, 108v (La Paz); 205v (Sicasica); 405, 413–17v (Omasuyos); 524, 529, 530 (Cochabamba); and AGNA, Sala 13, leg. 18.7.4, ff. 478v, 498 (Porco); 531 (Chayanta); 583v (Carangas).

31. For general complaints about the kurakas' inability to comply, see AGNA, Sala 9, leg. 10.3.7, ff. 81, 82, 85, 90, 93–93v (La Paz); 350 (Pacajes);

395, 395v, 399v, 424v (Omasuyos); 528, 534, 536, 560v (Cochabamba); and AGNA, Sala 13, leg. 18.7.4, ff. 478v, 479, 482 (Porco); 509, 528v, 529v (Chayanta). There was, furthermore, a great deal of competition among kurakas for those Indians who had been included on multiple rosters—AGNA, Sala 9, leg. 10.3.7, ff. 3v, 67–67v (La Paz); 532 (Cochabamba); and AGNA, Sala 13, leg. 18.7.4, f. 497v (Porco).

32. For kuraka flight, see AGNA, Sala 9, leg. 10.3.7, ff. 43 (La Paz); 155 (Larecaja); 509, 529, 560 (Cochabamba); and AGNA, Sala 13, leg. 18.7.4, ff. 501v (Chayanta); 586v, 597–600 (Carangas).

33. For attempts by kurakas to resign, see AGNA, Sala 9, leg. 10.3.7, ff. 16v, 61, 93–93v (La Paz); 160 (Larecaja); 403v, 419 (Omasuyos); 534–34v, 536v, 564v (Cochabamba); and AGNA, Sala 13, leg. 18.7.4, ff. 479, 480v, 484, 485, 491 (Porco); 503v (Chayanta). For jailings of kurakas, see AGNA, Sala 9, leg. 10.3.7, ff. 27, 44v, 47v, 50v, 52, 60v, 72, 83v, 84, 86, 90, 97, 98, 102, 104, 105 (La Paz); 189 (Misque); 434, 501v, 529, 530, 534v (Cochabamba); and AGNA, Sala 13, leg. 18.7.4, f. 578 (Paria).

34. AGNA, Sala 9, leg. 10.3.7, ff. 25, 108–109 (La Paz); 386–90 (Pacajes). See also ANB, M 126, no. 4 (summarized in the footnote in Chap. 6, p. 115). In the frontier regions, kurakas often had not been appointed, and those who had been named were only just establishing themselves. In Tomina and Pilaya y Paspaya, for example, the corregidores were overwhelmed from the very beginning (AGNA, Sala 9, leg. 10.3.7, ff. 113, and 121, 128, respectively). The corregidor-elect of Larecaja, moreover, refused to accept that post (AGNA, Sala 9, leg. 10.3.7, ff. 161v–66).

35. For complaints that the inclusion of new areas was especially damaging, see AGNA, Sala 9, leg. 10.3.7, ff. 5v (La Paz); 110–20v (Tomina); 121–21v, 123–23v (Pilaya y Paspaya); 468, 569–70v (Cochabamba); and AGNA, Sala 13, leg. 18.7.4, ff. 574–74v (Tarija).

36. For protests of the effects of Palata's program on the frontier settlements and references to Toledo's reasons for having exempted them, see AGNA, Sala 9, leg. 10.3.7, ff. 153–54, 158 (Larecaja); 193, 198, 229, 241–41v, 247, 249, 251v, 252, 332, 334 (Sicasica); 472, 562 (Cochabamba); and AGNA, Sala 13, leg. 18.7.4, ff. 574–74v (Tarija).

37. AGNA, Sala 9, leg. 10.3.7, and Sala 13, leg. 18.7.4. Four overviews of the entire process are (1) Archbishop Liñán y Cisneros to the Crown, Lima, Sept. 1, 1692, AGI, Charcas, leg. 271, no. 6; (2) the bishop of Cuzco to the Crown, Cuzco, Oct. 3, 1692, AGI, Charcas, leg. 271, no. 8; (3) the same bishop's report for the Conde de la Monclova, Cuzco, Mar. 19, 1691, AGI, Charcas, leg. 271, no. 8A (a copy); (4) the Conde de Canillas (Corregidor Pedro Luis Enríquez) to the Crown, Lima, Dec. 22, 1691, AGI, Charcas, leg. 273, no. 1.

38. Palata, "Advertencias" (cited in n. 20 above).

39. *Ibid.*

40. Noted by the viceroy in his relación of Dec. 18, 1689, in Hanke and

Rodríguez, eds., *Virreyes* (Perú), vol. 6, p. 239. Crahan, p. 412, claims that Palata's failures as viceroy were caused by the structures of the Hapsburg administration, and contends that he would have been more successful had he served under Charles III rather than Charles II. Ezquerra Abadía, pp. 492−95, says that Palata's chances for success were lowered significantly by his replacement so soon after his reforms were introduced. In the case of the general enumeration of Indians, Peru would probably have been better off had the viceroy been replaced sooner and had the administration worked less efficiently.

41. The Conde de la Monclova to the Crown, Lima, Mar. 15, 1690, AGI, Charcas, leg. 270, no. 33 (this letter is transcribed in Moreyra y Paz-Soldán and Céspedes de Castillo, eds., vol. 1, pp. 15−23). For the response of the Council of the Indies' fiscal to this report, see AGI, Charcas, leg. 270, no. 33A (Madrid, Mar. 27, 1693). The second wave of complaints is noted in a comprehensive summary by the Council of the Indies, Madrid, Feb. 1, 1697, AGI, Charcas, leg. 273, no. 21. The Duque de la Palata's secretary, Joseph Bernal, noted that many of the corregidores had suspended all action on the reforms until the Conde de la Monclova arrived (in his letter to the secretary of the Council of the Indies, Madrid, Nov. 2, 1692, AGI, Charcas, leg. 271, no. 9).

42. The complaints addressed to Monclova are to be found throughout AGNA, Sala 9, leg. 10.3.7, and Sala 13, leg. 18.7.4; see also the bishop of Cuzco's report for Monclova, Cuzco, Mar. 19, 1691, AGI, Charcas, leg. 271, no. 8A (a copy). Monclova commented on these letters in his Apr. 27, 1692, order reforming the mita, Lima, Apr. 27, 1692, BNB, MSS 4, ff. 279−87. Manuel de Ribero Leal to the Conde de la Monclova, Sipesipe, Nov. 11, 1690, AGNA, Sala 9, leg. 10.3.7, ff. 562−65v (includes the quoted passage on f. 563).

43. AGI, Charcas, leg. 270, no. 33.

44. The deputies of the Azogueros Guild to the Crown, Potosí, Aug. 21, 1692, AGI, Charcas, leg. 271, no. 7B. The three officials who reviewed the 1689 charter in La Plata (Corregidor Enríquez, President Mesía, and Archbishop González de Poveda—the ex-president) had predicted that the azogueros would be upset with the changes in their report to Palata of Oct. 19, 1688 (AGI, Charcas, leg. 270, no. 32A).

45. The Conde de la Monclova to the Crown, Lima, Dec. 31, 1691, AGI, Charcas, leg. 273, no. 3 (a general report on the enumeration, the 1689 repartimiento, and his efforts to resolve the problems caused by them); BNB, MSS 4, ff. 279−87; AGI, Charcas, leg. 273, no. 21. The reports of Fiscal Matías Lagúnez and the protector general are included in AGI, Charcas, leg. 272, first item (the second tome of a three-volume set sent to Madrid by the Conde de la Monclova; the first is AGI Charcas 271, last item; and the third is AGI Charcas 273, item following no. 29; for a complete description of these volumes, see Hanke and Rodríguez, eds., *Guía de las fuentes en el*

Archivo General de Indias, vol. 1, pp. 332–41. The three tomes were sent with Monclova's letter to the Crown, Lima, Aug. 15, 1692, AGI, Charcas, leg. 273, no. 4.

46. Fiscal Matías Lagúnez to the Crown, Lima, Sept. 15, 1692, AGI, Charcas, leg. 273, no. 5 (this is a summary of his arguments, to be found at much greater length in AGI, Charcas, leg. 272, first item). Arzáns, *Historia*, vol. 2, p. 363 (for Enríquez's role in saving the mita from extinction).

47. These twelve resolutions are described in BNB, MSS 4, ff. 279–87, and recounted in AGI, Charcas, leg. 273, no. 21.

48. The original order (of Lima, Apr. 24, 1692) is in AGNA, Sala 9, leg. 14.8.10, ff. 187–87v; the printed provisión is BNB, MSS 4, ff. 279–87. See also the Conde de la Monclova's follow-up declaration (a synthesis of the Apr. 27 provisión), Los Reyes, July 19, 1692, AGI, Charcas, leg. 273, no. 4A.

49. An eighteenth-century copy of Monclova's repartimiento (of Lima, Apr. 27, 1692), BNB, MSS 31, ff. 37–53; the general provisión of the viceroy, Lima, May 8, 1692, AGNA, Sala 9, leg. 14.8.10, ff. 50–145v; Monclova's provisión of Lima, May 6, 1692, BNB, MSS 31, ff. 53–64 (describing how the mitayos are to be employed at Potosí; this is also an eighteenth-century copy). A summary of the 1692 charter is also included in a letter from Corregidor Enríquez to the Azogueros Guild, Lima, Apr. 28, 1692, AGI, Charcas, leg. 271, no. 7D (a copy).

50. AGI, Charcas, leg. 271, no. 7D. Sánchez-Albornoz, *Indios y tributos*, p. 82, discusses the naming of Enríquez by the azogueros to be their representative in the junta. See also Arzáns, *Historia*, vol. 2, pp. 357–58. The Azogueros Guild said that Monclova had forced it to donate the 35,000 pesos to support the corregidor and his wife (AGI, Charcas, leg. 271, no. 7B).

51. The "república" of Potosí to the Crown, Potosí, Apr. 1, 1692, AGI, Charcas, leg. 271, no. 7A. The Azogueros Guild to the Conde de la Monclova, Potosí, Aug. 19, 1692, AGI, Charcas, leg. 271, no. 7C (a copy); the viceroy described their petition in his letter to the Crown, Lima, Oct. 21, 1693, AGI, Charcas, leg. 273, no. 10. The azogueros to the Crown, Potosí, Dec. 9, 1693, AGI, Charcas, leg. 273, no. 6.

52. The Conde de Canillas (Pedro Luis Enríquez) to the Conde de la Monclova, Potosí, Nov. 29, 1692, AGI, Charcas, leg. 271, no. 11B. Sánchez-Albornoz, *Indios y tributos*, pp. 79–83, describes the corregidor's work once he returned to Potosí, as do Arzáns, *Historia*, vol. 2, pp. 364–65, and AGI, Charcas, leg. 273, no. 21.

53. The Conde de Canillas (Enríquez) to the Crown, Potosí, Dec. 10, 1692, AGI, Charcas, leg. 271, no. 12. Transcript of the declarations of the capitán mayor de la mita and veedores that those who were denied mitayos in the 1692 repartimiento had committed abuses, whereas those who were allotted mitayos were meritorious (AGI, Charcas, leg. 273, no. 11A).

54. AGI, Charcas, leg. 271, no. 12. The corregidor sent along to the Crown testimony by the azogueros that they were happy with the com-

promise (AGI, Charcas, leg. 271, nos. 12A and 12B; the latter is dated Dec. 10, 1692). For the guild's side of the story, including its claim that the compromise was suggested by the corregidor and manifesting its continued displeasure with the compromise, see its letter of Dec. 9, 1693 (AGI, Charcas, leg. 273, no. 6).

55. The Conde de la Monclova to the Crown, Lima, Oct. 21, 1693, AGI, Charcas, leg. 273, no. 10; the viceroy relayed the corregidor's side of the story.

56. The Conde de la Monclova to the Crown, Lima, Aug. 15, 1692, AGI, Charcas, leg. 273, no. 4.

57. AGI, Charcas, leg. 273, no. 10. Secretary Antonio Ortiz de Otalora's acknowledgement of receipt by the Council of the Indies of Monclova's report was sent on Jan. 22, 1695 (AGI, Charcas, leg. 417, lib. 7, f. 149v). The archbishop's position paper, of Dec. 3, 1692, is AGI, Charcas, leg. 273, no. 11E.

58. Materials for and against Monclova's program arrived in Madrid, including a petition from "Los Caciques y enteradores de la Mita" to the Crown, n.d. (the envelope carries "1694," the year that it arrived in Spain), AGI, Charcas, leg. 273, no. 14, and an undated letter from the Azogueros Guild to the Crown, Potosí (also received in 1694), AGI, Charcas, leg. 273, no. 15. An order to gather materials for the Council's review is AGI, Charcas, leg. 273, no. 13 (dated Apr. 2, 1694). The minutes of its deliberations, Madrid, Jan. 18, 1697, AGI, Charcas, leg. 273, no. 19B. The search for a compromise—indeed, this entire process—is also discussed in AGI, Charcas, leg. 273, no. 21.

59. AGI, Charcas, leg. 273, no. 19B. "Reforma y prevensiones en los doce puntos" by the Council of the Indies, n.d. (ca. 1697), AGI, Charcas, leg. 273, no. 19C. The Conde de la Monclova to the Audiencia of La Plata, Lima, May 23, 1698, AGI, Charcas, leg. 273, no. 23 (relating the Council's decisions; a copy). The Council of the Indies also voted that the position of corregidor of Potosí should no longer be sold, and that all contracts with individuals for that position be cancelled, owing to the importance of the post to the economic well-being of the viceroyalty and the empire.

60. The Crown to the viceroy of Peru and Audiencia of Lima, Madrid, Feb. 18, 1697, AGI, Charcas, leg. 273, no. 23A (no. 27 is a draft; AGI, Charcas, leg. 417, lib. 7, ff. 196–214v, is a copy); royal cédula to the corregidor of Potosí, Madrid, Feb. 18, 1697, BNB, MSS 4, ff. 156–57 (a copy is AGI, Charcas, leg. 417, lib. 7, ff. 214v–19); royal cédula to the royal treasury officials of Potosí, Madrid, Feb. 18, 1697, BNB, MSS 4, f. 155 (a copy is AGI, Charcas, leg. 417, lib. 7, ff. 219–20v); report by the Audiencia of La Plata, La Plata, Aug. 16, 1698, AGI, Charcas, leg. 273, no. 25; report by the corregidor and royal treasury officials of Potosí, Potosí, July 7, 1698, AGI, Charcas, leg. 273, no. 24; report by the archbishop of Charcas, Tomina de la Frontera, July 3, 1698, AGI, Charcas, leg. 273, no. 26; and the royal

treasury officials of Potosí to the Crown, Potosí, Apr. 14, 1699, AGI, Charcas, leg. 273, no. 29.

CHAPTER 7

1. The works of Enrique Tandeter and Ramón Ezquerra Abadía are listed in the Bibliography. Tandeter's thesis, "La rente comme rapport de production et comme rapport de distribution," should appear in book form in the near future.

2. Ezquerra Abadía, pp. 496–97.

3. *Ibid.*, pp. 497–502 (Castillo), and 502–11 (Gómez García).

4. *Ibid.*, p. 497.

5. Tandeter, "Forced and Free Labour," p. 104.

6. *Ibid.*, pp. 102–3.   7. *Ibid.*, p. 103.

8. *Ibid.*, p. 125.   9. *Ibid.*, pp. 120, 124.

10. Klein, pp. 71–72.

11. Tandeter, "Forced and Free Labour," p. 100.

12. *Ibid.*, p. 110.   13. *Ibid.*, pp. 100–101, 115.

14. *Ibid.*, pp. 107–9.   15. *Ibid.*, pp. 99, 101.

16. *Ibid.*, pp. 106–7; Carmen; AGNA, Sala 9, leg. 27.2.2.

17. For a survey of recent works on the eighteenth-century Indian uprisings, see Leon G. Campbell, "Recent Research on Andean Peasant Revolts, 1750–1820," *Latin American Research Review*, 14:1 (1979).

Bibliography

ARCHIVAL SOURCES

Archivo General de Indias, Seville, Spain [AGI]. Microfilm copies of the following legajos were consulted in the University of Massachusetts, Amherst, Library:

Ramo	Legajo	Description
Charcas	266	Expedientes sobre la mita de Potosí; repartimientos de indios y reducción del trabajo de los mismos, 1634–63.
Charcas	267	Expedientes sobre la mita de Potosí y el repartimiento de indios de dicha mita, 1647–70.
Charcas	268	Expedientes, consultas y cartas sobre la mita de Potosí, y agravios a los indios que trabajan en ella, 1667–81.
Charcas	270	Expedientes sobre la mita de Potosí, y numeración general de los naturales, 1692.
Charcas	271	Expedientes sobre la reintegración de la mita de Potosí y la numeración de los indios, 1692.
Charcas	272	Alegaciones que se dieron el fiscal de la Audiencia de Lima y el protector general de los naturales del reino del Perú en defensa de los indios, pidiendo su alivio y desagravio, 1692.
Charcas	273	Expedientes sobre la mita de Potosí, 1693 a 1699. Cartas y expedientes sobre como encontró la mita de Potosí el Conde de la Monclova cuando tomó posesión del virreinato, así como lo ejecutado durante estos años de su gobierno, 1691–99.
Charcas	416	Registros de reales órdenes, nombramientos, gracias, etc., de la Audiencia de Charcas, 1577–1700, Libro 6.
Charcas	417	Registros de reales órdenes, nombramientos, gracias, etc., de la Audiencia de Charcas, 1577–1700, Libros 7–8.

Ramo	Legajo	Description
Charcas	420	Registros de reales órdenes, nombramientos, gracias, etc., de la Audiencia de Charcas, 1563–1699, Libros 8–9.

(For more complete descriptions of the contents of these legajos, see Hanke and Rodríguez, eds., *Guía de las fuentes en el Archivo General de Indias*, vol. 1, pp. 328–41, 392–93; please note that the last three legajos contain copies of orders.)

Archivo General de la Nación, Buenos Aires, Argentina [AGNA]. The following legajos from Salas 9 and 13 were consulted:

Sala	Legajo Title	Years	Legajo
9	Hacienda, Acuerdos del Real	1611–36	13.8.7
		1636–61	13.8.8
		1667–1710	13.8.9
9	Indios, Padrones de	1623–71	20.4.4
9	Lima y Buenos Aires. Ordenanzas de las Reales Audiencias de Charcas	1563–1784	15.2.4
9	Mendoza, Juan de (Marqués de Montesclaros). Ordenanzas	1609	45.6.2
9	Minas de Potosí. Código Carolino de Ordenanzas Reales		27.2.2
			27.2.3
9	Mita, ordenanzas de virreyes, Potosí	1683–1774	14.8.10
9	Omasuyo, Representaciones y quejas de las provincias de La Paz, Tomina, Pilaya, Mizque	1689–91	10.3.7
9	Padrones de indios de Alto Perú	1676	45.5.10
		1645–86	17.1.4
9	Pérez de Salazar, Alonso y Alfaro, Francisco de	1611–23	26.4.2
9	Perú, virreinato del	1684–1755	17.1.6
9	Potosí	1613–1750	6.2.5
9	Provisiones, cédulas, reales órdenes	1617–1796	25.4.32
9	Reales cédulas, órdenes, provisiones, decretos	1664–1802	25.4.33
13	Representaciones y quejas de las provincias, Porco, Chayanta, Tarija, Paria y Carangas	1689–90	18.7.4

Also consulted in the Archivo General de la Nación, Buenos Aires, were selected items from the collection of the Biblioteca Nacional. Leg. 42 included an "Informe del duque de la Palata, virrey del Perú, á su sucesor el conde de la Moncloba, sobre la situación del virreinato," Lima, Nov. 18, 1689. Leg. 181 included a "Real cédula para que los indios que están dispersos, pasados veinte años, puedan connaturalizarse en el paraje donde habitan . . . ," Madrid[?], Feb. 4, 1655; a "Real provisión para que los indios del Perú que vayan á Tucumán puedan connaturalizarse allí," Madrid[?], Feb. 4, 1655;

and a "Real cédula para que con los indios que se van reduciendo se formen nuevos pueblos," Madrid[?], Oct. 14, 1687.

Archivo General de la Nación, Lima, Peru [AGNP]. Three items were of particular interest: Derecho Indiano, C. 79, "Testimonio de los autos seguidos por D. Blas Ignacio Catacora, Cacique principal de Acora en la provincia de Chucuito, a fin de que se le acordasen las gracias y premios a que sus mayores se habían hecho acreedores por sus servicios al Rey, y su continua asistencia a la pesada mita de Potosí, expediente incompleto, 1625"; Derecho Indiano, C. 809, "Fragmento de un expediente sobre revisita de indios de la Villa de Potosí, efectuada por el General D. Fernando de Torres Mesía, Conde de Velayos, Corregidor y Justicia Mayor de dicha Villa, 1693"; Superior Gobierno, C. 92, "Testimonio de un Real Acuerdo de Justicia, expedido por el Secretario de Cámara D. Andrés de Valsanz de la Real Audiencia de los Charcas, por el que se estableció que el Situado del Reyno de Chile, se despachara de las Cajas Reales de Potosí, y se remitiera en reales y no en ropa a los soldados, para que percibieran su paga en dinero, de los 212 mil ducados situados, para el ejército de aquel Reyno. Plata que se entregaría en Potosí, por intermedio de quien fuera con Poder del Ejército de Chile, 1688."

Archivo Histórico de Potosí, Potosí, Bolivia [AHP]. The following legajos were consulted:

Ramo	Legajo	Description
Cajas Reales	47	Libro de tasas de Chuquito y otros pueblos, 1592–1604.
Cajas Reales	52	Libro de diligencias acerca del azogue, 1594–1618.
Cajas Reales	72	Padrón de los indios mitayos, 1600.
Cajas Reales	153	Libro real de acuerdos y diligencias tocantes a la real hacienda, 1614–21.
Cajas Reales	201	Libro real de provisiones, títulos y tomas de razón, 1624–29 (incompleto).
Cajas Reales	336	Libro real de bienes de difuntos, 1652–94.
Cajas Reales	418	Libro real de provisiones que empieza a correr a quince de noviembre de este año de mil seiscientos y sesenta y ocho, 1668–78.
Cajas Reales	484	Padrón de indios tributarios de los distintos pueblos de la provincia de Porco, 1687–88.
Cajas Reales	503	Libro donde se sientan las cartas que escribe su magestad a esta caja y las del gobierno superior de este reino y las respuestas y satisfacción que se da a todo con las del tribunal de cuentas y santa cruzada, 1651–74.

Archivo Nacional de Bolivia and *Biblioteca Nacional de Bolivia*, Sucre,

186   BIBLIOGRAPHY

Bolivia [ANB and BNB]. For a thorough description of these two institutions and the wealth of documentation that they contain, see Gunnar Mendoza L., "Guía de fuentes inéditas en el Archivo Nacional de Bolivia para el estudio de la administración virreinal en el distrito de la Audiencia de Charcas, años 1537–1700," in Hanke, Mendoza L., and Rodríguez, eds., *Guía de las fuentes en Hispanoamérica*, pp. 46–257. These are the collections used for this book:

Archivo Nacional:

Abbreviation	Collection
ACh.LA	Audiencia de Charcas. Libros de acuerdos.
C	Audiencia de Charcas. Correspondencia.
EC	Audiencia de Charcas. Expedientes.
M	Minas.
RC	Audiencia de Charcas. Reales cédulas.

Biblioteca Nacional:

Abbreviation	Collection
CPLA	Cabildo de Potosí. Libros de acuerdos.
MSS	Colecciones particulares de manuscritos, Rück, Manuscritos de Pedro Vicente Cañete.

Biblioteca Nacional del Perú, Lima, Peru [BNP]. These items were of special interest:

B39. "Testimonio de reales cédulas: 1° para que se envíen a Chile pobladores desde Potosí; 2° sobre la forma de procederse en la marca de los indios cautivos de Chile; 3° disposiciones acerca de la esclavitud; 4° instrucciones enviadas al Presidente interino de la Real Audiencia de La Plata, Juan Victorino Martínez; y 5° instrucciones al nuevo Gobernador de Huancavelica, Domingo Jáuregui, 1611–?

B492. "Reales provisiones expedidas en favor de los indios, Los Reyes," June 1654.

B516. "Memorial acerca de las mitas de los indios del Perú (por D. Pedro de Palacios Zerdán)." Buenos Aires, Nov. 1, 1664.

B575. "Paucarcolla. Autos sobre el despacho de la mita de Potosí e información de los caciques para su gran disipación, Villa de Concepción," Oct. 24, 1669.

B585. "Despacho de la mita de Potosí," Puno, Nov. 1673.

B614. "Relación de los indios mitimaes de Huarochirí, Lima," Dec. 3, 1642.

B684. "Expediente sobre la petición presentada por el Oidor de la Real Audiencia, D. Andrés de Villela a fin de que se practique una visita a las minas de la jurisdicción de Lima y Chuquisaca, 1646."

B956. "Cuaderno y padrón de los indios mitimaes en esta ciudad de Chucuito de la parcialidad de Hanansaya . . . , 1686."

B1535. "Cuaderno donde se asienta la plata que viene de Potosí, La Paz y Arequipa este año de 1641," Lima, July 8, 1641.

BIBLIOGRAPHY   187

PRINTED AND SELECTED MANUSCRIPT SOURCES

Acosta, José de. *Obras de P. José de Acosta.* Ed. Francisco Mateos. Biblioteca de Autores Españoles, no. 73. Madrid, 1954.

AGI, AGNA, AGNP, AHP: see preceding section, "Archival Sources."

Alvares Reyero, Francisco. "Relacion dada al Virrey de Lima por d[n] . . . del natural delos Indios de Potosí sus vestimentas, las horas quetrabajan &a y el importe dela plata sacada de aquel cerro con los quintos q[e] han dado à S. M. y tributos delos indios fecha á 1° de Junio de 1670," *Revista de la Biblioteca Nacional* (Buenos Aires), 9 (1943), pp. 336–65.

ANB: see preceding section, "Archival Sources."

Andrien, Kenneth J. "Reform, Resistance, and Imperial Decline in Seventeenth-Century Lima." Paper presented at the 97th Annual Meeting of the American Historical Association, Dec. 28, 1982.

Angulo, Andrés de. "Relacion o ressumen de las rraciones y pareceres que sse han dado sobre que sse quitte y cesse la mitta forzada de yndios para las minas de el Zerro de Potosi" (Madrid, May 3, 1673), AGI, Charcas, leg. 268, no. 36.

Argentina. Archivo General de la Nación. *Indice temático general de unidades archivonómicas del período colonial—Gobierno.* Coleccíon auxiliares heurísticos, serie índices, no. 2. Buenos Aires, 1978.

———. Biblioteca Nacional. *Catálogo por órden cronológico de los manuscritos relativos a América existentes en la Biblioteca Nacional de Buenos Aires.* 2 vols. Buenos Aires, 1905–6.

———. ———. *Segundo catálogo por órden cronológico de los manuscritos relativos a América en la Biblioteca Nacional de Buenos Aires.* Buenos Aires, 1944.

Arzáns de Orsúa y Vela, Bartolomé. *Historia de la Villa Imperial de Potosí.* Ed. Lewis Hanke and Gunnar Mendoza L. 3 vols. Providence, R.I., 1965.

———. *Tales of Potosí.* Trans. Frances M. López-Morillas; ed. R. C. Padden. Providence, R.I., 1975.

Arze Aguirre, René. *Documentos sobre la historia de Bolivia existentes en el Archivo General de la Nación Argentina (índice parcial).* La Paz, 1975.

———. "Guía sumaria para el investigador del Archivo de La Paz," *Boletín del Archivo de La Paz,* año 4, no. 6 (1979), pp. 3–10.

Assadourian, Carlos Sempat. "La producción de la mercancía dinero en la formación del mercado interno colonial. El caso del espacio peruano, siglo xvi," in Enrique Florescano, ed., *Ensayos sobre el desarrollo económico de México y América Latina (1500–1975)* (Mexico City, 1979), pp. 223–92.

Ayanz, Antonio de. "Breve Relación de los agravios que reciven los indios que ay desde cerca del Cuzco hasta Potosí . . . (1596)," in Rubén Vargas Ugarte, ed. *Pareceres jurídicos en asuntos de Indias (1601–1718),* pp. 35–88.

Bakewell, Peter J. *Miners of the Red Mountain: Indian Labor in Potosí, 1545–1650.* Albuquerque, 1984 (used in manuscript form).

———. "Registered Silver Production in the Potosí District, 1550–1735," *Jahrbuch für Geschichte von Staat, Wirtschaft und Gesellschaft Lateinamerikas* (Cologne), 12 (1975), pp. 67–103.

———. *Silver Mining and Society in Colonial Mexico: Zacatecas, 1546–1700.* Cambridge, Eng., 1971.

———. "Technological Change in Potosí: The Silver Boom of the 1570's," *Jahrbuch für Geschichte von Staat, Wirtshaft und Gesellschaft Lateinamerikas* (Cologne), 14 (1977), pp. 57–77.

Ballesteros Gaibrois, Manuel. *Descubrimiento y fundación del Potosí.* Zaragoza, Spain, 1950.

———. "Notas sobre el trabajo minero en los Andes, con especial referencia a Potosí (s. XVI y ss.)," in *La minería hispana e iberoamericana,* pp. 529–57.

Baquíjano y Carrillo, Joseph. "Historia del descubrimiento del cerro de Potosí, fundación de su Imperial Villa, sus progresos y actual estado," *Mercurio Peruano* (Lima), Jan. 10, 13, and 17, 1793; facsimile ed., Lima, 1964, pp. 25–48.

Bargalló, Modesto. *La minería y la metalurgía en la América española durante la época colonial.* Mexico City, 1955.

Barnadas, Josep M. *Charcas: orígenes históricos de una sociedad colonial.* La Paz, 1973.

———. "Una polémica colonial: Potosí, 1579–1684," *Jahrbuch für Geschichte von Staat, Wirtschaft und Gesellschaft Lateinamerikas* (Cologne), 10 (1973), pp. 16–70.

Basadre, Jorge. *El conde de Lemos y su tiempo.* Lima, 1945.

———. "El Régimen de la Mita," *Letras* (Lima), 8 (1937), pp. 325–64.

Beltrán y Rózpide, Ricardo, ed. *Colección de las memorias o relaciones que escribieron los virreyes del Perú.* Madrid, 1921.

Benino, Nicolás del. "Relación muy particular del cerro y minas de Potosí y de su calidad y labores . . . dirigida a don Francisco de Toledo, virrey del Perú, en 1573," in Marcos Jiménez de la Espada, ed., *Relaciones geográficas de Indias.—Perú,* vol. 1, pp. 362–71.

Biscay, Acarete du. "An Account of a Voyage up the River de la Plata and thence over Land to Peru (c. 1660)," in Irving Leonard, ed., *Colonial Travelers in Latin America* (New York, 1972), pp. 125–43.

BNB, BNP: see preceding section, "Archival Sources."

Brading, D. A., and Harry E. Cross, "Colonial Silver Mining: Mexico and Peru," *The Hispanic American Historical Review,* 52 (1972), pp. 545–79.

Campo y de la Rynaga, Nicolás Matías del. *Memorial apologético, histórico, jurídico y político.* Lima, 1672.

Cañedo-Arguelles Fabrega, Teresa. "Efectos de Potosí en la estructura de una provincia mitaya: Pacajes a mediados del siglo XVII." Thesis for the degree of Licenciatura, Universidad de Sevilla, 1976.

Cañete y Domínguez, Vicente. *Descripción geográfica, histórica, física, y natural de la Villa Imperial y Cerro Rico de Potosí* [1789]. Potosí, 1952.

Capoche, Luis. *Relación general de la Villa Imperial de Potosí* [1585]. Ed. Lewis Hanke. Biblioteca de Autores Españoles, no. 122. Madrid, 1959.

Cardozo, Efraim. "La Audiencia de Charcas y la facultad de gobierno," *Humanidades* (La Plata, Arg.), 25 (1936), pp. 137–56.

Carmen, María del. "Una polémica en torno a la mita de Potosí a fines del siglo xviii," *Revista de Indias* (Madrid), 30 (1970), pp. 131–215.

Castañeda Delgado, Paulino. "El tema de las minas en la ética colonial española," in *La minería hispana e iberoamericana*, pp. 330–54.

Castillo, Pedro Antonio del. "Libro y relacion sumaria Que de orden del . . . Duque de la Palata . . . Virey . . . de estos reinos Y Provincias del Peru . . . A formado D^n Pedro Antonio del castillo . . . De todo lo obrado en [el Perú], assi por el dho señor Duque Como por los demas ministros de su M. que entendieron en la numeracion general de los Yndios del dho reyno que en Virtud de Zedulas suias Se hisso el ano pasado de 1684= . . . Para ymforme e Instrucion de los ministros de su M. que entendieron en este Govierno y de los de su R.^1 Y supremo consejo de Yndias" (ca. 1690), AGI, Charcas, leg. 270, no. 33C.

Céspedes del Castillo, Guillermo. "La visita como institución indiana," *Anuario de Estudios Americanos* (Seville), 3 (1946), pp. 984–1025.

Chacón Torres, Mario. "El Archivo Histórico de Potosí," *Boletín del Archivo de La Paz*, año 3, no. 5 (1978), pp. 27–32.

Cobb, Gwendolin Ballantine. "Potosí, a South American Mining Frontier," in *Greater America: Essays in Honor of Herbert Eugene Bolton* (Berkeley, Calif., 1945), pp. 39–58.

———. "Potosí and Huancavelica: Economic Bases of Peru, 1545 to 1640." Ph.D. diss., Univ. of Calif., Berkeley, 1947.

———. *Potosí y Huancavelica. Bases económicas, 1545–1640*. Trans. Jorge Muñoz Reyes. La Paz, 1977.

———. "Supply and Transportation for the Potosí Mines, 1545–1640," *The Hispanic American Historical Review*, 29 (1949), pp. 25–45.

Cole, Jeffrey A. "An Abolitionism Born of Frustration: The Conde de Lemos and the Potosí Mita, 1667–73," *The Hispanic American Historical Review*, 63 (1983), pp. 307–33.

———. "The Potosí Mita under Hapsburg Administration. The Seventeenth Century." Ph.D. diss., Univ. of Mass., Amherst, 1981.

———. "Viceregal Persistence versus Indian Mobility: The Impact of the Duque de la Palata's Reform Program on Alto Perú, 1681–1692," *Latin American Research Review*, 19, no. 1 (1984), pp. 37–56.

Colección de documentos inéditos para la historia de España. 112 vols. Madrid, 1842–95.

Cook, Noble David. "The Indian Population of Peru, 1570–1620." Ph.D. diss., Univ. of Texas, Austin, 1973.

———, ed. *Tasa de la visita general de Francisco de Toledo.* Lima, 1975.

Crahan, Margaret E. "The Administration of Don Melchor Navarra y Rocafull, Duque de la Palata: Viceroy of Peru, 1681–1689," *The Americas,* 27 (1971), pp. 389–412.

Crespo Rodas, Alberto. *La guerra entre Vicuñas y Vascongados (Potosí, 1622–1625).* Lima, 1956.

———. "La 'Mita' de Potosí." *Revista Histórica* (Lima), 22 (1955–56), pp. 169–82.

———. "El reclutamiento y los viajes en la 'mita' del cerro de Potosí," in *La minería hispana e iberoamericana,* pp. 467–82.

"Descripción de la villa y minas de Potosí. Año de 1603," in Marcos Jiménez de la Espada, ed., *Relaciones geográficas de Indias.—Perú,* vol. 1, pp. 372–85.

Diffie, Bailey W. "Estimates of Potosí Mineral Production, 1541–1555," *The Hispanic American Historical Review,* 20 (1940), pp. 275–82.

Dobyns, Henry F. "An Outline of Andean Epidemic History to 1720," *Bulletin of the History of Medicine,* 37, no. 6 (Nov./Dec. 1963), pp. 493–515.

Domínguez Ortiz, Antonio. *The Golden Age of Spain, 1516–1659.* Trans. James Casey; ed. John Parry and Hugh Thomas. London, 1971.

Elliott, J. H. *Imperial Spain, 1469–1716.* New York, 1963.

Escobedo Mansilla, Ronald. *El tributo indígena en el Perú (siglos XVI–XVII).* Pamplona, 1979.

Evans, Brian M. "Census Enumeration in Late Seventeenth-Century Alto Perú: The Numeración General of 1683–1684," in David J. Robinson, ed., *Studies in Spanish American Population History* (Boulder, 1981), pp. 25–44.

Ezquerra Abadía, Ramón. "Problemas de la mita de Potosí en el siglo XVIII," in *La minería hispana e iberoamericana,* pp. 483–511.

Fox, K. V. "Pedro Muñiz, Dean of Lima, and the Indian Labor Question (1603)," *The Hispanic American Historical Review,* 42 (1962), pp. 63–88.

Fuente, Rodrigo de la. "Relación del cerro de Potosí y su descubrimiento," in Marcos Jiménez de la Espada, ed., *Relaciones geográficas de Indias.—Perú,* vol. 1, pp. 357–61.

Fuentes, Manuel A., ed. *Memorias de los virreyes que han gobernado el Perú durante el tiempo del coloniaje español.* 6 vols. Lima, 1859.

Gibson, Charles. *The Black Legend: Anti-Spanish Attitudes in the Old World and the New.* New York, 1971.

———. *The Inca Concept of Sovereignty and the Spanish Administration in Peru.* Austin, 1948.

Goldwert, Marvin. "La lucha por la perpetuidad de las encomiendas en el Perú virreinal, 1550–1600," *Revista Histórica* (Lima), 22 (1955–56), pp. 336–60.

Hamilton, Earl J. *American Treasure and the Price Revolution in Spain, 1501–1650.* Cambridge, Mass., 1934.

Hanke, Lewis. "Como estudiar el Derecho Indiano," in *Homenaje a Jorge Basadre*. Lima, 1978.

———. *The Imperial City of Potosí. An Unwritten Chapter in the History of Spanish America*. The Hague, 1956.

———. "Luis Capoche and the History of Potosí, 1545–1585," *Inter-American Economic Affairs*, 12, no. 2 (1958), pp. 19–51.

———. "A Modest Proposal for a Moratorium on Grand Generalizations: Some Thoughts on the Black Legend," *The Hispanic American Historical Review*, 51 (1971), pp. 112–27.

———. "The Portuguese in Spanish America, with Special Reference to the Villa Imperial de Potosí," *Revista de Historia de América* (Mexico City), 61 (1961), pp. 1–48.

———. "The Social History of Potosí," in *La minería hispana e ibero-americana*, pp. 451–65.

———. "Viceroy Francisco de Toledo and the Just Titles of Spain to the Inca Empire," *The Americas*, 3 (1946), pp. 3–19.

Hanke, Lewis, and Celso Rodríguez, eds. *Guía de las fuentes en el Archivo General de Indias para el estudio de la administración virreinal española en México y en el Perú, 1535–1700*. 3 vols. Cologne, 1977.

———. *Los virreyes españoles en América durante el gobierno de la Casa de Austria*. 12 vols. Biblioteca de Autores Españoles, nos. 273–77 (México, vols. 1–5), 280–86 (Perú, vols. 1–7). Madrid, 1978–80.

Hanke, Lewis, Celso Rodríguez, and Gunnar Mendoza L., eds. *Guía de las fuentes en Hispanoamérica para el estudio de la administración virreinal española en México y en el Perú, 1535–1700*. Washington, D.C., 1980.

Haring, Clarence Henry. "American Gold and Silver Production in the First Half of the Sixteenth Century," *The Quarterly Journal of Economics*, 29 (1915), pp. 433–79.

———. *The Spanish Empire in America*. New York, 1947.

———. *Trade and Navigation between Spain and the Indies in the Time of the Hapsburgs*. Cambridge, Mass., 1918.

Helmer, Marie. "Comércio e contrabando entre Bahía e Potosí no século XVI," *Revista de História* (São Paulo), 15 (1953), pp. 195–210.

———. "La encomienda à Potosí d'après un document inédit," *Proceedings of the XXXth International Congress of Americanists*, 36 (Cambridge, Eng., 1952), pp. 235–38.

———. "Un tipo social: el 'minero' de Potosí," *Revista de Indias* (Madrid), 16 (1956), pp. 85–92.

Heredia Herrera, Antonia. "Los cedularios de oficio y partes del Consejo de Indias: sus tipos documentales (siglo XVII)," *Anuario de Estudios Americanos* (Seville), 29 (1972), pp. 1–60.

Hermosa Virreira, Walter. *Breve historia de la minería en Bolivia*. La Paz, 1979.

Holmes, Garrick Wilson. "The Indian Miner in Colonial Potosí. Sketch for a

Study of Urbanization in the Andes." M.A. Thesis, Columbia Univ., 1959.

Jiménez de la Espada, Marcos, ed. *Relaciones geográficas de Indias.—Perú.* 3 vols. Biblioteca de Autores Españoles, nos. 183–85. Madrid, 1965.

Keen, Benjamin. "The Black Legend Revisited: Assumptions and Realities," *The Hispanic American Historical Review,* 49 (1969), pp. 703–19.

———. "The White Legend Revisited: A Reply to Professor Hanke's 'Modest Proposal,'" *The Hispanic American Historical Review,* 51 (1971), pp. 336–55.

———, ed. *Readings in Latin American Civilization, 1492 to the Present.* 2d ed. Boston, 1967.

Keith, Robert G. "Encomienda, Hacienda and Corregimiento in Spanish America: A Structural Analysis," *The Hispanic American Historical Review,* 51 (1971), pp. 431–46.

Klein, Herbert S. *Bolivia, The Evolution of a Multi-Ethnic Society.* New York, 1982.

Konetzke, Richard, ed. *Colección de documentos para la historia de la formación social de Hispanoamérica (1493–1810).* 3 vols. Madrid, 1953–58.

Kubler, George. "The Quechua in the Colonial World," in Julian H. Steward, ed., *Handbook of South American Indians* (7 vols.; New York, 1946–59), vol. 2, pp. 331–410.

Levillier, Roberto, ed. *La Audiencia de Charcas, Correspondencia de presidentes y oidores.* 3 vols. Madrid, 1918–22.

———. *Gobernantes del Perú. Cartas y papeles, siglo XVI.* 14 vols. Madrid, 1921–26.

Lizarraga, Reginaldo de. "Descripción breve de toda la tierra del Perú (1605)," in *Historiadores de Indias* (Nueva Biblioteca de Autores Españoles, no. 15.; Madrid, 1909), pp. 554–59.

Lohmann Villena, Guillermo. *El corregidor de indios en el Perú bajo los Austrias.* Madrid, 1957.

———. *Las minas de Huancavelica en los siglos XVI y XVII.* Seville, 1949.

———. "La minería en el marco del virreinato peruano. Invenciones, sistemas, técnicas y organización industrial," in *La minería hispana e iberoamericana,* pp. 639–55.

———, ed. "Un informe veraz sobre la situación del virreinato en 1640," *Revista Histórica* (Lima), 23 (1957), pp. 278–95.

Lynch, John. *Spain Under the Hapsburgs.* Vol. II: *Spain and America, 1598–1700.* New York, 1969.

Málaga Medina, Alejandro. "El Virrey Don Francisco de Toledo y la reglamentación del tributo en el virreinato del Perú," *Anuario de Estudios Americanos* (Seville), 29 (1972), pp. 597–623.

Malca Olguín, Oscar. "Ordenanzas para corregidores del XIII virrey del Perú, Don Diego Fernández de Córdoba, Marqués de Guadalcázar—Año 1626," *Revista del Archivo Nacional del Perú,* 19 (1955), pp. 155–81.

Martínez Arzans y Vela, Nicolás. *Historia de la Villa Imperial de Potosí*. La Paz, 1975.

Matienzo, Juan de. *Gobierno del Perú* [1567]. Ed. Guillermo Lohmann Villena. Lima, 1967.

Mendiburu, Manuel de. *Diccionario histórico-biográfico del Perú*. 2d ed. Ed. Evaristo San Cristóval. 11 vols. Lima, 1931–35.

Mendoza L., Gunnar. "Archivo de Potosí. Guía preliminar de la documentación del coloniaje, 1551–1825." Typescript; Potosí, 1958.

———. "Fuentes inéditas para la historia de Potosí, con referencia especial al Archivo de Potosí y al Archivo Nacional de Bolivia," in Bartolomé de Arzáns de Orsúa y Vela, *Historia de la Villa Imperial de Potosí*, vol. 3, pp. 492–500.

———. "Guía de documentos en el Archivo Nacional de Bolivia y la Biblioteca Nacional de Bolivia para el estudio de la mano de obra minera durante el coloniaje, años 1549–1825." Typescript; Sucre, 1962.

———. Guía de documentos en el Archivo Nacional de Bolivia y la Biblioteca Nacional de Bolivia para el estudio de la minería en Bolivia durante el coloniaje, años 1549–1825." Typescript; Sucre, 1962.

———. "Guía de fuentes inéditas en el Archivo Nacional de Bolivia para el estudio de la administración virreinal en el distrito de la Audiencia de Charcas, años 1537–1700," in Hanke, Rodríguez, and Mendoza L., eds., *Guía de las fuentes en Hispanoamérica para el estudio de la administración virreinal española en México y en el Perú, 1535–1700*, pp. 46–255.

Mesía Venegas, Alfonso. "Memorial del P. Alfonso Mesía Venegas, sobre la cédula del servicio personal de los indios. 1603," in Rubén Vargas Ugarte, ed., *Pareceres jurídicos en asuntos de Indias (1601–1718)*, pp. 94–115.

La minería hispana e iberoamericana. Contribución a su investigación histórica. Vol. I of *Ponencias del VI Congreso Internacional de Minería*. León, Spain, 1970.

Moore, Sally Falk. *Power and Property in Inca Peru*. New York, 1958.

Moreyra y Paz-Soldán, Manuel. "Introducción a documentos y cartas de la Audiencia y del Virrey Marqués de Montesclaros," *Revista Histórica* (Lima), 19 (1952), pp. 203–63.

———, and Guillermo Céspedes del Castillo, eds. *Virreinato Peruano. Documentos para su historia. Colección de cartas de virreyes. Conde de la Monclova*. 3 vols. Lima, 1954–55.

Múzquiz de Miguel, José Luis. *El Conde de Chinchón*. Madrid, 1945.

Padden, R. C. "Introduction," in Bartolomé Arzáns de Orsúa y Vela, *Tales of Potosí*, pp. xi–xxix.

"Pareceres de los Padres de la Compañía de Jesús de Potosí. 1610," in Rubén Vargas Ugarte, ed., *Pareceres jurídicos en asuntos de Indias (1601–1718)*, pp. 116–31.

Parry, J. H. *The Spanish Seaborne Empire*. New York, 1966.

Pereyra, Carlos. "La mita peruana en el calumnioso prólogo de las 'Noticias Secretas,'" *Revista de Indias* (Madrid), 2, no. 6 (1941), pp. 5–37.

Pérez Bustamante, Ciriaco. "Las minas en los grandes geógrafos del período hispánico," in *La minería hispana e iberoamericana*, pp. 295–306.

Pérez de Tudela y Bueso, Juan. "El problema moral en el trabajo minero del indio (siglos XVI y XVII)," in *La minería hispana e iberoamericana*, pp. 352–71.

Phelan, John Leddy. "Authority and Flexibility in the Spanish Imperial Bureaucracy," *Administrative Science Quarterly* (Ithaca, N.Y.), 5 (1960), pp. 7–65.

———. *The Kingdom of Quito in the Seventeenth Century. Bureaucratic Politics in the Spanish Empire.* Madison, Wisc., 1967.

Polo, José Toribio, ed. *Memorias de los virreyes del Perú: Marqués de Mancera y Conde de Salvatierra.* Lima, 1899.

Prieto, Carlos. *La minería en el Nuevo Mundo.* Madrid, 1968.

Ramírez del Aguila, Pedro. *Noticias políticas de Indias* [1639]. Ed. Jaime Urioste Arana. Sucre, 1978.

Ramos Pérez, Demetrio. "Ordenación de la minería en hispanoamérica durante la época provincial (siglos XVI, XVII y XVIII)," in *La minería hispana e iberoamericana*, pp. 373–97.

Rasnake, Roger Neil. "The *Kurahkuna* of Yura: Indigenous Authorities of Colonial Charcas and Contemporary Bolivia." Ph.D. diss., Cornell Univ., 1982.

Real Academia de Historia. *Mapas españoles de América. Siglos XV–XVII.* Madrid, 1951.

Riva-Agüero, José de la, ed. "Descripción anónima del Perú y de Lima a principios del siglo XVII, compuesta por un judío portugués y dirigida a los estados de Holanda," *Revista Histórica* (Lima), 21 (1954), pp. 9–36.

Rodríguez-Rivas, Daniel Alonso. "La legislación minera hispano-colonial y la intrusión de labores," in *La minería hispana e iberoamericana*, pp. 657–68.

Romero, Florencia de. "El Fondo del Archivo de la Biblioteca Municipal de Oruro," *Boletín del Archivo de La Paz*, año 3, no. 5 (1978), pp. 3–13.

Rosenblat, Angel. *La población indígena y el mestizaje en América.* 2 vols. Buenos Aires, 1954.

Rowe, John Howland. "Inca Culture at the Time of the Spanish Conquest," in Julian H. Steward, ed., *Handbook of South American Indians* (7 vols.; New York, 1946–59), vol. 2, pp. 183–330.

———. "The Incas Under Spanish Colonial Institutions," *The Hispanic American Historical Review*, 37 (1957), pp. 155–99.

Sánchez-Albornoz, Nicolás. *Indios y tributos en el Alto Perú.* Lima, 1978.

———. "Migraciones internas en el Alto Perú. El saldo acumulado en 1645," *Historia Boliviana* (Cochabamba), 2, no. 1 (1982), pp. 11–19.

———. "Mita, migraciones y pueblos. Variaciones en el espacio y en el tiempo. Alto Perú, 1578–1692." Typescript.

Sandoval y Guzmán, Sebastián de. *Pretensiones de la Villa Imperial de Potosí.* Madrid, 1634.

Schäfer, Ernst. *El Consejo Real y Supremo de las Indias: su historia, organización y labor administrativa hasta la terminación de la Casa de Austria.* 2 vols. Seville, 1935–47.

Simon, K. G., Victor Engelbert, and H. J. Anders. "The Man-eating Mountain," *Geo,* 1 (1979), pp. 72–90.

Sluiter, Engel, ed. "Francisco López de Caravantes' Historical Sketch of Fiscal Administration in Colonial Peru, 1533–1618," *The Hispanic American Historical Review,* 25 (1945), pp. 224–56.

Sociedad Geográfica y de Historia 'Potosí.' *Indice analítico. Archivo de documentos en la Casa Real de Moneda. Potosí.* Buenos Aires, 1944.

Solórzano Pereira, Juan de. *Política Indiana* [1648]. Ed. Francisco Ramiro de Valenzuela. 5 vols. Biblioteca de Autores Españoles, nos. 252–56. Madrid, 1972.

Stein, Stanley J., and Barbara H. Stein. *The Colonial Heritage of Latin America. Essays on Economic Dependence in Perspective.* New York, 1970.

Stern, Steve J. *Peru's Indian Peoples and the Challenge of Spanish Conquest: Huamanga to 1640.* Madison, Wisc., 1982.

Subieta Sagárnaga, Luis. "Institución de la Mita, estudio histórico," *Boletín de la Sociedad Geográfica y de Historia de Potosí,* 39, no. 11 (1951), pp. 97–123.

Tandeter, Enrique. "Forced and Free Labour in Late Colonial Potosí," *Past & Present,* 93 (1981), pp. 98–136.

———. "Mineros de 'week-end.' Los ladrones de minas de Potosí," *Todo es Historia* (Buenos Aires), 15, no. 174 (1981), pp. 32–46.

———. "La rente comme rapport de production et comme rapport de distribution: le cas de l'industrie minière de Potosí, 1750–1826." Thesis (3ᵉ cycle en Histoire), Ecole des Hautes Etudes en Sciences Sociales, Paris, 1980.

TePaske, John J. "Recent Trends in Quantitative History: Colonial Latin America," *Latin American Research Review,* 10, no. 1 (1975), pp. 51–62.

———, ed. *Three American Empires.* New York, 1967.

Trenti Rocamora, José Luis. *Catálogo de documentos del Museo Histórico Nacional.* 3 vols. Buenos Aires, 1952.

Tudela de la Orden, José. "La minería y la metalurgía de la América española en los manuscritos de las bibliotecas de España," in *La minería hispana e iberoamericana,* pp. 679–89.

Ulloa, Antonio de. *Relación histórica del viaje a la América meridional* [1748]. 2 vols. Madrid, 1978.

Valera, Francisco de. *Propuesta, y parecer, que hace y ofrece al Excelentísimo Señor Doctor Don Melchor de Liñán y Cisneros . . . sobre el mejor cumplimiento de la cédula de Su Magestad de 8 de julio del año de 1676.* Lima, 1680.

Vargas Ugarte, Rubén. *Historia general del Perú.* 6 vols. Lima, 1966–71.

———, ed. *Pareceres jurídicos en asuntos de Indias (1601–1718).* Lima, 1951.

Vázquez de Espinosa, Antonio. *Compendium and Description of the West Indies.* Trans. C. U. Clark. Washington, D.C., 1942.

Vázquez Machicado, José. *Catálogo de documentos referentes a Potosí en el Archivo de Indias de Sevilla.* Potosí, 1964.

Whitaker, Arthur P. *The Huancavelica Mercury Mine. A Contribution to the History of the Bourbon Renaissance in the Spanish Empire.* Cambridge, Mass., 1941.

Wiedner, David L. "Forced Labor in Colonial Peru," *The Americas,* 16 (1960), pp. 357–83.

Zavala, Silvio. *Hispanoamérica septentrional y media. Período colonial.* Mexico City, 1953.

———. *Las instituciones jurídicas en la conquista de América.* 2d ed. Mexico City, 1971.

———. *New Viewpoints on the Spanish Colonization of America.* 2d ed. New York, 1968.

———. *El servicio personal de los indios en el Perú.* 3 vols. Mexico City, 1978–80.

———. *Servidumbre natural y libertad cristiana.* Buenos Aires, 1944.

Index

Abolition of the mita, 58f, 125–31 *passim*; by Bolívar, 1; proposed by government officials, 64, 66, 71, 79, 93n, 96–105 *passim*, 119

Abuses: of the mita, 22, 26, 57–64 *passim*, 71f, 80–100 *passim*, 119–27 *passim*, 131; of mitayos, 24–34 *passim*, 58–63 *passim*, 68, 72, 116, 123; of kurakas, 28, 43–44, 57f, 92, 124. *See also* Indios de faltriquera

Acosta, José de, 24

Administration: division of authority in, 21–22, 68–69, 103, 128; and problems with the mita, 44, 68–69, 77, 89, 96, 124, 128; roots of ineffectiveness of, 61, 90, 128, 130, 136; exaggeration/hyperbole as gambit of, 66, 71, 88, 121, 127, 130; and problems with responsibility, 100–103 *passim*, 128; and viceroy, 122, 130; conservatism of, 128–30 *passim*. *See also* Audiencias of La Plata and Lima; Corregidores; Council of the Indies; Crown; Phelan thesis; Viceroys

Agia, Miguel de, 66

Alba [de Aliste], Conde de [Luis Enríquez de Guzmán], 90–97 *passim*, 104, 129f

Alcabala, 52

Alcalde mayor de minas, 14, 30, 79

Alternatives to the mita, 5, 29–30, 57–67 *passim*, 64n, 66n, 100. *See also* Slaves

Amalgamation (refining process), 1, 4–9 *passim*, 55, 123. *See also* Mercury; Production of silver

Anava, Pedro, 34

Andrada Sotomayor, Pedro, 32

Annual draft, 17, 25, 28, 37, 76, 90, 111, 117, 132

Apiris, 17, 23 ff, 30f, 47–51 *passim*, 57, 76, 123–26 *passim*. *See also* Mingas; Mitayos

Archbishops of Charcas, 98f, 105–7 *passim*, 118f

Archbishops of Lima, 105, 105n, 119

Arequipa, 12, 33, 35

Arica, 18, 48

Arusi, Domingo, 35

Arusi, Pedro Alata [a.k.a. Pedro Gualpa], 34–35

Asangaro, 17, 36, 38, 42, 75

Asillo, 36
Audiencia of Charcas, *see* Audiencia of La Plata
Audiencia of La Plata, 19, 30–37 *passim*, 53 f, 83, 121, 128; oidores of, 6, 63, 95, 131–32; opposition to the mita of, 19, 33, 54, 64; rulings and cases heard by, 31–36 *passim*, 43–44, 115 n; presidents of, 37, 40, 68, 72, 77–84 *passim*, 88–99 *passim*, 105 ff, 118, 128, 130; and conflict with Lima officials, 69–70; and support for Oruro, 70–71; and corregidores of Potosí, 70, 128
Audiencia of Lima, 2, 19, 96, 116, 131 f; as interim head of government, 70, 97; and conflict with Audiencia of La Plata, 70; as Real Acuerdo, 91
Audiencia of Quito, 70, 95
Aullagas, 49
Ayanz, Antonio de, 26 n
Ayllus, 2–15 *passim*, 27, 32, 67, 80, 85, 107, 113, 116
Aymaras, 12, 17
Aymaya, 115 n
Azero, Juan, 31
Azogue, *see* Mercury
Azogueros, 8–22 *passim*, 46, 68, 77, 87–102 *passim*, 109, 116, 123–28 *passim*; and kurakas, 19, 80; and encomenderos, 22, 64 f, 72, 127; and changing production realities, 25–26, 56, 80, 123; petitions, proposals, and threats of, 25, 51–60 *passim*, 72, 80–84 *passim*, 105, 118, 124; and distribution of mitayos, 30, 71–72, 81, 98; and lack of new concessions, 36–37, 42–43, 56–57, 124; financial problems of, 46–49, 62, 90, 124;

privileges of, 46–47, 65; and moneylenders and silver merchants, 46–50 *passim*; and competitors, 49, 58, 61, 70, 125; and violence, 67, 78, 80, 93, 93 n, 99, 124, 129 f; and 1633 repartimiento, 79–84 *passim*; and 1689 repartimiento, 116, 118; and 1692 repartimiento, 116–19 *passim*. *See also* Abuses; Azogueros Guild
Azogueros Guild, 42, 44, 52, 54, 81–88 *passim*, 119, 124–27 *passim*, 132 f; intraguild problems of, 47, 84–85; and government officials, 49–53 *passim*, 81–90 *passim*

Barreteros, 25, 30
Basques, 50
Bautista Catari, Juan, 34
Bishop-elect of Concepción (assails the mita), 101 n
Black Legend, 58
Blacks, 28, 128. *See also* Slaves
Bolívar, Simón, 1
Bourbons, 130–36 *passim*

Cabezas de ingenio, 46, 46 n, 81, 133. *See also* Mills (silver)
Cabildo of Potosí, 50, 52
Caciques, *see* Kurakas
Cajíamarca, Gerónimo, 40
Calancha, Antonio de la, 26 n
Calcha, 43
Callao, 69
Campo y de la Rynaga, Nicolás Matías del, 59–60, 102 f
Canas, *see* Canas y Canches
Canas y Canches, 7–12 *passim*, 17, 38–42 *passim*, 75
Cañete, Marqués de [Andrés Hurtado de Mendoza], 2
Cañete, Marqués de [García Hur-

Corregidores de indios, 2–5 *passim*, 33f, 51, 54, 70, 115n, 125; responsibilities of, under the mita, 15, 67, 92, 100, 112–15, 121; and use of Indian labor, 27, 77, 106, 125; of Porco, 34; of Asangaro, 36; of Paucarcolla, 39; of Colquemarca, Desaguadero, Chayanta, and Paria, 42; as census takers, 94; and Palata's revitalization program, 106–12 *passim*

Corregidores of Potosí, 40–47 *passim*, 91, 99, 128, 131; distribution of mitayos by, 9–12, 30; jurisdiction of, over the mita, 12, 68, 70, 89, 131; and mita deliveries, 15, 36f, 56, 67–70 *passim*; questioning of capitanes enteradores in 1690, 34, 39; ordered to establish resident labor force, 64; and conflicts with Audiencia of La Plata, 70; role as broker, 79, 85; and Palata, 105–7; on 1693 committee, 118. *See also individual corregidores by name*; Local government officials

Corregimientos: distinguished from provinces, 91, 91n; new ones included in mita, 94–97 *passim*, 103–6 *passim*, 110–13 *passim*, 129, 131

Council of the Indies, 44, 52f, 80–82 *passim*, 87–106 *passim*, 112, 128–30 *passim*; and 1570's investigation of the mita, 19–20; and program of 1650's, 88–94 *passim*, 104, 112, 114–15, 128; and the Conde de Lemos, 98, 101f; and 1690's debate, 119–21; and 1732 proposal that mita be abolished, 132

Criollos, 14

Crown: and its colonists, 2, 65,

78–79, 127–30 *passim*; and concern for Indians, 3, 19–22 *passim*, 63, 66, 78–79, 87, 96, 102–3, 119, 121, 126–35 *passim*; and kurakas, 15, 43; and support for the mita, 20, 55, 64; and azogueros, 22, 51–60 *passim*, 65, 72, 80–87 *passim*, 102, 124–27 *passim*, 132. *See also* Administration; Cédulas; Council of the Indies; Royal fifth; *and individual monarchs by name*

Cruz, Francisco de la, 37–39, 43, 91–93, 126–30 *passim*

Cuzco, 7–14 *passim*

Debt peonage, 17, 57

Dejación, 83f

Depopulation, 28, 32, 49, 72, 109, 124f; and the mita, 26, 26n, 44, 54–60 *passim*, 66, 79, 124f. *See also* Population

Desaguadero, 42

Desmontes, *see* Tailings

Díaz de Lopidana, Juan, 63

Diezmo, 25

Disease, 23–24, 28, 32, 44, 63, 111, 124

Drought, 47, 69, 103n

Dutch, 69, 92

Elites, 22, 64, 66, 78–79, 127, 129, 135f. *See also* Azogueros; Chacareros; Encomenderos; Estancieros

Encomenderos, 2–3, 64f, 127

Encomienda, 2f, 65; and the mita, 22, 72

Enríquez, Martín, 24–25, 62, 72

Enríquez, Pedro Luis, 33, 115n, 116–19 *passim*

Entero, 15, 36

Epidemics, *see* Disease

Esquilache, Príncipe de [Francisco